1992 – 2012
UNITED NATIONS
DECLARATION ON
Minority
Rights

Promoting and Protecting Minority Rights

A Guide for Advocates

UNITED NATIONS

UNITED NATIONS
HUMAN RIGHTS
OFFICE OF THE HIGH COMMISSIONER

Geneva and New York, 2012

Note

The designations employed and the presentation of the material in this publication do not imply the expression of any opinion whatsoever on the part of the Secretariat of the United Nations concerning the legal status of any country, territory, city or area, or of its authorities, or concerning the delimitation of its frontiers or boundaries.

*

*   *

Symbols of United Nations documents are composed of capital letters combined with figures. Mention of such a figure indicates a reference to a United Nations document.

HR/PUB/12/7
Sales No. E.13.XIV.1
ISBN 978-92-1-154197-7
eISBN 978-92-1-056280-5

Foreword

I am delighted that this publication, *Promoting and Protecting Minority Rights: A Guide for Minority Rights Advocates*, comes before you as we celebrate the twentieth anniversary of the adoption of the Declaration on the Rights of Persons Belonging to National or Ethnic, Religious and Linguistic Minorities.

This anniversary gives us the opportunity to look back on the 20 years of promoting the Declaration and use that experience to plan and strategize for the future, to decide how best to bring this Declaration further to the fore of human rights discussions taking place all over the world and discuss its implementation. It is our hope that the *Guide* will be a true vade mecum, assisting civil society to engage even more effectively in this important and immense task.

Whether we are talking about democracy-building following the uprisings in North Africa and the Middle East or ensuring human rights in the context of the global economic downturn; about sustainable development in the context of the 2012 United Nations Conference on Sustainable Development ("Rio+20") or about guaranteeing effective participation of minorities, including minority women and girls, in all spheres of life, worldwide; minority issues need to maintain their rightful place on the agendas of decision makers.

In this anniversary year, my Office is increasing its engagement on minority rights even further. We are organizing a series of subregional and regional events to address most topical minority issues and we pursue a range of awareness-raising activities. We are taking the lead in the formation and coordination of the United Nations Network on Racial Discrimination and Protection of Minorities, a new platform aiming to enhance cooperation and dialogue on minorities across the United Nations system. All this is in addition to already established work on minority rights, which includes field-presence engagement on minority issues, capacity-building for minority rights activists through the Minorities Fellowship Programme, supporting the mandate of the Independent Expert on minority issues and the annual Forum on Minority Issues. Please visit our website to make sure you have all the latest information on these activities.

It is our role as human rights defenders to ensure that the rights of national or ethnic, religious and linguistic minorities are highlighted and taken into account. We hope that this *Guide* will prove to be a valuable tool for minority rights advocates, helping them place minority rights on the agenda, where this has not yet been done, or make sure they stay there and are adequately addressed.

In the international, regional and national discussions framed by the "all human rights for all" principle, we must work together to make sure that minorities are not left out. Towards this end, the *Guide* explains, in a reader-friendly way, who are the main actors working on minority issues in the United Nations and in key regional organizations, and what are the best ways of engaging them.

Minorities enrich the societies of each and every country in the world. Through working on guaranteeing their rights, our chief aims must be that no one will be afraid to self-identify as a member of a minority, fearing disadvantage will come out of that decision; that persons belonging to minorities will be guaranteed protection of their existence and identity; and that they will benefit from the principles of effective participation and non-discrimination. Let this publication guide us in working towards making this a reality for all persons belonging to minorities, everywhere.

Navi Pillay

United Nations High Commissioner for Human Rights

Acknowledgements

The Office of the United Nations High Commissioner for Human Rights wishes to express its sincere thanks to Hurst Hannum, Professor of International Law at the Fletcher School of Law and Diplomacy, for his valuable contribution to the preparation of this *Guide*. In addition, special mention and thanks are due to our United Nations partners and regional organizations that have contributed to the publication.

Contents

INTRODUCTION

Today, issues related to the rights of persons belonging to minorities may be found in nearly every human rights instrument and forum. The United Nations and other intergovernmental organizations recognize that minority rights are essential to protect those who wish to preserve and develop values and practices which they share with other members of their community. They also recognize that members of minorities make significant contributions to the richness and diversity of society, and that States which take appropriate measures to recognize and promote minority rights are more likely to remain tolerant and stable.

The present *Guide* offers information related to norms and mechanisms developed to protect the rights of persons belonging to national, ethnic, religious or linguistic minorities. It includes detailed information about procedures and forums in which minority issues may be raised within the United Nations system and in regional systems. By focusing on the work related to minorities and by also covering selected specialized agencies and regional mechanisms, the present *Guide* complements information contained in *Working with the United Nations Human Rights Programme: A Handbook for Civil Society* (OHCHR, 2008), which provides practical guidance on the United Nations human rights mechanisms in general.[1] The information contained in the *Guide* is accurate as of 1 January 2012.

It is hoped that this *Guide* will be useful in assisting minority advocates to make full and effective use of existing international mechanisms and, ultimately, to promote and protect the rights guaranteed under international instruments.

1 Available from www.ohchr.org/EN/AboutUs/CivilSociety/Pages/Handbook.aspx (accessed 29 November 2012). The *Handbook* is available in Arabic, Chinese, English, French, Russian and Spanish; online, it is also available in Farsi, Georgian and Nepali. An associated DVD was produced in 2011.

PART ONE
MINORITY RIGHTS FOCUS IN THE UNITED NATIONS

CHAPTER I

OVERVIEW: DEVELOPMENT OF MINORITY RIGHTS IN INTERNATIONAL LAW

Summary: The first significant attempt to identify internationally recognized minority rights was through a number of "minority treaties" adopted under the auspices of the League of Nations. With the creation of the United Nations, attention initially shifted to universal human rights and decolonization. However, the United Nations has gradually developed a number of norms, procedures and mechanisms concerned with minority issues, and the 1992 United Nations Declaration on the Rights of Persons belonging to National or Ethnic, Religious and Linguistic Minorities is the fundamental instrument that guides the activities of the United Nations in this field today.

The concepts of "minority" and "majority" are relatively recent in international law, although distinctions among communities have obviously existed throughout history. Some political systems did grant special community rights to their minorities, although this was not generally based on any recognition of minority "rights" per se. The millet system of the Ottoman Empire, for example, allowed a degree of cultural and religious autonomy to non-Muslim religious communities, such as Orthodox Christians, Armenians, Jews and others. The French and American revolutions in the late eighteenth century proclaimed the free exercise of religion as a fundamental right, although neither directly addressed the broader issue of minority protection. The 1815 Congress of Vienna, which dismantled the Napoleonic Empire, recognized minority rights to some extent, as did the 1878 Treaty of Berlin, which recognized special rights for the religious community of Mount Athos.

Most international legal-political concerns during the nineteenth century, however, were directed towards justifying the unification of linguistic "nations" based on the principle of self-determination, rather than the protection of minority groups as such. As the lure of nationalism grew, people who did not share the ethnic, linguistic or religious identity of the majority within their country were increasingly under threat. The consolidation of States along linguistic lines, expansion of trade and increasing need for literate populations who could work successfully in the context of the industrial revolution placed pressures on smaller or less powerful communities to conform to dominant linguistic and cultural norms. By the time of the outbreak of the First World War in 1914, national or minority concerns were at the forefront of international politics, at least in Europe.

The League of Nations

Following the end of the First World War, minority issues became a central concern for the League of Nations. A series of so-called minority treaties was adopted to protect certain specified groups, addressing many of their key concerns.

Among the protections commonly included were the rights to equality and non-discrimination; the right to citizenship if a person commonly resident in a new State (or a State with new borders) so wished; the right to use one's own language in public and private; the right of minorities to establish their own religious, cultural, charitable and educational institutions; an obligation on the State to provide an "equitable" level of financial support to minority schools, in which instruction at the primary level would be in the minority's mother tongue; and entrenchment of laws protecting minorities so that they could not be changed by subsequent statutes.

Although the supervisory system established by the League was political rather than legal and did not permit aggrieved minorities to engage States on an equal or adversarial footing, it did provide certain oversight through the League's Secretariat. Almost any person or group could bring a situation to the attention of the League and the Secretariat could also investigate situations on its own initiative. The ultimate sanction was public discussion in the League Council and, potentially, the adoption of a resolution calling upon a State to take particular action. Some treaties, such as that which created the Free City of Danzig, provided for access to the Permanent Court of International Justice (the predecessor of today's International Court of Justice), and the Court delivered a number of important advisory opinions on minority issues.[2]

Although the scope of minority treaties was limited – they applied only to a small number of defeated or new States and there was no agreement that minority rights were universally applicable – their significance should not be underestimated. They had concrete implications for minorities within the State, and they constituted an important step in the development of international minority rights and human rights law. In particular, the acceptance of the principle of international interest in and supervision of the fate of minorities within States was a major breakthrough in the development of international law, which in some ways presaged the later promotion of broader human rights by the United Nations.

The United Nations

The Charter of the United Nations makes no mention of minority rights per se, but it does include several provisions on human rights, including Article 1 (3), which identifies as one of the purposes of the United Nations the achievement of international cooperation "in promoting and encouraging respect for human rights and for fundamental freedoms for all without distinction as to race, sex, language, or religion".

In 1948, the General Assembly adopted the Universal Declaration of Human Rights, which articulated the content of human rights in much greater detail and remains one of the most important international human rights documents: its anti-discrimination provisions and other articles are of central importance also for persons belonging to minorities. While the General Assembly was unable to agree on any formulation in the Declaration concerning minority rights per se, it did note that the United Nations "cannot remain indifferent to the fate of minorities". It added, in the same resolution that proclaimed the Universal Declaration, that it was "difficult to adopt a uniform solution for this complex and delicate question [of minorities], which has special aspects in each State in which it arises."[3]

---

2 See, in particular, Permanent Court of International Justice, *Rights of Minorities in Upper Silesia (Minority Schools), Germany v. Poland*, Judgment No. 12, 26 April 1928; *Questions Relating to Settlers of German Origin in Poland*, Advisory Opinion, Series B No. 6, 10 September 1923; *The Greco-Bulgarian "Communities"*, Advisory Opinion, Series B No. 17, 31 July 1930; *Access to German Minority Schools in Upper Silesia*, Advisory Opinion, Series A./B. No. 40, 15 May 1931; *Minority Schools in Albania*, Advisory Opinion, Series A./B. No. 62, 6 April 1935.

3 Resolution 217 C(III).

While many argued that issues related to minorities would be best addressed through a combination of respect for individual human rights and the growing attention being paid to the right of colonial territories to self-determination, the United Nations did address minority issues in a number of specific cases. For example, the 1948 Convention on the Prevention and Punishment of the Crime of Genocide prohibits the destruction of "a national, ethnical, racial or religious group, as such". In 1947, the Sub-Commission on Prevention of Discrimination and Protection of Minorities was created as a sub-body of the Commission on Human Rights and an influential study on that issue prepared for the Sub-Commission by Special Rapporteur Francesco Capotorti was published in 1979.[4] In the 1960s, three important treaties were adopted that also addressed minority rights. In 1960, the United Nations Educational, Scientific and Cultural Organization (UNESCO) adopted the Convention against Discrimination in Education, which recognized the right of minority group members to carry out their own educational activities, including establishing their own schools and teaching their own language. In 1965, the United Nations adopted the International Convention on the Elimination of All Forms of Racial Discrimination, which prohibits any distinction "based on race, colour, descent, or national or ethnic origin". In 1966, the International Covenant on Civil and Political Rights included in article 27 a specific provision concerned with minorities, a principal legal tool to advance minority rights. The Convention and the Covenant are discussed more fully in chapter V.

While these developments were important, advancing the protection of minority rights received more attention as the cold war ended. The importance of minority rights and their contribution to the stability of States was increasingly recognized in the work of international institutions, including in Central and Eastern Europe and in the former Soviet Union.

In Europe, an important breakthrough came in 1990, when a review meeting of the Conference on Security and Co-operation in Europe (now the Organization for Security and Co-operation in Europe (OSCE), see chap. XIII) adopted a declaration on human rights, democracy, the rule of law and minority rights. This so-called Copenhagen Document commits the (now) 56 participating States of OSCE to a wide range of minority rights. Although the Copenhagen Document is a political declaration, its impact has been significant and it helped to pave the way for the legally binding Framework Convention for the Protection of National Minorities, adopted by the Council of Europe in 1994. These and other initiatives of the Council of Europe and OSCE are discussed in chapters XII and XIII respectively.

At the United Nations, a declaration on minority rights was under discussion for over a decade before the General Assembly adopted the Declaration on the Rights of Persons Belonging to National or Ethnic, Religious and Linguistic Minorities (Minorities Declaration) in 1992 (see annex I). The Minorities Declaration contains progressive language, including as regards minority participation in the political and economic life of the State. In addition, the preamble recognizes that protecting minority rights will "contribute to the political and social stability of States in which they live" and, in turn, "contribute to the strengthening of friendship and cooperation among peoples and States".

Among its more noteworthy substantive provisions are:

Article 1

> 1. States shall protect the existence and the national or ethnic, cultural, religious and linguistic identity of minorities within their respective territories and shall encourage conditions for the promotion of that identity. [...]

4 *Study on the Rights of Persons Belonging to Ethnic, Religious and Linguistic Minorities*, reprinted as Human Rights Study Series No. 5 (United Nations publication, Sales No. E.91.XIV.2).

Article 2

[...]

2. Persons belonging to minorities have the right to participate effectively in cultural, religious, social, economic and public life.

3. Persons belonging to minorities have the right to participate effectively in decisions on the national and, where appropriate, regional level concerning the minority to which they belong or the regions in which they live, in a manner not incompatible with national legislation. [...]

Article 4

[...]

2. States shall take measures to create favourable conditions to enable persons belonging to minorities to express their characteristics and to develop their culture, language, religion, traditions and customs, except where specific practices are in violation of national law and contrary to international standards. [...]

In 1995, the Commission on Human Rights authorized the Sub-Commission to establish a five-member working group to "[r]eview the promotion and practical realization" of the Declaration, "[e]xamine possible solutions to problems involving minorities ... [and recommend] further measures, as appropriate, for the promotion and protection of the rights of persons belonging to national or ethnic, religious and linguistic minorities".[5] The Working Group on Minorities held 12 sessions between 1995 and 2006 and provided a venue for representatives of minorities to raise issues within the United Nations and enter into dialogue directly with States. The Working Group achieved a great deal, not only in conceptualizing the rights of persons belonging to minorities but also by establishing good practices and other measures to promote and protect minorities.[6] In 2005 the Working Group adopted the Commentary on the Declaration (see annex I).

The position of Independent Expert on minority issues was created by the Commission on Human Rights in 2005. Further to the creation of the Human Rights Council in 2006, the Forum on Minority Issues was established in 2007. The work of the Independent Expert and other special procedures is discussed in greater detail in chapter IV, and the Forum in chapter III.

The United Nations has further contributed to developing standards for the protection of minorities with the adoption of the 1981 Declaration on the Elimination of All Forms of Intolerance and of Discrimination Based on Religion or Belief;[7] the appointment of special rapporteurs by the Commission on Human Rights in the 1980s to consider aspects of religious intolerance and discrimination; and a 1993 report by the Sub-Commission on "the possible ways and means of facilitating the peaceful and constructive solution of problems involving minorities".[8] In 2001, the United Nations Secretary-General appointed a Special Adviser on the Prevention of Genocide, who seeks and receives information related to his or her mandate, particularly early-warning information.[9] States Members of the United Nations adopted the 2005 World Summit Outcome, which notes that "the promotion and protection of the rights of persons belonging to national or

5 Resolution 1995/24, para. 9.

6 Documents considered by the Working Group are available from www.ohchr.org/EN/Issues/Minorities/Pages/TheformerWGonMinorities.aspx (accessed 29 November 2012).

7 General Assembly resolution 36/55. See also D. J. Sullivan, "Advancing the freedom of religion or belief through the UN Declaration on the Elimination of Religious Intolerance and Discrimination", *American Journal of International Law*, vol. 82 (1988), p. 487.

8 E/CN.4/Sub.2/1993/34 and Adds. 1–4.

9 See www.un.org/en/preventgenocide/adviser/index.shtml (accessed 29 November 2012).

ethnic, religious, and linguistic minorities contribute to political and social stability and peace and enrich the cultural diversity and heritage of society".[10]

It is also important to note that, in addition to the development of minority rights, the United Nations has actively pursued distinct work on the human rights of indigenous peoples. This work culminated in the Declaration on the Rights of Indigenous Peoples, a landmark document drafted with strong input from representatives of indigenous peoples and adopted by the General Assembly in September 2007.

The 2001 Durban World Conference against Racism, Racial Discrimination, Xenophobia and Related Intolerance (Durban Conference) and the Durban Review Conference held in 2009 reaffirmed non-discrimination as a core human rights principle and recommended various measures towards securing additional protection against racism. The Durban Declaration and Programme of Action proposes concrete actions to combat racism, racial discrimination, xenophobia and related intolerance; addresses a wide range of issues; and contains far-reaching recommendations and practical measures regarding various groups which suffer from discrimination. Specific recommendations are formulated to combat discrimination against Africans and people of African descent, Asians and persons of Asian descent, indigenous peoples, migrants, refugees, minorities, Roma and other groups.

Several recommendations are made towards equal treatment of minorities and their enjoyment of human rights and fundamental freedoms without discrimination of any kind. The Durban Declaration and Programme of Action recognizes that victims often suffer from multiple or aggravated forms of discrimination based on sex, language, religion, political or other opinion, social origin, property, birth or other status. The Durban Review Conference provided an opportunity to assess and accelerate progress on the implementation of measures adopted under the Durban Declaration and Programme of Action. Its Outcome Document essentially reaffirms the commitments contained in the Durban Declaration and Programme of Action.

Two intergovernmental mechanisms and two expert mechanisms were subsequently created: the Intergovernmental Working Group on the Effective Implementation of the Durban Declaration and Programme of Action, the Ad Hoc Committee on the elaboration of complementary standards, the Independent Eminent Experts' Group and the Working Group of Experts on People of African Descent. The last is discussed more fully in chapter IV.

Throughout the above developments, a persistent challenge for minority advocates within the United Nations and other intergovernmental bodies has been the lack of agreement on just what a "minority" is. The difficulties in arriving at an agreed definition have at times overshadowed substantive consideration of minority rights, and the adoption of the Minorities Declaration became possible only after a decision was taken to proceed without defining the persons to whom it would apply. One of the most widely cited definitions is that proposed by Special Rapporteur Francesco Capotorti. In his 1979 report, he defined a minority as "[a] group numerically inferior to the rest of the population of a State, in a non-dominant position, whose members – being nationals of the State – possess ethnic, religious or linguistic characteristics differing from those of the rest of the population and show, if only implicitly, a sense of solidarity, directed towards preserving their culture, traditions, religion or language".

In 1984, in the course of deliberations that would eventually lead to the adoption of the Minorities Declaration in 1992, the Commission on Human Rights requested the Sub-Commission to revisit the definition. After surveying various national and international precedents, Sub-Commission member Jules Deschenes submitted the following definition, which did not differ substantially from that by Mr. Capotorti:

[10] General Assembly resolution 60/1, para. 130.

> A group of citizens of a State, constituting a numerical minority and in a non-dominant position in that State, endowed with ethnic, religious or linguistic characteristics which differ from those of the majority of the population, having a sense of solidarity with one another, motivated, if only implicitly, by a collective will to survive and whose aim is to achieve equality with the majority in fact and in law.[11]

This proposal was simply forwarded to the Commission without having been approved by the Sub-Commission, and the Commission's Working Group eventually decided to postpone further consideration of definitional questions and to proceed to elaborate the substantive articles of the draft declaration. While some elements of these definitions have often been challenged, notably the references to citizenship or nationality of the State concerned, they reflect the consensus that any definition of "minority" must include both objective factors (such as the existence of shared ethnicity, language and religion) and subjective factors (e.g., that individuals identify themselves as members of a minority group). It is also widely accepted that whether or not a minority exists is a question of fact and does not depend on a formal determination by the State.[12]

Article 27 of the International Covenant on Civil and Political Rights refers to "ethnic, religious or linguistic" minorities. Instruments adopted by the Conference on Security and Co-operation in Europe and the Council of Europe, on the other hand, refer only to "national" minorities. The Minorities Declaration has the broadest scope, encompassing persons belonging to "national or ethnic, religious and linguistic minorities"; it also refers to the protection of "cultural" identity.

The Human Rights Committee, in its general comment No. 23 (1994), addresses definitions only indirectly. It observes that "it is not relevant to determine the degree of permanence that the term 'exist' connotes" and goes on to adopt the expansive view that article 27 applies to everyone belonging to one of the named categories of minorities and present within a country, including "migrant workers or even visitors".

Further information

A great number of books have been written on the development of minority rights. Among those which pay particular attention to the United Nations and/or international mechanisms are: *Mechanisms for the Implementation of Minority Rights* (ECMI Minority Issues Handbook series, Council of Europe, 2004); R. M. Letschert, *The Impact of Minority Rights Mechanisms* (T. M. C. Asser Press, 2005); G. Pentassuglia, *Minorities in International Law* (Council of Europe, 2002); P. Thornberry, *International Law and the Rights of Minorities* (Oxford, 1991); and M. Weller, ed., *Universal Minority Rights: A Commentary on the Jurisprudence of International Courts and Treaty Bodies* (Oxford, 2007).

---

[11] E/CN.4/Sub.2/1985/31 and Corr. 1.

[12] This point is supported by the Human Rights Committee. See its general comment No. 23 (1994) on the rights of minorities, para. 5.2.

CHAPTER II

THE OFFICE OF THE UNITED NATIONS HIGH COMMISSIONER FOR HUMAN RIGHTS

Summary: The High Commissioner for Human Rights has the lead responsibility within the United Nations system for implementing the United Nations human rights programme. The High Commissioner plays an important role in promoting and protecting human rights through public statements, dialogue with Governments, liaison with United Nations and other bodies, and by ensuring that human rights, including minority rights, remain an integral part of the work of the United Nations. The High Commissioner can give voice to minorities facing discrimination. The Office of the United Nations High Commissioner (OHCHR) services the main United Nations human rights bodies and mechanisms, and ensures that minority issues are regularly placed on the international human rights agenda.

Minority rights advocates who have concerns about the protection of minority rights may contact OHCHR directly. The Office works on minority issues through its global, thematic work and more than 50 field presences. The section most concerned with minority rights issues is the Indigenous Peoples and Minorities Section, based in Geneva. OHCHR field presences enable minorities to communicate directly with United Nations staff and participate in relevant programming, training and monitoring activities. Increasingly, OHCHR features minority issues in its regular involvement with, for example, the United Nations Human Rights Council and its special procedures, the human rights treaty bodies and the universal periodic review process.

Under the direction of the High Commissioner for Human Rights, OHCHR has the mandate to promote and protect all human rights for all people. It works to build awareness of and respect for human rights, to assist States to uphold human rights in accordance with international human rights law and to empower individuals to claim their rights. OHCHR is headquartered in Geneva, with an office in New York and a network of more than 50 field presences around the world, many of which work actively on minority issues.

OHCHR is proactive in advocating for minority rights. Consistently focusing on the human rights of persons belonging to minority groups, it strives to have their issues mainstreamed throughout the United Nations system and by many different stakeholders. The High Commissioner often speaks out on behalf of minorities, giving them a stronger voice.[13]

The United Nations High Commissioner for Human Rights is the official with "principal responsibility" for United Nations human rights activities. In summary, the mandate of the High Commissioner is to:

- Promote and protect all human rights for all people;
- Make recommendations to the competent bodies of the United Nations system for improving the promotion and protection of all human rights;
- Promote and protect the right to development;
- Provide technical assistance for human rights actions and programmes;

[13] See www.ohchr.org/en/NewsEvents/Pages/NewsSearch.aspx?PTID=HC&NTID=STM (accessed 29 November 2012).

- Coordinate United Nations human rights education and public information programmes;
- Play an active role in removing obstacles to the realization of human rights and preventing the continuation of human rights violations;
- Engage in dialogue with Governments in order to help secure respect for all human rights;
- Enhance international cooperation;
- Coordinate human rights promotion and protection activities throughout the United Nations system;
- Rationalize, adapt, strengthen and streamline the United Nations human rights machinery.[14]

OHCHR focuses its work on:

- Standard-setting – contributing to the development of international norms to advance human rights protection and entitlement;
- Monitoring – ensuring that these standards are implemented in practice;
- Implementation – identifying early-warning signs of human rights crises and deteriorating situations and, where possible, offering technical assistance to Governments, and deploying staff and resources, to contribute to the prevention and addressing of human rights violations.

OHCHR Management Plan 2012-2013: Working for Results highlights minority issues through one of its thematic priorities, countering discrimination.[15] OHCHR places this priority at the heart of its continued advocacy, technical assistance and capacity-building work.

The work of OHCHR is based on dialogue and cooperation with Governments, legislatures, courts, national institutions and civil society, with regional and international organizations, and within the United Nations system itself. Its work on minority issues encompasses:

- Technical support to Governments;
- Capacity-building for Government officials and non-governmental organization (NGO) representatives and other minority rights advocates;
- Substantive work which contributes to international minority rights standard-setting;
- Mainstreaming and advancing the promotion and protection of minority rights throughout the United Nations system and in the field;
- Cooperating with all relevant stakeholders, including providing a platform for the exchange of experience and information (the Forum on Minority Issues, discussed in chap. III).

The structure of OHCHR is illustrated in figure I. OHCHR provides substantive and secretariat support to the various United Nations human rights bodies (described in detail in chaps. III-V) as they fulfil their standard-setting and monitoring duties.

The Human Rights Council Branch serves as the Secretariat of the Human Rights Council and a number of its mechanisms. The Council is the key United Nations intergovernmental body responsible for human rights. It addresses violations, reviews States' human rights records, works to prevent human rights abuses, responds to emergencies, serves as an international

[14] For the formal mandate, see General Assembly resolution 48/141.

[15] See www2.ohchr.org/english/ohchrreport2011/web_version/ohchr_mp_2012_2013_web_en/index.html#/home (accessed 29 November 2012).

forum for human rights dialogue and makes recommendations to the General Assembly for the development of international human rights law (see chap. III).

The Special Procedures Branch supports the work of the special procedures, that is, individuals or expert groups appointed by the Council to monitor human rights in various countries or in relation to specific issues. OHCHR assists these independent experts as they carry out thematic work, conduct visits to the field, receive and consider complaints from victims of human rights violations and appeal to States on behalf of victims (see chap. IV).

The Human Rights Treaties Division provides legal research and secretariat support to the core human rights treaty bodies (see chap. V). Treaty bodies or committees are composed of independent experts who monitor States parties' compliance with their treaty obligations through examining periodic reports, issuing recommendations and general comments and (for some committees) considering individual complaints of treaty violations.

The Field Operations and Technical Cooperation Division (FOTCD) provides substantive and administrative support to the work of the more than 50 human rights field presences, generally coordinates the development and implementation of OHCHR work at country level and manages OHCHR technical cooperation programmes. The Division is one of the most important points of entry (along with the Civil Society Section) for minority rights activists as it can offer advice on country-specific situations. Minority rights defenders are also an invaluable source of information on the situation of the minorities to which they belong.

The Research and Right to Development Division provides legal and policy advice and undertakes substantive research on a broad range of thematic human rights issues. The Indigenous Peoples and Minorities Section (IPMS) is situated within this Division. It works at both international and national levels to improve human rights protection for persons belonging to minorities through strategies such as strengthening relevant legislation, policies and practices and undertaking capacity-building activities, while also promoting the Minorities Declaration and other key human rights standards. The Division works on matters such as the rule of law; the administration of justice; and issues relating to poverty, development, discrimination and the rights of vulnerable groups. It develops methodological tools and learning resources, and engages with stakeholders, disseminating research findings, providing advice and training, undertaking needs assessments, and designing and assisting in the implementation of capacity-building projects at country level.

The Civil Society Section is the main entry point for civil society actors wishing to contact OHCHR headquarters. It provides information and advice on a broad range of issues, advises on policies and strategies to enhance cooperation, and develops tools to assist civil society in engaging with the United Nations human rights bodies and mechanisms.

The New York office of OHCHR represents the High Commissioner in New York.[16] It works for the effective integration of human rights norms and standards in the decision-making and operational activities of intergovernmental and inter-agency bodies based at United Nations headquarters. It also leads efforts to end discrimination based on sexual orientation and gender identity.[17]

---

[16] See www.ohchr.org/EN/NewYork/Pages/Overview.aspx (accessed 29 November 2012).

[17] Since the Minorities Declaration is devoted to national or ethnic, linguistic and religious minorities, persons of particular sexual orientation or identity (e.g., lesbian, gay, bisexual, transgender or intersexual) fall under its scope when they are also members of a national or ethnic, linguistic and religious minority, in which case efforts aimed at guaranteeing their human rights require addressing multiple discrimination issues.

Promotion and protection of minority rights

Based on the universality of human rights and the fundamental principle of equality and non-discrimination, the High Commissioner strives to promote and protect the human rights of all, everywhere. The promotion and protection of the rights of persons belonging to minorities is therefore an integral responsibility and significant priority of the High Commissioner and OHCHR, including field presences.[18] More specifically, the High Commissioner is called upon to promote implementation of the principles contained in the Minorities Declaration and to engage in a dialogue with Governments concerned for that purpose.[19]

During such ongoing dialogue and country visits, the High Commissioner regularly discusses problems and possible solutions concerning situations involving minorities with both Government and civil society representatives. The High Commissioner and OHCHR also actively provide guidance and support to other bodies and organs of the United Nations. This includes follow-up on minority-related resolutions of bodies such as the General Assembly and the Human Rights Council and on the recommendations of treaty bodies, the universal periodic review, the Forum on Minority Issues and special procedures, including the Independent Expert on minority issues (see chaps. III-V). In 2012, for example, OHCHR organized a Human Rights Council panel and a range of other activities to mark the twentieth anniversary of the adoption of the Minorities Declaration.

OHCHR also leads inter-agency work on minorities. It coordinates the United Nations Network on Racial Discrimination and Protection of Minorities established by the Secretary-General in 2012 to advance system-wide collaboration in this area.

The Groups in Focus Section of the Special Procedures Branch services the Forum on Minority Issues and the mandate of the Independent Expert on minority issues. The work of the Independent Expert, including cooperation with minority rights advocates, is described in detail in chapter IV.

IPMS seeks to have key human rights standards (notably the Minorities Declaration and the Declaration on the Rights of Indigenous Peoples) more consistently reflected in national laws, policies and practices, and in the programmes and activities of the United Nations. It does so through thematic research, advice, awareness-raising and capacity-building.

IPMS is also responsible for preparing the annual report of the High Commissioner on the rights of persons belonging to national or ethnic, religious and linguistic minorities, presented to the Human Rights Council.[20] The report summarizes the main developments in the work of the United Nations human rights bodies and mechanisms, including OHCHR, which contribute to the promotion and implementation of rights provided for under the Minorities Declaration.

IPMS produces a newsletter on the activities of OHCHR and developments pertaining to minorities, and pursues thematic work on such areas as the representation and participation of minorities in policing.[21] Close cooperation with OHCHR field presences is essential in order to respond to demands for targeted assistance on minority issues and to raise awareness among NGOs and other stakeholders.

[18] General Assembly resolution 48/141. OHCHR press releases on minority issues are available from www.ohchr.org/EN/NewsEvents/Pages/NewsSearch.aspx?MID=IE_Minorities (accessed 29 November 2012).

[19] General Assembly resolution 49/192.

[20] Reports to the Human Rights Council are available from ap.ohchr.org/documents/sdpage_e.aspx?s=93 (accessed 29 November 2012).

[21] See www.ohchr.org/EN/Issues/Minorities/Pages/NewsletterArchives.aspx (accessed 29 November 2012).

IPMS is often the first point of contact at OHCHR for minority advocates and it facilitates their interaction with the rest of the Office and the United Nations system.

Minorities Fellowship Programme

IPMS organizes an annual Minorities Fellowship Programme, which provides intensive human rights training for minority representatives at OHCHR headquarters in Geneva to increase their knowledge of the United Nations system, instruments and mechanisms.[22] The fellows attend briefing sessions on international human rights instruments and mechanisms and observe relevant sessions of human rights bodies. They are also introduced to the mandates and activities of other organizations within the United Nations system (including those discussed in chaps. VI–X). The programme involves individual and group assignments, including preparation of presentations on human rights issues in the fellows' respective communities. The fellows learn about the country-focused work of OHCHR and practical ways of strengthening national human rights protection systems. They can also establish contacts with NGOs and intergovernmental organizations. The five-week programme, begun in 2005 and currently conducted in English and Arabic, has built the capacity of more than 65 representatives from different ethnic, religious and linguistic minority communities to work more effectively on minority issues. Many fellows have since conducted further training within their communities.

In 2011, IPMS piloted the position of Senior Minority Fellow, through which a member of a national or ethnic, religious and linguistic minority who has relevant experience and education gains practical knowledge and work experience by directly contributing to the programmes and activities of IPMS.

Former fellows have created a practical tool, the Minority Profile and Matrix on the human rights situation of minorities, by which minority advocates can present information to their own Governments, national human rights institutions, regional organizations and the United Nations. It indicates current legislation, policies and practices; identifies avenues for data collection, analysis and application; suggests ways of improving specific situations; offers a checklist of human rights challenges facing minorities; pinpoints trends and situations which may fuel conflict and violence; and develops a common language for sharing information and good practices.[23]

In 2006, OHCHR supported a project submitted by a former minority fellow from a Romani community in Bulgaria. The project enabled his organization, Roma Together, to organize a training workshop in Polski Trambesh for local Romani representatives. The workshop recommended that the municipal council set up a standing body of local minority representatives to provide policy input on minority issues, which was accepted by the mayor and the municipal council. A council on ethnic and demographic issues was subsequently established, offering a forum for consultation on local programmes and strategies targeting Roma. As a result, addressing issues facing the local Romani community became a priority in municipal policy; in 2009, the municipality allocated approximately 350,000 euros for activities aimed at the integration of the Romani minority.

A number of funds and grants are managed by OHCHR (see chap. IX of *Working with the United Nations Human Rights Programme: A Handbook for Civil Society*).

[22] See www.ohchr.org/EN/Issues/Minorities/Pages/Fellowship.aspx (accessed 29 November 2012).

[23] E/CN.4/Sub.2/AC.5/2006/3.

OHCHR work in the field

Over the years, OHCHR has increased its presence in the field, which is coordinated by FOTCD (see fig. II). FOTCD comprises five geographic teams which ensure country expertise and, among other activities, support the country mandates of special procedures (see chap. IV). The teams also serve as entry points to OHCHR for both its own offices and civil society within particular countries. Desk officers, each responsible for a number of countries in a region, are important contacts for minority advocates. Their roles include supporting the mainstreaming of human rights (including minority rights) in the Common Country Assessment/United Nations Development Assistance Frameworks (CCA/UNDAFs); providing information to treaty bodies and special procedures on the human rights situation (including that of minorities) in the countries for which they have responsibility; collecting and analysing such information and preparing relevant reports; assisting in transmitting and processing individual cases of alleged violations under thematic mechanisms; assisting in the adaptation of materials related to human rights education in the countries concerned; and maintaining an awareness of human rights educational and information activities.

FOTCD desk officers are the main source of information and advice on country-specific work for minority advocates, while minority advocates are an invaluable source of information for desk officers. Desk officers can also help minority advocates connect with the other parts of OHCHR, both at headquarters and in the field.

FOTCD and field presences maintain regular contact with civil society organizations, including those working on minority issues, in order to better understand the human rights situation in a country or region and ensure that communication and consultation mechanisms between Government bodies and minority groups are in place. *Minority advocates are encouraged to contact the geographic sections of FOTCD and to maintain regular contact with the desk officer for the country of interest.* The National Institutions and Regional Mechanisms Section in FOTCD is another important contact point as it facilitates partnership between civil society, national human rights institutions and other relevant actors to advance the promotion and protection of human rights at country level.

It is through its field presences that OHCHR can most directly contribute to addressing human rights violations and issues. Work in the field allows OHCHR to better understand human rights issues and to establish direct and continuous dialogue and partnership with all relevant actors – Government counterparts, national institutions, civil society, the United Nations system and regional organizations – with a view to improving the human rights situation. On this basis, OHCHR can develop and implement technical cooperation programmes which are adapted to the needs of:

- National authorities, so they are aware of their human rights obligations and can design effective remedies to overcome obstacles to the realization of human rights;
- Rights holders, so they are better protected;
- Government officials and civil society, to increase their capacity to address human rights concerns.

The work of OHCHR at the country level is aimed at preventing, reducing and addressing human rights violations through dialogue with the authorities and other relevant counterparts, and through strengthening the national human rights protection systems.

Thus, OHCHR assists efforts to harmonize national legislation and practice with States' international obligations under international human rights law, and advises on the establishment and functioning of independent national human rights institutions. It also works with and provides human rights training and technical advice to the judiciary, parliament, police and the military, for example. Field presences also provide advice to national counterparts on cooperation with United Nations human rights mechanisms – treaty bodies, special procedures and the universal periodic review. OHCHR also develops programmes for human rights education and conducts capacity-building within civil society, from which minority rights advocates can also benefit.

There are four types of human rights field presences: OHCHR country offices, OHCHR regional offices, human rights components of peace missions and human rights advisers to United Nations country teams. In addition, OHCHR deploys rapid-response missions in response to emerging human rights crises (see fig. II), by providing surge capacity to human rights field presences when requested to support United Nations Resident Coordinators (see below), or technical and logistical support to missions mandated by the Human Rights Council or the Secretary-General.

Country offices

OHCHR country offices are established by agreement with the host Government. They reflect the mandate of the High Commissioner, including human rights observation, protection, technical cooperation and public reporting.

Persons belonging to minorities or minority groups can submit information about alleged human rights violations to a country office. While no particular form is required, the special procedures model questionnaires provide guidance and assistance in the preparation of communications.[24]

A letter or other communication containing sufficiently detailed and verified information, together with the name and contact details of the sender, should suffice in the first instance. Depending on the relevant context and available mechanisms for redress in a given country or situation, the country office may take action by, for example:

- Advising the complainant(s) on redress available domestically and/or transmitting the complaint to the competent national authorities;
- Informing the authorities and formulating recommendations on concrete measures which might be adopted in a particular case or cases, when, in the opinion of the office, the national procedures do not provide effective redress;
- Making recommendations to the national authorities for protection measures for victims and witnesses of human rights violation(s) (although the office is not a prosecuting body and does not substitute for the State in its obligation to investigate human rights violations);
- Assisting with the referral of complaints to appropriate United Nations human rights bodies and mechanisms;
- Referring the complainant(s) to non-governmental support groups, welfare organizations, hotlines, etc.;
- Directly addressing individual cases in meetings and discussions with Government representatives.

Country offices also support States in following up the recommendations of special procedures and treaty bodies, and on matters relating to the universal periodic review. They organize awareness-raising and training activities, and provide technical advice, in support of the submission of NGO or shadow reports to treaty bodies, specific information and reports to the Special Procedures Branch, and civil society stakeholder submissions during the universal periodic review process. Organizations working on minority issues can benefit from such activities.

[24] See www.ohchr.org/EN/HRBodies/SP/Pages/QuestionnairesforsubmittingInfo.aspx (accessed 29 November 2012).

OHCHR has 11 country offices (in Bolivia (Plurinational State of), Cambodia, Colombia, Guatemala, Guinea, Mauritania, Mexico, Nepal, Togo, Tunisia and Uganda) and two stand-alone offices, in Kosovo and the Occupied Palestinian Territory.

Regional offices

Regional offices are also established on the basis of an agreement with the host Government, and cover countries where there is no other OHCHR field presence. They complement the expertise of country presences by providing support on institutional and thematic issues in terms of capacity-building, fact-finding, advocacy and other activities. They focus on cross-cutting regional human rights concerns. They also support Governments with special procedures, follow-up on recommendations made by treaty bodies and matters relating to the universal periodic review. They work closely with regional and subregional NGOs and intergovernmental organizations, including in relation to the work of United Nations human rights mechanisms.

OHCHR has 10 regional offices, in East Africa (Addis Ababa), Southern Africa (Pretoria), West Africa (Dakar), South-East Asia (Bangkok), the Pacific (Suva), the Middle East (Beirut), Central Asia (Bishkek), Europe (Brussels), Central America (Panama City) and South America (Santiago de Chile). It also has a regional human rights centre in Central Africa (Yaoundé) and a human rights training and documentation centre for South-West Asia and the Arab region (Doha).

Human rights components of peace missions

OHCHR provides support to human rights components in United Nations peace missions. Based on Security Council resolutions establishing the relevant peace mission, the mandates of human rights components include human rights monitoring and investigation as well as technical cooperation.

Fifteen United Nations peace missions have a human rights component: UNAMA (Afghanistan), BNUB (Burundi), BINUCA (Central African Republic), UNOCI (Côte d'Ivoire), MONUSCO (the Democratic Republic of the Congo), UNIOGBIS (Guinea-Bissau), MINUSTAH (Haiti), UNAMI (Iraq), UNMIL (Liberia), UNSMIL (Libya), UNIPSIL (Sierra Leone), UNPOS (Somalia), UNMISS (South Sudan), UNAMID (Darfur, Sudan) and UNMIT (Timor-Leste).

Human rights advisers to United Nations country teams

The Resident Coordinator system encompasses all organizations of the United Nations system concerned with operational activities for development, regardless of their formal presence in the country. The system aims to bring United Nations agencies together to improve the efficiency and effectiveness of operational activities at country level. Human rights advisers are deployed at the request of the Resident Coordinator in a country and assist him or her, and the United Nations country team, to integrate human rights into their programmes and activities. They also advise on strategies to strengthen national human rights capacities; advise and provide training to independent national human rights institutions; build networks with and provide practical support to civil society actors; and provide operational support to human rights training and/or national capacity-building activities.

Resident Coordinators lead United Nations country teams in more than 130 countries and are the designated representatives of the United Nations Secretary-General for development operations. Working closely with Governments, Resident Coordinators and country teams promote the interests and mandates of the United Nations system.

OHCHR has 18 human rights advisers, in Ecuador, the former Yugoslav Republic of Macedonia, Honduras, Kenya, Madagascar, the Republic of Moldova, Niger, Papua New Guinea, Paraguay, the Russian Federation, Rwanda, Serbia, the South Caucasus region (based in Tbilisi and covering Georgia, Azerbaijan and Armenia), Sri Lanka, Tajikistan, Ukraine and West Africa (based in Dakar).

OHCHR field presences

There are a number of ways in which minority rights advocates might work with the OHCHR field presences. For example, they can alert OHCHR to deteriorating human rights situations and emerging trends concerning their communities; provide information to OHCHR on local, national and regional human rights developments; work in partnership with OHCHR on human rights seminars, workshops, training programmes and projects to raise awareness of human and minority rights; help OHCHR promote the ratification of human rights treaties and their implementation; bring to the attention of OHCHR the existence of discriminatory legislation, policies and practices; work with OHCHR and other counterparts on developing technical advice, programmes and activities to address issues pertaining to minority rights; and jointly organize activities aimed at furthering the promotion and protection of minority rights, in particular promoting the implementation of the Minorities Declaration.

Human rights field presences, in turn, contribute in many ways to the promotion and protection of the rights of persons belonging to minorities. The focus and content of such contributions vary, but may include, for example:

- Ensuring that specific attention is paid to the situation of minority groups in all monitoring activities;
- Identifying challenges to the realization of human rights by minorities in local contexts and working towards finding solutions;
- Identifying and addressing gaps in the protection of rights to which minorities are entitled;
- Ensuring that laws relating to minority rights and related issues are consistent with international human rights standards, including the Minorities Declaration, and that these standards are fully reflected in legislative initiatives;
- Encouraging the collection and analysis of data disaggregated along ethnic, religious and gender lines in order to better inform policymaking;
- Facilitating dialogue between minorities and Government officials at the central and local levels, including creating country-specific consultative structures for minorities where they do not presently exist;
- Working with minority advocates and other stakeholders towards the implementation of recommendations issued by human rights treaty bodies and special procedures, and those developed within the universal periodic review process, including facilitating their translation into local and minority languages;
- Working with the media towards more inclusive and unbiased reporting regarding minorities;
- Suggesting programmes and actions to enable minorities to express and develop their culture, language, religion, traditions and customs;
- Helping to ensure that persons belonging to minority groups have access to information relating to public policies and decisions that affect them, and facilitating the participation of minorities in decision-making;
- Facilitating dialogue with minority groups at the national, regional and local government levels;
- Facilitating capacity-building and networks for exchange of information and coordination of activities among minority rights advocates;

- Preparing and disseminating information materials regarding minority issues, including in minority languages;
- Facilitating the participation of minorities in the development, design, implementation and evaluation of United Nations programmes, particularly through United Nations advisory or consultative bodies;
- Working towards ensuring that minorities are able to benefit equitably from development and economic progress;
- Promoting positive measures to increase access for persons belonging to minority groups to educational opportunities and jobs;
- Assisting in the reform of discriminatory processes or electoral systems.

The OHCHR country office in the Plurinational State of Bolivia has established countering discrimination as one of its priorities. It focuses on Afro-descendant people, actively promoting their increased participation in the design and implementation of public policies. It has also been encouraging minority groups to increasingly use international, regional and national human rights mechanisms, through capacity-building and awareness-raising initiatives and facilitating dialogue among the different stakeholders.

Contacts and further information

Postal address
Office of the United Nations High Commissioner for Human Rights (OHCHR)
Palais des Nations
8-14 Avenue de la Paix
CH-1211 Geneva 10
Switzerland

Tel: 41 22 917 9220
E-mail: InfoDesk@ohchr.org
Website: www.ohchr.org

Visiting addresses
Palais Wilson
52 Rue des Pâquis
1201 Geneva
Switzerland

OHCHR-Motta
48 Avenue Giuseppe Motta
1202 Geneva
Switzerland

Key entry points to OHCHR for minority rights advocates are:

Indigenous Peoples and Minorities Section
Tel: 41 22 917 92 20

Fax: 41 22 928 90 66

E-mail: minorities@ohchr.org

Civil Society Section

Tel: 41 22 917 96 56

E-mail: civilsociety@ohchr.org

FOTCD teams:

Africa Section

Tel: 41 22 928 96 94

E-mail: au@ohchr.org

Middle East and North Africa Section

Tel: 41 22 928 91 53

E-mail: mena@ohchr.org

Asia-Pacific Section

Tel: 41 22 928 96 59

E-mail: apu@ohchr.org

Europe and Central Asia Section

Tel: 41 22 928 92 94

E-mail: enaca@ohchr.org

Americas Section

Tel: 41 22 928 91 67

E-mail: lac@ohchr.org

National Institutions and Regional Mechanisms Section

Tel: 41 22 928 94 67

E-mail: niu@ohchr.org

The OHCHR website provides a detailed overview of the human rights activities of the United Nations. Further information on how civil society can engage with OHCHR may be found in: *Working with the United Nations Human Rights Programme: A Handbook for Civil Society.*

Figure I. OHCHR organizational chart

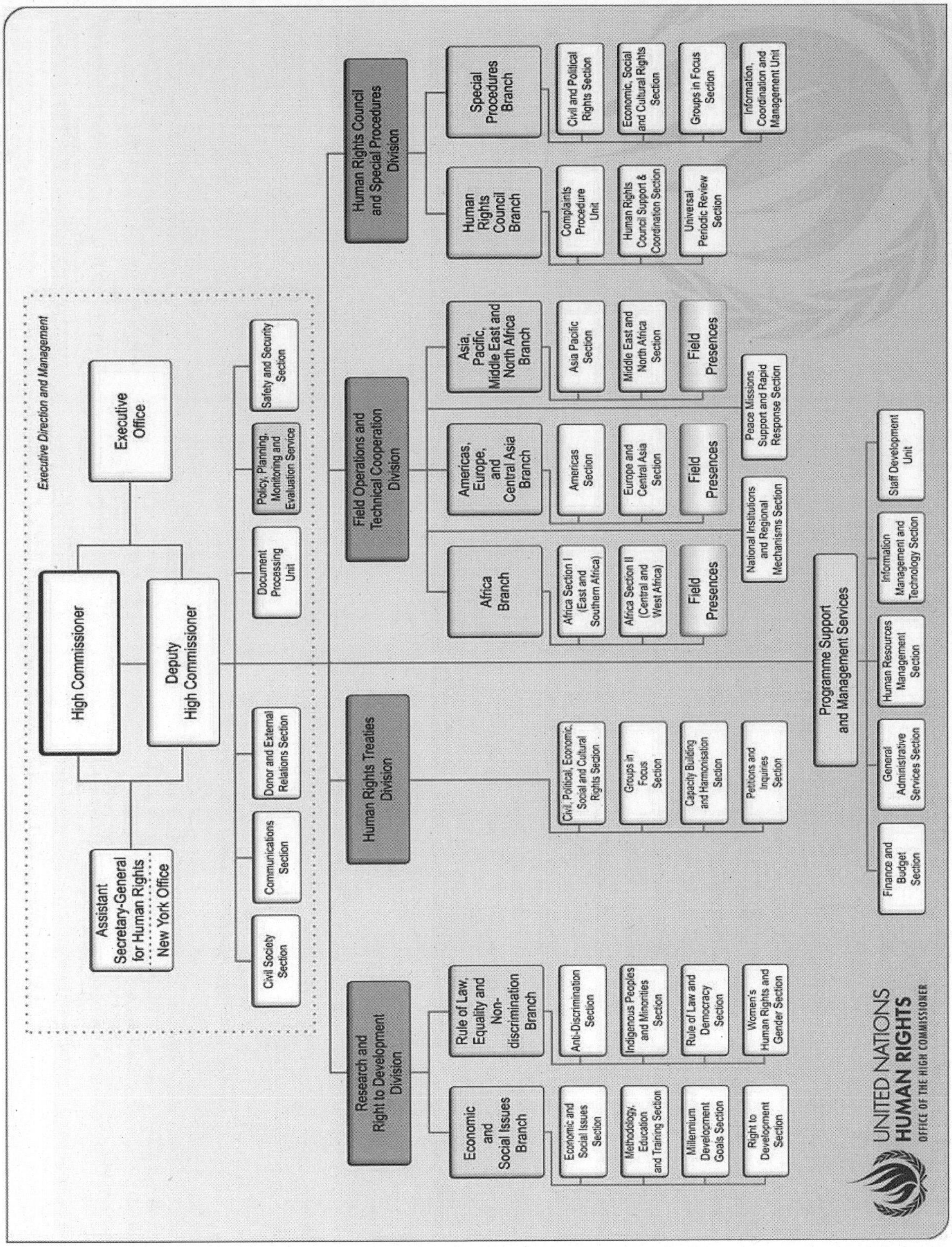

Figure II. OHCHR presences worldwide

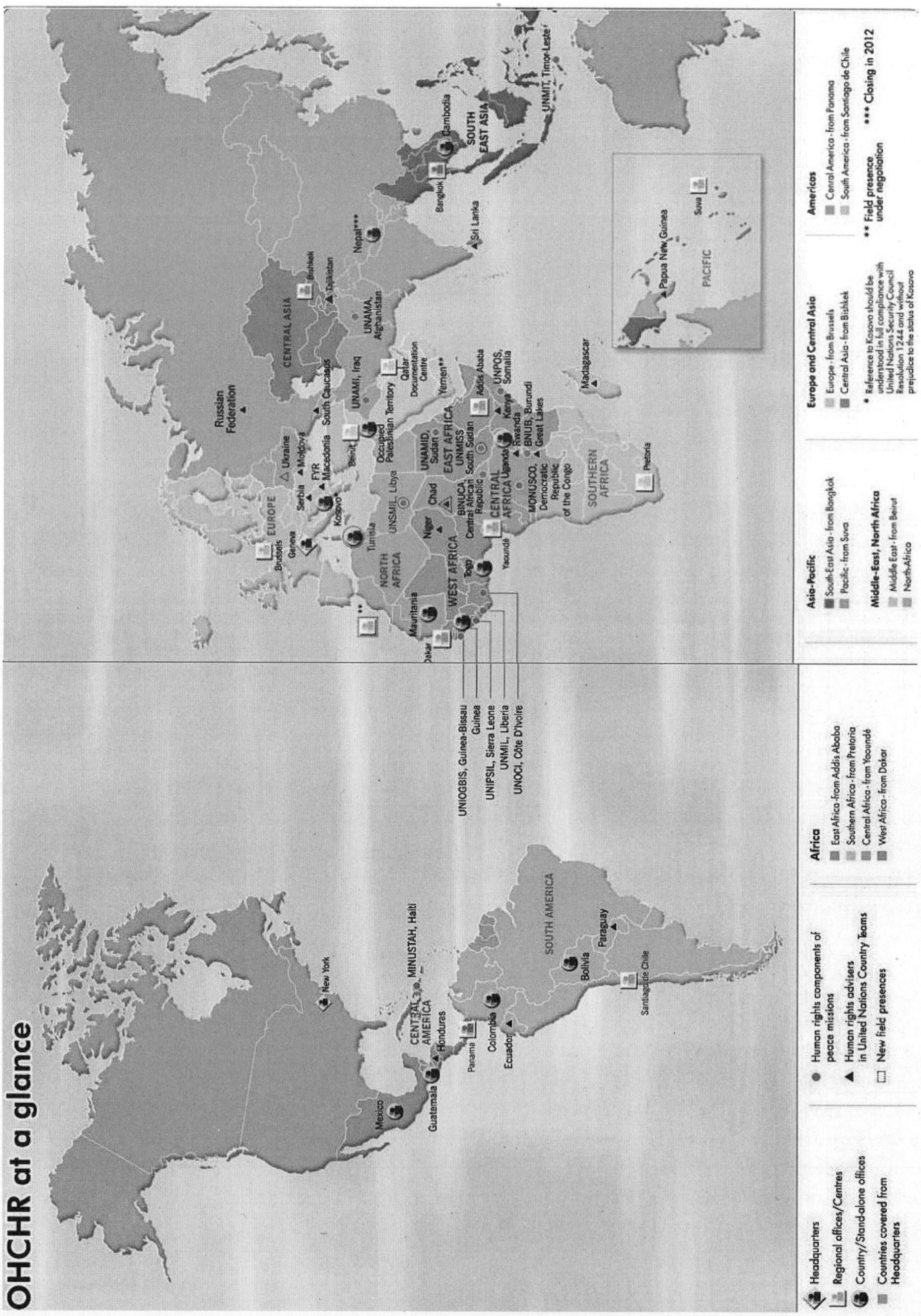

The boundaries and the names shown and the designations used on this map do not imply official endorsement or acceptance by the United Nations.

CHAPTER III

THE HUMAN RIGHTS COUNCIL AND ITS SUBSIDIARY BODIES

Summary: The Human Rights Council is the most important intergovernmental human rights body in the United Nations. It provides a number of avenues through which various concerns, including minority rights, may be made known to United Nations experts and Government representatives. Among the relevant human rights mechanisms established by the Council is the Forum on Minority Issues, which meets annually to discuss particular thematic issues relevant to minorities; the universal periodic review, which considers the human rights situation in every State Member of the United Nations every four and a half years; and the complaint procedure, under which communications alleging a consistent pattern of gross violations of the human rights of minorities may be submitted to the Council for consideration.

This chapter provides information about the work of the Human Rights Council and its subsidiary organs (see fig. III), and offers advice on how minorities can participate in their meetings or otherwise raise awareness of issues of particular concern to minorities. The special procedures system of independent experts and other mechanisms created and/or assumed by the Council is described separately in chapter IV.

Figure III. Human Rights Council organizational chart

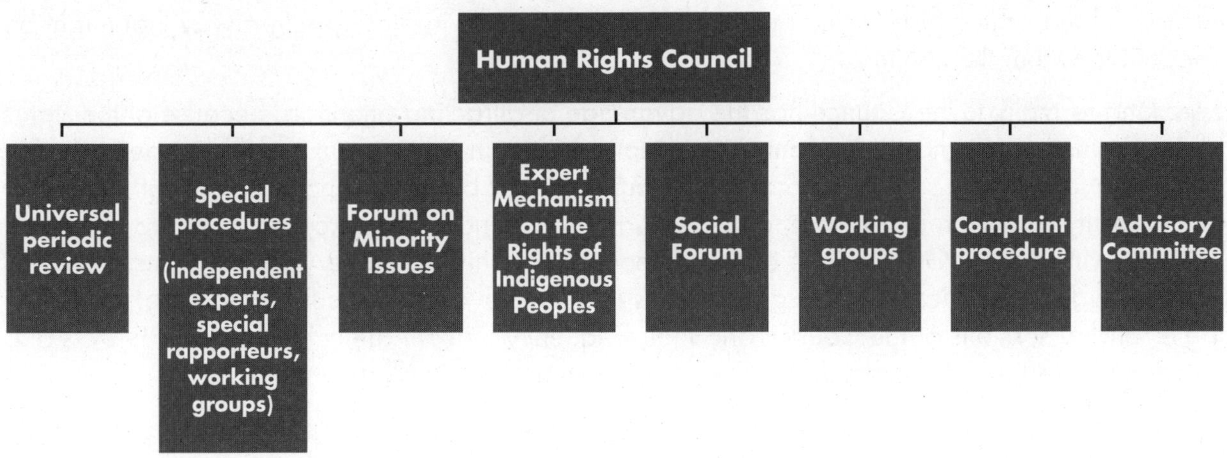

The Human Rights Council

The Council is the successor to the Commission on Human Rights, which it replaced in 2006.[25] The Council is composed of 47 Member States, each represented by a Government delegation. Members of the Council are elected by majority vote through a secret ballot in the General Assembly. A candidate's human rights record is taken into account: "members elected to the Council shall uphold the highest standards in the promotion and protection of human rights". The term of service is three years and members are not eligible for immediate re-election after two consecutive terms. Membership is distributed among the regional groups; Africa has 13 members; Asia, 13; Latin America and the Caribbean, 8; Western Europe and other States, 7; and Eastern Europe, 6.

[25] General Assembly resolution 60/251.

The Council holds at least three regular sessions annually, for a total of no fewer than 10 weeks. The main session takes place in March. The Council can hold special sessions upon the request of a member State, if supported by at least one third of the membership. To date, the Council has held 18 such sessions, the subjects of which have addressed country-specific situations in the Syrian Arab Republic, the Middle East, the Democratic Republic of the Congo, Darfur, Haiti, Myanmar, the Sudan, Sri Lanka, Côte d'Ivoire and Libya, as well as thematic topics, such as the impact of the world financial crisis on human rights and the global food crisis. The Council adopts a number of resolutions and decisions each year, and its sessions attract a large number of observer States, representatives of United Nations specialized agencies and regional institutions, NGOs and others. Those resolutions which express concern over or even condemnation of the human rights situation in a particular country are usually the subject of intense debate and lobbying by States.

Notwithstanding the Council's intergovernmental nature, NGOs are essential in providing it with information. Many of the human rights issues addressed by the Council (and its predecessor, the Commission on Human Rights) have benefited from the forward-thinking initiatives and advocacy of NGOs.

The Council can be used as a venue for initiating dialogue with States which can subsequently be continued at country level. Given that Government delegations often operate on instructions from their capital, discussions between the Council and the relevant foreign ministry is often as effective as having a delegation appear in Geneva. On the other hand, only the actual presence of minority rights advocates will enable response to last-minute developments or unexpected resistance. The presence of minority advocates in a United Nations forum might also increase the chances of the United Nations having a fruitful dialogue with the State concerned. The "neutral" territory of the United Nations can make it easier to engage in dialogue in a way that might be impossible within the country.

Speaking formally to the Council has the advantage of attracting attention, because of the status of the Council as the most important United Nations human rights forum and the wide audience that it provides. At the same time, however, your issue will be competing with a great number of others for the attention of States and the media. The Council is an excellent place to meet and network with other NGOs, and it offers a good opportunity to make your concerns known to a much wider constituency, although progress is often slow and difficult to measure. However, the extended sessions of the Council and their frequency make it difficult for smaller NGOs and those not based in Geneva to participate on a regular basis in all the meetings.[26]

Statements in the Council are normally made in the order in which representatives ask to speak, with priority given to members of the Council, observer States and organizations, and thereafter to NGOs which have consultative status with the United Nations Economic and Social Council. Only these NGOs can be accredited to participate in sessions of the Human Rights Council as observers. Organizations applying for consultative status with the Economic and Social Council must respond to a questionnaire and provide detailed information about their structure, finances and other matters. The application process and other matters relating to NGOs are handled by the Non-Governmental Organizations Section of the Department of Economic, Social and Cultural Affairs in New York.[27]

Once accredited as observers, NGOs in consultative status enjoy a number of prerogatives within the participatory arrangements provided for by the Council. They are able to submit

[26] Human Rights Council sessions are webcast live; see www.unmultimedia.org/tv/webcast/c/un-human-rights-council.html (accessed 29 November 2012).

[27] Economic and Social Council resolution 1996/31. See http://esango.un.org/civilsociety/ (accessed 29 November 2012).

written statements to the Council ahead of a given session; make oral interventions during all substantive items of the Council agenda; participate in interactive dialogues with special procedure mandate-holders; and organize "parallel events" on issues relevant to the work of the Council.[28] In addition, the President of the Human Rights Council and its secretariat hold regular NGO briefings throughout the sessions. NGOs in consultative status should request accreditation for their representatives to attend Council sessions and meetings of other United Nations bodies, pursuant to procedures set forth by the Economic and Social Council and the bodies themselves. These procedures are not onerous, but complying with them does require a certain degree of planning and prior notification.

While lack of consultative status can be a serious impediment for those wishing to work within the United Nations system, it is usually relatively easy to consult with accredited NGOs and provide them with information. Collaboration among NGOs is common, and many statements to the Council are delivered jointly by a number of NGOs. Several Geneva-based NGOs which can assist with practical arrangements as well as advice on how to participate most effectively in Council meetings are listed at the end of this chapter. Perhaps the best known international NGO focusing on minority issues is the London-based Minority Rights Group International (see annex II).

Universal periodic review

The universal periodic review (UPR) was mandated in 2006 by General Assembly resolution 60/251, which created the Human Rights Council. The resolution instructed the Council to "undertake a universal periodic review, based on objective and reliable information, of the fulfilment by each State of its human rights obligations and commitments in a manner which ensures universality of coverage and equal treatment with respect to all States". A year later, the Council adopted an "institution-building package" which remains the guide for its work.[29] This package details the specifics of the universal periodic review – a unique mechanism that emphasizes State responsibility to respect and implement human rights and fundamental freedoms.

The universal periodic review is a State-driven process of peer review of the human rights situation in every State Member of the United Nations. After its first four-year cycle it was extended to every four and a half years. It is substantively based on human rights obligations contained in the Charter of the United Nations, Universal Declaration of Human Rights and human rights instruments to which the State is a party. The principles on which the universal periodic review is based include establishment of "a cooperative mechanism based on objective and reliable information and on interactive dialogue" with the State under consideration and promotion of the "universality, interdependence, indivisibility and interrelatedness of all human rights". In addition, it is designed not to be overly burdensome on States and not to absorb "a disproportionate amount of time, human and financial resources". It seeks the "improvement of the human rights situation on the ground", enhancement of State capacity and cooperation, thus offering an opportunity to highlight the situation of persons belonging to minorities in a country and advocate for the implementation of their rights.

The timing of a review depends on when the Member State was reviewed in the first review cycle.[30] The review is conducted in two stages. The first consists of a three-and-a-half-hour oral dialogue with the State in an open-ended working group of the Council. Discussion is based

28 *Working with the United Nations Human Rights Programme: A Handbook for Civil Society*, pp. 90–94.

29 Resolution 5/1; see A/HRC/5/21.

30 The order of review in the second cycle (2012-2016) is available from www2.ohchr.org/SPdocs/UPR/UPR-FullCycleCalendar_2nd.doc (accessed 29 November 2012).

on three reports: (1) a report prepared by the State under review; (2) comments specific to the reviewed State from treaty bodies, special procedures and other United Nations entities, compiled by OHCHR; and (3) information from other stakeholders, including national human rights institutions and civil society actors, also compiled by OHCHR. The last two are limited to 10 pages each.

The outcome emphasizes cooperation and full involvement of the State. The working group adopts an "outcome" document, which includes a summary of the review process, conclusions and recommendations, and any voluntary commitments that the State may make. The Council in plenary adopts the outcome sometime after the review, giving the State an opportunity to determine which of the recommendations it accepts and which it does not. The outcome also includes recommendations which need further examination. It is neither an assessment nor an evaluation of whether or not the State is living up to its human rights obligations.

NGOs and other stakeholders may submit information for inclusion in the compilation prepared by OHCHR (the third of the above-mentioned reports), but they can only observe, and not participate in, the working group session – provided they have consultative status with the Economic and Social Council. At the plenary Council session, United Nations entities and stakeholders, including national human rights institutions and NGOs, have the opportunity to make "general comments" before the outcome is adopted.[31]

Since the universal periodic review addresses the entire range of human rights issues, minority rights are rarely at the forefront of debates. However, the situations of minorities have been raised on a number of occasions, for example, regarding Roma in Slovakia, Tibetans and Uyghurs in China, Oromos in Ethiopia and various minorities in Viet Nam. It is worthwhile, therefore, for minority advocates to contribute written information to OHCHR prior to a review of a State. It also needs to be noted that the second review cycle will focus on implementation of the recommendations made in the first review. The NGO information should therefore concentrate on any recommendations on minorities made in the first review and their implementation (or lack of implementation).

NGOs can also contact the Government of a member State of the Council, directly or indirectly, to request that its representative include a relevant minority issue among its recommendations. At the very least, the universal periodic review reinforces the principle that every State has human rights obligations, and reinforces the declarations in the Charter of the United Nations and Universal Declaration of Human Rights that all rights are to be enjoyed "without distinction as to race, sex, language or religion".

As is true for many United Nations and other international mechanisms, the full potential of the universal periodic review can be realized only if civil society contributes to the process and publicizes its outcome at home. Even if they are couched in general terms, the recommendations accepted by the State, and any additional commitments that the State may make, should help minority rights advocates to raise their human rights concerns with the authorities.

Forum on Minority Issues

The Forum on Minority Issues was established pursuant to Human Rights Council resolution 6/15, to provide a platform for promoting dialogue and cooperation on issues pertaining to national or ethnic, religious and linguistic minorities, and contributing to the work of the Independent Expert on minority issues (see chap. IV).[32] Each session of the Forum considers a particular theme and is

[31] Technical guidelines for stakeholders' submissions are available from www.ohchr.org/EN/HRBodies/UPR/Documents/TechnicalGuideEN.pdf (accessed 29 November 2012).

[32] See www2.ohchr.org/english/bodies/hrcouncil/minority/forum.htm (accessed 29 November 2012).

chaired by a different expert on minority issues, appointed by the President of the Human Rights Council. The Independent Expert is responsible for guiding Forum sessions, preparing its annual two-day meetings, making recommendations to the Human Rights Council for thematic subjects to be considered, and reporting on the thematic recommendations of the Forum to the Council.

The Forum's mandate is to "identify and analyse best practices, challenges, opportunities and initiatives for the further implementation of the Declaration". It seeks to provide concrete and tangible outcomes in the form of thematic recommendations of practical value to all stakeholders. In its first four sessions, the Forum dealt respectively with the themes of education, effective political participation, effective participation in economic life, and guaranteeing the rights of minority women and girls. The Forum's recommendations, drafted by the Independent Expert based on discussions at the session, are presented to the Human Rights Council and posted on the Forum's website, as is a summary of the discussions. Forum sessions, which are held at the United Nations in Geneva, include formal presentations by invited panellists and oral interventions by other participants. All participants – whether they be Government representatives, NGOs, minority advocates or individual experts – are given an opportunity to speak. Interventions during the annual sessions may be directed to various aspects of the theme under discussion and may describe specific situations relevant to the topic, offer examples of good practices or provide scholarly analysis.

As the only annual United Nations meeting dedicated to minority issues, the Forum offers a unique opportunity for engagement and dialogue with a wide range of stakeholders, including representatives of Member States, United Nations specialized agencies, human rights treaty bodies, intergovernmental and regional organizations, NGOs, national human rights institutions, minority representatives, academics, experts and representatives of civil society. The Forum is open to active participation by all stakeholders and pursues creative collaborations and ways of engaging. To participate in Forum sessions, pre-registration with the OHCHR Secretariat is required, but there are few restrictions and NGOs are not required to have consultative status with the Economic and Social Council in order to attend.

The Forum on Minority Issues also offers an opportunity for minority advocates, experts and States to share experiences and opinions informally, and is one means of ensuring that minority issues remain on the Council's agenda. Suggestions for annual themes, discussion panellists or other matters may be given to the Independent Expert on minority issues and/or the OHCHR staff who support the mandate (e-mail minorityforum@ohchr.org).

Working Groups and other subsidiary organs

The work of the Human Rights Council is not limited to its periodic sessions in Geneva. The Council establishes working groups, in particular with the aim of drafting new standards, such as that which drafted the Optional Protocol to the International Covenant on Economic, Social and Cultural Rights, which was opened for signature in September 2009. Working groups of the Council include those related to the Durban process, such as the Intergovernmental Working Group on the Effective Implementation of the Durban Declaration and Programme of Action, the Ad Hoc Committee on the elaboration of complementary standards and the Working Group of Experts on People of African Descent (see chap. IV). NGO participation in working groups is often less formal than participation in plenary sessions of the Council. The OHCHR website provides a calendar of meetings.

The Council also convenes an annual three-day meeting of its Social Forum, which offers the opportunity for open and interactive dialogue among Governments, independent experts, intergovernmental organizations and, in particular, members of civil society. Originated by the former Sub-Commission on the Promotion and Protection of Human Rights for the purpose of discussing economic, social and cultural rights, the Social Forum discusses issues linked with the national and international environment needed for the promotion of the enjoyment of all human rights by all. Recent discussions have addressed themes such as the right to development, the impact of climate change, negative impacts of economic and financial crises on efforts to combat poverty, and the role of women in the fight against poverty and the right to participation. Discussions at the Social Forum may address issues of particular importance to minorities and hence minorities are encouraged to take active part in its preparation and organization.[33]

The Expert Mechanism on the Rights of Indigenous Peoples, created by the Council in resolution 6/36, meets annually for up to five days.[34]

Complaint procedure

The complaint procedure of the Human Rights Council addresses "consistent patterns of gross and reliably attested violations of all human rights and all fundamental freedoms occurring in any part of the world and under any circumstances". It is based on the former Commission's procedure 1503, improved to ensure that it is impartial, objective, efficient, victim-oriented and conducted in a timely manner.

The complaint procedure of the Human Rights Council is the only universal complaint procedure covering all human rights and fundamental freedoms in all States Members of the United Nations. Communications under this procedure are not tied to the acceptance of treaty obligations by the State concerned or the existence of a special procedures mandate. However, the procedure does not provide a remedy for individual violations, nor does it provide compensation.

The key requirement for a communication under the complaint procedure is that it must involve a "consistent pattern of gross and reliably attested human rights violations", not simply an individual case, except where the communication alone or in combination with other communications appears to reveal a consistent pattern of gross and reliably attested violations of human rights and fundamental freedoms.

A minority rights NGO could invoke the procedure in a situation of persistent de facto discrimination or discriminatory legislation, provided that the alleged violations were sufficiently serious.

Submission and consideration of complaints

In order to be admissible under the Human Rights Council complaint procedure, a communication (i.e., complaint) should include:

- Identification of the person(s) or organization(s) submitting the communication (this information will be kept confidential, if requested); anonymous complaints are not admissible;
- Description of the relevant facts in as much detail as possible, providing names of alleged victims, dates, location and other evidence;
- The purpose of the complaint and the rights allegedly violated;
- Explanation of how the case may reveal a pattern of gross and reliably attested human rights violations rather than individual violations;
- Details of how domestic remedies have been exhausted, or explanation of how such remedies would be ineffective or unreasonably prolonged.

33 See www.ohchr.org/EN/Issues/Poverty/SForum/Pages/SForumIndex.aspx (accessed 29 November 2012).

34 See www.ohchr.org/EN/Issues/IPeoples/EMRIP/Pages/EMRIPIndex.aspx (accessed 29 November 2012).

A communication should not use language deemed to be abusive or insulting. In addition, it should not refer to a case that appears to reveal a consistent pattern of gross and reliably attested violations of human rights already being dealt with by a special procedure, treaty body or other United Nations or similar regional complaints procedure in the field of human rights. Furthermore, the complaint should not be manifestly politically motivated and its object should be consistent with the Charter of the United Nations, the Universal Declaration of Human Rights and other applicable instruments in the field of human rights law. It must not be exclusively based on reports disseminated by mass media.

Stage 1: Initial screening

The OHCHR Secretariat together with the Chair of the Working Group on Communications screens all communications as they arrive, on the basis of admissibility criteria, and discards those found to be "manifestly ill founded" or anonymous. If a communication is not screened out, the author receives a written acknowledgement and the communication is sent to the State concerned for reply.

Stage 2: Working Group on Communications

The Working Group on Communications is made up of appointed members of the Human Rights Council Advisory Committee and is mandated to meet at least twice a year for five days each session. It examines complaints which have passed the initial screening stage and any replies received from States, with a view to bringing to the attention of the Working Group on Situations any particular situation that appears to reveal a consistent pattern of gross and reliably attested violations of human rights and fundamental freedoms.

Stage 3: Working Group on Situations

The Working Group on Situations is composed of five members of the Human Rights Council, who serve in their personal capacity, and is mandated to meet at least twice a year, for five days each session, to consider situations referred to it. It produces a report for the Council on consistent patterns of gross and reliably attested violations and makes specific recommendations on action to be taken. Alternatively, it may decide to keep a situation under review or to dismiss a case.

Stage 4: Human Rights Council

The Council considers situations brought to its attention by the Working Group on Situations in closed plenary meetings as frequently as necessary, but at least once a year. The report of the Working Group on Situations is examined in a confidential manner, unless the Council decides otherwise. Based on its consideration of a situation, the Council may take any of the following actions, usually in the form of a resolution or decision:

- To discontinue considering the situation when further consideration/action is not warranted;
- To keep the situation under review and request the State concerned to provide further information within a reasonable period of time;
- To keep the situation under review and appoint an independent and highly qualified expert to monitor the situation and report back to the Council;
- To discontinue reviewing the matter under the confidential complaint procedure in order to take up public consideration of the same;
- To recommend to OHCHR to provide technical cooperation, capacity-building assistance or advisory services to the State concerned.

The authors of communications and the States concerned are informed of the proceedings at all key stages of the complaint procedure.

All material provided by individuals and States, as well as the decisions taken at the various stages of the procedure, remain confidential. This also applies to situations that have been discontinued.

Communications submitted under the complaint procedure should be addressed to:

Human Rights Council Branch
Complaint Procedure Unit
OHCHR-UNOG
1211 Geneva 10
Switzerland
Fax: 41 22 917 90 11
E-mail: CP@ohchr.org

Advisory Committee

The Advisory Committee of the Human Rights Council replaces the former Sub-Commission on the Promotion and Protection of Human Rights. It consists of 18 experts, who serve in their personal capacity for renewable three-year terms. The experts are nominated by States (which are encouraged to consult with civil society before doing so) and elected by the Council. The Committee convenes for one or two sessions each year, for a maximum of 10 working days.

The Committee provides research-based advice on a variety of thematic issues, upon request by the Council. It may also make proposals to the Council for enhancing its procedural efficiency or for further research. During its first two cycles, the Committee initiated research on a number of thematic issues. It submitted to the Council a draft declaration on human rights education and training, as well as reports on discrimination in the context of the right to food. Member States and observers – including States which are not members of the Council, specialized agencies, other intergovernmental organizations, national human rights institutions and NGOs in consultative status with the Economic and Social Council – are encouraged to participate in the work of the Advisory Committee; interested NGOs should contact the OHCHR Secretariat. The degree of participation is similar to that pertaining to the Human Rights Council (see above).[35]

Contacts and further information

Various NGOs can facilitate your stay in Geneva and participation in Council sessions. Among them are:

International Service for Human Rights
(for information on coverage of minority issues at all United Nations meetings, training and strategy)
Tel: 41 22 919 71 00
Fax: 41 22 919 71 25
E-mail: ishr@worldcom.ch
Website: www.ishr.ch

Mandat International
(for accommodation, word-processing, documentation, office space, fax and e-mail services and photocopying)
Tel: 41 22 959 88 55
Fax: 41 22 959 88 51
E-mail: info@mandint.org

[35] Specific rules for NGOs are spelled out at www2.ohchr.org/english/bodies/hrcouncil/advisorycommittee/ngo_participation.htm (accessed 29 November 2012).

Website: www.mandint.org

Geneva International Welcome Centre
(for accommodation and information on hospitals, doctors, banks, restaurants and other services)

Tel: 41 22 918 02 70
Fax: 41 22 918 02 79
Website: www.cagi.ch/en.php

There are several publications which describe the bodies and procedures discussed in this chapter in greater detail, although most do not deal specifically with minorities. These include: *Working with the United Nations Human Rights Programme: A Handbook for Civil Society.*

CHAPTER IV

THE UNITED NATIONS SPECIAL PROCEDURES

Summary: "Special procedures" is a term that covers a wide range of mechanisms of the Human Rights Council to address either specific country situations or thematic issues. Special procedures have developed into one of the most effective ways of mobilizing the resources of the United Nations to respond to specific human rights concerns. In practice, special procedures are specific persons or working groups. Their mandates vary, as do their activities. This chapter focuses on the special procedures which are most relevant to minority issues, including the Independent Expert on minority issues; the Special Rapporteur on freedom of religion or belief; the Special Rapporteur on contemporary forms of racism, racial discrimination, xenophobia and related intolerance; the Independent Expert in the field of cultural rights; and the Working Group of Experts on people of African descent.

Special procedures receive their mandates from the Human Rights Council. Their activities include investigating and reporting annually on human rights issues, and offering recommendations for measures to be taken, including through technical assistance, to address those problems. Special procedures take action upon individual complaints, conduct studies, help to interpret international human rights law, provide advice on technical cooperation at the country level, and engage in outreach and general promotional and educational activities. Unlike United Nations treaty bodies, special procedures can be resorted to even if a State has not ratified a relevant instrument or treaty, and it is generally not necessary to have exhausted domestic remedies in order to access them. NGOs and minority advocates may contact the mechanisms directly (through the OHCHR Secretariat) with information, suggestions, questions or proposals for action. Despite their limited financial and human resources, special procedures provide one of the most valuable points of contact on minority rights issues.

Special procedures go by a variety of designations; they may be working groups, special rapporteurs, independent experts or representatives or, in a few cases, (special) representatives of the Secretary-General. These titles do not reflect any hierarchy or indicate different levels of authority. Of primary importance is each procedure's mandate, which is defined by the resolution creating the procedure.[36]

Country-specific mandates usually call on mandate holders to examine, monitor, advise and publicly report on human rights situations in specific countries or territories. In November 2012 there were 10 such mandates.[37] The Council takes the initiative to create new procedures for particular States only under extraordinary circumstances.

There are 36 *thematic* mandates, each concerned with a particular issue.[38] While persons belonging to minorities may be affected by any of these issues, of particular relevance is the Independent Expert on minority issues, and, for example, the special procedures on migrants, freedom of opinion and expression, human rights defenders, indigenous peoples, education and countering terrorism. The mechanisms on freedom of religion or belief, people of African

[36] It is important to note that many of the special procedures not discussed in this chapter also address minority issues in their work, as they are able to identify thematic issues related to their mandates and highlight both areas of concern and positive examples of State action.

[37] See www.ohchr.org/EN/HRBodies/SP/Pages/Countries.aspx (accessed 29 November 2012).

[38] See www.ohchr.org/EN/HRBodies/SP/Pages/Themes.aspx (accessed 29 November 2012).

descent, contemporary forms of racism and cultural rights also regularly pay attention to minority concerns. These mechanisms are discussed more fully below.

All mandate holders of the special procedures serve in their personal capacity, and do not receive a salary or other financial compensation for their work from the United Nations.[39] They are not United Nations staff members but are supported by OHCHR; they enjoy diplomatic immunity when they are carrying out their mandate. Over the past few years, special procedures have been trying to enhance their coordination and coherence as a system of independent experts, through a coordination committee that supports the harmonization of their working methods and advocates on behalf of the system.

The independence of special procedures is crucial to their ability to fulfil their functions impartially. A code of conduct reiterates this independence and calls upon States to cooperate with special procedures, but it also emphasizes that special procedures are to focus exclusively on the respective mandate, maintain the trust of stakeholders (including States), seek to engage in a dialogue with States and ensure that full consideration is given to State responses.[40]

Some special procedures intervene directly with States through *communications* on specific allegations of violations of human rights which fall within their mandates. An intervention can relate to a human rights violation that has already occurred, is ongoing or has a high risk of occurring. The process usually involves sending a letter to the State concerned requesting information and comments on the allegation and, where necessary, that preventive or investigatory action be taken.

Upon receiving information about an alleged violation, special procedures send a letter of allegation or urgent appeal to the Government. *Letters of allegation* are based on information relating to ongoing or non-urgent issues of concern and seek to obtain information from and the views of a State. *Urgent appeals* normally reflect more immediate concern about alleged violations and may call for immediate action by a State to cease acts that allegedly violate human rights or to protect an individual or group from harm. In 2011, 645 communications were sent to 131 States; 72 per cent were joint communications involving several mandates, a practice that is becoming increasingly common.

The decision to intervene directly is at the discretion of the special procedure mandate holder and will depend on the criteria established by him or her, the authority granted under the mandate and the requirements of the code of conduct. The criteria will generally relate to the reliability of the source, the credibility of information received and the degree of detail provided. However, because the criteria and the means of taking action upon receipt of a complaint vary, it is necessary to submit a communication in accordance with the specific requirements established by each special procedure.

For a communication to be assessed, it must identify the alleged victim(s), perpetrators of the violation, and date and place of the incident, and provide a detailed description of the incident in which the alleged violation occurred. While the identification of the person or organization submitting a communication may be kept confidential upon request, it must be indicated with the communication. Other details pertaining to the alleged violation may be required by the relevant thematic mandates (e.g., past and present places of detention of the victim, medical certificate based on examination of the victim, identification of witnesses to the alleged violation, any measures undertaken to seek redress locally, etc.). Communications which contain abusive

[39] A visual directory of special procedures, including e-mail addresses, is available from www2.ohchr.org/english/ohchrreport2011/web_version/media/pdf/18_Visual_directory_of_special_procedures.pdf (accessed 29 November 2012).

[40] Human Rights Council resolution 5/2.

language or are obviously politically motivated are not considered. To facilitate the consideration of reported violations, several mandates have developed questionnaires for those who wish to report.[41] However, communications are considered even if they are not submitted on such a questionnaire.

Several of the thematic mechanisms have a specific submission format, including those mandates which allow "urgent actions". These include the Special Rapporteur on extrajudicial, summary or arbitrary executions; the Special Rapporteur on violence against women; the Working Group on Arbitrary Detention; the Working Group on Enforced and Involuntary Disappearances; the Special Rapporteur on the promotion and protection of the right to freedom of opinion and expression; and the Special Representative on human rights defenders.

Developments subsequent to a report should always be brought to the attention of the rapporteur, expert or group, irrespective of whether they tend to disprove or confirm the allegation. This helps the mechanism to act more effectively and avoid mistakes. It is important to note that communications and responses received from Governments are confidential, until they are reported by mandate holders to the Human Rights Council. From 2011, all mandate holders' communications are compiled by country in alphabetical and chronological order in common reports, presented at each regular session of the Council.

For specific information on communication procedures, consult the web page of the particular special procedure.[42] The special procedures may be contacted as follows:

Quick Response Desk, Special Procedures Branch
Office of the United Nations High Commissioner for Human Rights (OHCHR)
Palais des Nations
8-14, Avenue de la Paix
CH-1211 Geneva 10
Switzerland
Fax: 41 22 917 90 06
E-mail: SPBInfo@ohchr.org (for general inquiries and information)
urgent-action@ohchr.org (for individual cases only).

Communications should indicate in the subject line of the e-mail or fax, or on the cover of the envelope, which special procedure is being addressed. As the contact address for communications is the same for all special procedures, clearly indicate the main subject or purpose of the correspondence; this will prompt a more timely response. It is also essential to indicate whether the correspondence is for the purpose of submitting information on a thematic issue or an individual complaint.

Other types of information or requests (e.g., an invitation to attend a conference or a request to meet the mandate holders) should be addressed to the general e-mail address above, or to the generic addresses of individual mandates (available on the special procedures website).

Mandate holders may carry out *country visits* to investigate the human rights situation at the national level or in pursuit of a thematic mandate, but such a visit may take place only with the agreement of the State concerned. Mandate holders typically write a letter of request to visit the country, and, if agreed, the State extends an invitation to visit. Currently, 89 States have issued

41 See www.ohchr.org/EN/HRBodies/SP/Pages/QuestionnairesforsubmittingInfo.aspx (accessed 29 November 2012).

42 The home page for all the special procedures is www2.ohchr.org/english/bodies/chr/special/index.htm (accessed 29 November 2012).

"standing invitations" to all mandates, which indicates their willingness in principle to invite any special procedure mandate at a mutually agreed time.[43]

Standing invitations are often issued or pledged when a State declares its candidacy for the Human Rights Council or while it is being reviewed under the universal periodic review. Mandate holders commonly undertake two or three country visits each year and base their selection of countries to which they request an invitation according to a range of criteria.

Country visits allow experts to assess the country's general human rights situation and to review institutional, legal, judicial and administrative developments as they pertain to their respective mandates. Experts usually meet with national and local authorities, including the executive, the judiciary and Members of Parliament; human rights institutions; NGOs; civil society organizations; and victims of human rights violations or their representatives. They often meet with local media representatives at the end of their mission, to issue preliminary observations that they will have discussed with the Government. A mission report including findings and recommendations is made public and submitted to the Council.

Country visits are an important tool for minority advocates. They can create momentum for further work on the ground, give visibility to minority issues and provide an opportunity for change at the domestic level. They are also an opportunity to voice minority concerns in international forums without having to travel to Geneva. Minority advocates can become involved in country visits at three different stages. First, they may make suggestions and send a request for a country visit to a mandate holder explaining why such a mission would be relevant to the mandate, desirable and timely. Second, once a country visit has been agreed, minority advocates can advise the mandate holder on where to go, whom to meet and what to address. They can also inform and prepare their organizations and communities to make the most of their interaction with the mandate holder. Third, they can suggest recommendations that would be useful for their communities. Fourth, they can disseminate the report, monitor its implementation and report back to the mandate holder.

Special procedures submit *annual reports* to the Council; some mechanisms are also requested to present an interim report to the United Nations General Assembly, which meets from September to December. The annual reports discuss the working methods, theoretical analysis, general trends and developments with regard to the mandate, and may contain general or specific recommendations; reports on country visits are usually presented as addenda. Reports have also contained summaries of communications transmitted to Governments.

Special rapporteurs or representatives, experts and Chairs of working groups hold *annual meetings*, which provide an opportunity for the special procedures to meet and exchange views with representatives of States, the Bureau of the Council, the United Nations Secretariat, NGOs, agencies, funds and programmes. The Special Procedures Branch of OHCHR serves as the secretariat for these meetings, during which there is also a joint meeting with Chairs of the human rights treaty bodies. Much of the discussion is concerned with enhancing working methods and improving coordination and cooperation among these mechanisms, which in turn may have an impact on relationships between the mechanisms and States and NGOs, respectively.

The Independent Expert on minority issues

While a number of United Nations human rights bodies and mechanisms are concerned with issues of discrimination, racism or xenophobia – frequently experienced by minorities – the Independent Expert on minority issues is requested to specifically consider the situation of

[43] See www.ohchr.org/EN/HRBodies/SP/Pages/Invitations.aspx (accessed 29 November 2012).

national, ethnic, religious and linguistic minorities and the rights of such groups.[44] Thus, the Independent Expert on minority issues should be a key focal point for the Council's activities on issues related to minorities.

Mandate of the Independent Expert

The mandate of the Independent Expert on minority issues is one of over 30 thematic human rights mandates. It was created in 2005 by the former Commission on Human Rights, extended for the first time in 2008 by the Human Rights Council and renewed again by its resolution 16/6. The resolution requests the Independent Expert to:

- Promote the implementation of the Declaration on the Rights of Persons Belonging to National or Ethnic, Religious and Linguistic Minorities, including through consultations with Governments, taking into account existing international standards and national legislation concerning minorities;
- Identify best practices and possibilities for technical cooperation with the Office of the United Nations High Commissioner, at the request of Governments;
- Apply a gender perspective in his or her work;
- Cooperate closely, while avoiding duplication, with existing relevant United Nations bodies, mandates and mechanisms and with regional organizations;
- Take into account the views of non-governmental organizations on matters pertaining to his or her mandate;
- Guide the work of the Forum on Minority Issues, as decided by the Council in its resolution 6/15;
- Submit annual reports on his or her activities to the Council, including recommendations for effective strategies for the better implementation of the rights of persons belonging to minorities.

The Independent Expert is clearly called upon to fully engage with organizations working in the field of minority issues at all levels, from local to international and both governmental and non-governmental. This, of course, includes the voices of minorities themselves, which are fully taken into account in every aspect of the work of the mandate.

The mandate holder

The Independent Expert is required to be independent from any Government or organization and serves in his or her individual capacity. Ms. Gay McDougall (of the United States of America) was the first holder of the mandate of Independent Expert on minority issues, between July 2005 and July 2011. Ms. Rita Izsák (of Hungary), also a participant in the Minorities Fellowship Programme, was appointed the second holder of the mandate and assumed her functions on 1 August 2011.

Scope of the mandate

In addition to the mandate, the Independent Expert is guided and informed by international standards relating to the rights of minorities, particularly the 1992 Declaration on the Rights of National or Ethnic, Religious and Linguistic Minorities. The Expert is also informed by international treaties that have provisions specifically relating to minority rights, including article 27 of the International Covenant on Civil and Political Rights and article 30 of the Convention on the Rights of the Child. Of course, the rights guaranteed to individuals in all other United Nations human rights conventions apply equally to members of minority groups. The work

[44] See www.ohchr.org/EN/Issues/Minorities/IExpert/Pages/IEminorityissuesIndex.aspx (accessed 29 November 2012).

of treaty-monitoring bodies (discussed in chap. V) is also valuable, including authoritative interpretations of standards relevant to minorities and minority rights. The Expert is also informed by and cooperates closely with regional human and minority rights instruments and mechanisms.

Based on the international standards relating to minority rights mentioned above, the first holder of the mandate, Gay McDougall, identified four broad areas of concern relating to minorities around the world:

- Protecting a minority's existence, including protection of its physical integrity and prevention of violence and genocide;
- Protecting and promoting the cultural and social identity of persons belonging to minorities, including the right of individuals to choose which ethnic, linguistic or religious groups they wish to be identified with, and the right of those groups to affirm and protect their collective identity and to reject forced assimilation;
- Ensuring the rights to non-discrimination and equality, including ending structural or systemic discrimination and the promotion of affirmative action when required;
- Ensuring effective participation of members of minorities in public life, especially with regard to decisions that affect them.

The Independent Expert recognizes the collective dimension of minority rights. This is important for the promotion and protection of minority identity and visibility; for the informed participation of minority groups in decisions that affect them, their rights and resources; and for securing collective claims such as those to linguistically and culturally appropriate education, land and other shared assets, to be enjoyed in community with other persons belonging to the minority group in question.

The Minorities Declaration identifies only national or ethnic, religious and linguistic minorities as falling within its scope. However, the Independent Expert can consider issues with regard to people belonging to other marginalized groups, such as those with disabilities, or issues relating to sexual orientation where they intersect with the issues and rights of persons belonging to national or ethnic, religious and linguistic minorities. Some persons belonging to minorities may face multiple and intersectional discrimination; for example, minority women and those who belong to an ethnic minority and live with disability may face unique challenges.

While indigenous peoples may also constitute numerical minorities, issues concerning indigenous peoples may be more appropriately taken up by the Special Rapporteur on the rights of indigenous peoples and other United Nations mechanisms specifically mandated to address their rights, including the Expert Mechanism on the Rights of Indigenous Peoples.

The Independent Expert on minority issues recognizes that minorities are not homogenous groups and that it is crucial to recognize the diversity that exists within every minority group. Explicit recognition should be given to the life experiences of minority women and children, the elderly and others who may face particular issues and challenges. Consequently, the first Independent Expert devoted particular attention in all aspects of her work to the situation of women and children belonging to minority groups.

Minority women

The Independent Expert is required under (his or) her mandate to apply a gender perspective in her work. Indeed, since its creation the mandate has highlighted that denial or violation of rights may manifest itself differently in the experiences of men and women, girls and boys. Minority women and girls may face multiple forms of discrimination based on both their minority status and their gender. Multiple or intersectoral discrimination may make women and girls particularly vulnerable to violation and denial of their rights in both public and private life. Women may face particular obstacles to equality both from wider society and within their own communities.

The Independent Expert encourages NGOs and States to provide information on the specific situations of minority women and the problems they face in their country, region or locality. Such information might relate to, for example, violence against minority women, unequal access to quality education, underrepresentation of minority women in public and political life, discrimination against minority women in employment, and the burdens faced by minority women supporting families in poverty. Such information has led the Independent Expert to make specific recommendations in her thematic and country reports, calling on States to address issues faced by minority women.

To ensure that women's concerns are addressed, the Independent Expert has developed the practice during country visits of holding forums specifically dedicated to minority women, in which women can share their experiences and views and thereby contribute to recommendations formulated by the Independent Expert. In addition, the fourth session of the Forum on Minority Issues (see chap. III) specifically focused on guaranteeing the rights of minority women.

Minority children

Article 30 of the Convention on the Rights of the Child guarantees that the same rights set forth in article 27 of the International Covenant on Civil and Political Rights also apply to children. The Independent Expert seeks to collaborate closely with the Committee on the Rights of the Child and share expertise with that body, particularly in regard to issues such as education, health, adequate housing and trafficking. In the course of country visits, the Independent Expert also seeks to hear the views and perspectives of children and young people, by visiting schools, universities and youth facilities.

In the field of education, the Independent Expert has been concerned that minority children often lack equal access to quality education. They may also face obstacles and challenges even where they do have access, such as lack of instruction in their own minority language, which puts them at a disadvantage in relation to other children. Minorities also commonly report that school curricula, text books and approaches to teaching frequently neglect minority culture and history, and the contributions of minorities to wider society. In 2008, the first session of the Forum on Minority Issues was devoted to the issue of minorities and the right to education, and produced comprehensive recommendations on this subject.

Methods of work

The Independent Expert employs diverse working methods in fulfilment of her mandate, with the aim of making the most effective and timely use of limited resources. The methods of work are informed by the practices of other special procedures mandates, with due regard for the particular features of the mandate provided in Human Rights Council resolution 16/6. Activities are focused on direct and constructive engagement and consultation with specific Governments, including through country visits and communications, and on thematic work that provides analysis, guidance and thematic recommendations which are relevant to all States.

Country visits

One of the most valuable tools available to the Independent Expert is the ability to conduct country visits at the invitation of States, in order to consult on minority issues in situ and to engage with States directly on the implementation of the Minorities Declaration. The findings and recommendations of the Independent Expert's official visits are submitted to the Human Rights Council and discussed during an annual Interactive Dialogue with the Council, States concerned and other interested United Nations Member States.

There may be many different motivations for visiting a particular country. These include the mandate holder having received information raising concern over the situation of minority groups there. Equally, the Independent Expert may seek to visit a country where a constructive political environment exists in which the Government demonstrates a willingness to protect and promote the rights of minorities. This offers the possibility of studying both challenges and positive practices in relation to minority issues which the Independent Expert may wish to share with other States.

The Independent Expert has a global mandate that commits him or her to conduct visits to all regions. By the end of her mandate in July 2011, the first Independent Expert had visited Hungary, Ethiopia, France, the Dominican Republic, Guyana, Greece, Kazakhstan, Canada, Colombia, Viet Nam, Rwanda and Bulgaria.

NGOs play a vital role in country visits and are consulted by the Independent Expert during planning, the visit itself and preparation of the report and recommendations. Indeed, NGOs can play a valuable role in encouraging States to accept a visit request from the Independent Expert or another mandate. NGOs are an important source of information relating to the situation of minorities and minority issues, and the Independent Expert meets with them during the course of country visits. NGOs often assist with facilitating visits to and consulting with minority communities. NGOs frequently use the reports and recommendations of the Independent Expert to assist them in their domestic and international advocacy work on behalf of minority communities, and their work is essential in following up on the Expert's activities.

Communications

The Independent Expert welcomes information, including allegations of violation(s) of the human rights of minorities and on minority issues, from a variety of sources, including NGOs, minority organizations, intergovernmental organizations and other United Nations bodies concerned with the protection of human rights. The Independent Expert analyses information received and decides whether or not to take action, and the nature of that action. Letters of allegation and urgent appeals to specific States are frequently inspired by information received by NGOs and minority communities themselves.

In most instances, the mandate of the Independent Expert focuses communications on situations affecting wider minority communities and which have an impact on numerous members of minority groups, rather than addressing individual cases. For example, communications have been sent which concern the planned or imminent eviction of a minority community from their homes or land, and the alleged detention or ill-treatment of numerous members of a minority due to their legitimate human rights activities on behalf of their community. However, all information received is treated on its merits and the Expert will consider action on cases concerning individuals belonging to minority communities who have faced violation of their rights as a result of their minority identity. Communications commonly reflect the four broad areas of concern identified above; they may also be related to the thematic work undertaken by the mandate. In addition, the Independent Expert often issues joint communications with other mandate holders where appropriate.

The role of the Independent Expert in identifying "best" or "successful" practices and opportunities for technical cooperation by OHCHR requires a form of engagement with States that differs from the monitoring and reporting function of some other mandates. Hence, the Independent Expert may request information from a State about its legislation, policy and practice in relation to a particular minority issue. The Independent Expert also values information from NGOs which identifies positive practices by States and other actors in regard to minority issues.

Thematic studies

An important part of the work of the Independent Expert is to conduct thematic studies relevant to minority issues in any region. The Expert selects specific issues upon which to focus in consultation with various constituencies, including NGOs, and in response to priorities which emerge in the course of the mandate. These studies include analysis of global minority issues and recommendations to United Nations Member States and others, and form the thematic content of the Expert's annual report to the Human Rights Council.

In 2006, the Expert conducted a thematic study on minorities in the context of poverty alleviation and reduction strategies and the Millennium Development Goals.[45] In 2007, she undertook research and convened a seminar on the issue of minorities and discriminatory denial or deprivation of citizenship.[46] In 2010, she presented a report to the General Assembly and the Human Rights Council focusing on the role of minority rights in conflict prevention.[47]

NGOs contribute to the thematic work of the Independent Expert in various ways. NGOs from all regions have attended the Forum on Minority Issues (discussed in chap. III) and have contributed specialized knowledge to conferences and seminars convened by the Independent Expert. If unable to attend, NGOs may provide written materials and research either before an event or as soon as possible after it has taken place. Regional conferences and seminars convened by the Independent Expert and OHCHR provide further opportunities for NGOs to contribute to the mandate. In compiling studies, the Independent Expert has used information provided by NGO experts on both the challenges facing minorities and positive practices. NGO analyses and suggestions have also contributed to the formulation of thematic recommendations in the annual reports of the Independent Expert to the Council.

Additional activities

In common with other special procedures mandate holders, the Independent Expert conducts a number of additional activities in support of the mandate and to promote implementation of the Minorities Declaration. The Independent Expert may issue press releases or public statements in order to highlight situations of concern; attend conferences and other public events, including those organized by NGOs in their countries or regions; deliver speeches and statements; and participate in training sessions on minority rights standards and protection mechanisms.

The Forum on Minority Issues (discussed in chap. III) meets annually for two working days allocated to thematic discussions. The Independent Expert on minority issues is required by the resolution to guide the work of the Forum, prepare its annual meetings and report on the thematic recommendations of the Forum to the Human Rights Council. Thus, the Independent Expert has an important role in the thematic work of the Forum and a strong and cooperative relationship is established between the only two mechanisms of the United Nations system dedicated to minority issues.

The Independent Expert actively promotes implementation of the Forum's recommendations, including through country visits, regional seminars and conferences.

Providing information to the Independent Expert

Information received by the Independent Expert is given careful consideration and may be disseminated to United Nations staff who deal with related issues or have country-specific responsibilities within OHCHR. As is true of all mandate holders, the Independent Expert

[45] A/HRC/4/9.

[46] A/HRC/7/23.

[47] A/65/287.

preserves confidentiality of sources of testimonies, if divulging them might cause harm to those involved.

In submitting information, include all relevant documentation in support of the issues being brought to the attention of the Independent Expert (e.g., recent reports of NGOs or research bodies, national or international media reports, or electronic links to such sources).

All communications relevant to the mandate of the Independent Expert should be addressed to:

Office of the United Nations High Commissioner for Human Rights (OHCHR)
Palais des Nations
8-14, Avenue de la Paix
CH-1211 Geneva 10
Switzerland

E-mail: minorityissues@ohchr.org

Minority representatives are also encouraged to follow relevant news and share information on the Independent Expert's Facebook page. However, communication via Facebook does not qualify as official submission; formal communication must be made via the mandate's official e-mail or postal address.

Other relevant mechanisms

In addition to the Independent Expert on minority issues, a number of the Council's special thematic mechanisms are of particular relevance to members of minorities and minority advocates. A brief description of four of these mechanisms follows, and each is described more fully on the OHCHR website. Of particular note is the fact that both the Special Rapporteur on freedom of religion or belief, and the Special Rapporteur on contemporary forms of racism, racial discrimination, xenophobia and related intolerance may contact States directly regarding allegations that rights that fall within their respective mandates are being violated, and may request that they adopt measures necessary to ensure that the rights are respected and individuals protected. Information may be provided to all the special procedures mandate holders at any time, so long as it is well documented, presented in a manner that can be readily understood by the mandate holders and appropriately related to the terms of the mandate.

Special Rapporteur on freedom of religion or belief

Although many people think primarily of national or ethnic groups when they think of "minorities", discrimination against religious minorities is also a serious problem around the world. The Special Rapporteur on freedom of religion or belief was created in 1986, originally as the Special Rapporteur on religious intolerance; the name was changed in 2000. The Special Rapporteur's mandate includes the authority to transmit urgent appeals to States on individual cases where freedom of religion or belief has been violated; undertake on-site fact-finding missions, upon the invitation of a Government; and submit an annual report to and engage in an "interactive dialogue" at the Human Rights Council, as do all of the special procedures mandate holders.

A model questionnaire has been developed for individual complaints to the Special Rapporteur, the objective of which is "to have access to precise information on alleged violations of freedom of religion or belief". While use of the questionnaire is not mandatory, it is strongly recommended. The Special Rapporteur has also developed a framework for communications that details the applicable international legal standards, arranged by subtopics such as freedom to change one's religion, the right to manifest one's religion or belief and the relationship between this freedom and other human rights.[48]

The Special Rapporteur conducted 32 country visits; reports on each are annexed to the annual report to the Council. Among the specific issues addressed in recent thematic reports are the situation of persons in vulnerable situations, the situation of persons with atheistic and non-theistic beliefs, and discrimination against members of religious minorities and new religious movements. The reports reveal that members of many religious minorities suffer from discrimination through policies, legislation and State practices, sometimes even leading to arbitrary detention and extrajudicial killings. Their vulnerable situation is aggravated when Governments target religious minorities by registering names and scrutinizing these people. In addition, violent acts or threats thereof are often perpetrated by non-State actors, either from different religious communities or from within the same community, without an adequate response from the State authorities. The Special Rapporteur has recommended that government officials be adequately trained in human rights standards and that particular attention should be paid to freedom of religion or belief. More generally, States should ensure that education is designed to encourage wider knowledge in society at large of the history, traditions, language and culture of the various religious minorities existing within their territory. Furthermore, States should ensure an equitable allocation of resources, including broadcasting frequencies, among public service, commercial and community media, so that the media as a whole represent the full range of cultures, communities and opinions in society.

To contact the Special Rapporteur, e-mail freedomofreligion@ohchr.org or urgent-action@ohchr.org (with Special Rapporteur on freedom of religion or belief in the subject line).

Special Rapporteur on contemporary forms of racism, racial discrimination, xenophobia and related intolerance

Established in 1993 by the Commission on Human Rights, the Special Rapporteur on contemporary forms of racism, racial discrimination, xenophobia and related intolerance (known as the Special Rapporteur on racism) engages in a wide range of activities related to the mandate. The Special Rapporteur has been entrusted with a broad mandate "to gather, request, receive and exchange information and communications with all relevant sources, on all issues and alleged violations falling within the purview of his/her mandate, and to investigate and make concrete recommendations, to be implemented at the national, regional and international levels". The Special Rapporteur visited 34 countries between 1994 and 2010; reports on these missions are included as addenda to the Special Rapporteur's annual reports to the Human Rights Council. The Special Rapporteur has also in recent years been requested by the Council to present specific reports on "the manifestations of defamation of religions, and in particular on the serious implications of Islamophobia, on the enjoyment of all rights by their followers" (2009, 2008); "political platforms which promote or incite racial discrimination" (2007); and "the situation of Muslim and Arab peoples in various parts of the world" (2006).

Upon the renewal of the mandate in 2008,[49] the Human Rights Council requested the Special Rapporteur to focus on 15 issues, some of which may be of relevance to the situation of minorities. These include incidents of contemporary forms of racism and racial discrimination against persons belonging to minorities; situations of persistent racial discrimination against persons

[48] The framework is available from www.ohchr.org/EN/Issues/FreedomReligion/Pages/Standards.aspx; the model questionnaire is available from www.ohchr.org/EN/Issues/FreedomReligion/Pages/Complaints.aspx (both accessed 29 November 2012).

[49] Human Rights Council resolution 7/34; the mandate was extended in 2011 by Human Rights Council resolution 16/33.

belonging to different racial and ethnic groups; racist and violent movements directed at Arab, African, Christian, Jewish, Muslim and other communities; the persistent and chronic inequalities faced by racial groups in various societies; best practices in the elimination of racism; follow-up to the Durban Declaration and Programme of Action and the promotion of mechanisms to combat racism; the role of human rights education in promoting tolerance; respect for cultural diversity; incitement to hatred and instances of racially motivated hate speech; xenophobic political platforms; the impact of counter-terrorism measures on the rise of racism, including racial profiling; institutional racism and racial discrimination; and measures taken by Governments to remedy the situation of victims of racism.

Upon receiving "reliable and credible information", the Special Rapporteur has the authority to transmit an "allegation letter" or "urgent appeal" to a State, in order to induce the national authority to investigate the incident(s) or individual cases brought to its attention. The Special Rapporteur does not require submission of a particular form, but communications should include, at a minimum, identification of the alleged victim(s) and the alleged perpetrator(s) of the violation; identification of the person(s) or organization(s) submitting the communication (this information will be kept confidential); date and place of the incident; and a detailed description of the circumstances of the incident in which the alleged violation occurred. These communications generally remain confidential until a summary of them, along with any replies received from the State concerned, is published in the Special Rapporteur's annual communications report.

To contact the Special Rapporteur, e-mail racism@ohchr.org or urgent-action@ohchr.org (with Special Rapporteur on contemporary forms of racism, racial discrimination, xenophobia and related intolerance in the subject line).

Independent Expert in the field of cultural rights

This is one of the newer special procedure mandates, created by the Human Rights Council in 2009. In the mandate, as set out in Council resolution 10/23, there is no explicit authority for the Independent Expert to communicate with States urgently with respect to alleged violations of cultural rights. However, States are called upon "to cooperate with and assist the Independent Expert in the discharge of his or her mandate, to provide him or her with all the necessary information requested by him or her and to give serious consideration to responding favourably to his or her requests to visit their countries".

The Expert is requested to:

- Identify best practices in the promotion and protection of cultural rights at the local, national, regional and international levels;
- Identify possible obstacles to the promotion and protection of cultural rights and submit proposals and/or recommendations to the Council on possible actions in that regard;
- Work in cooperation with States in order to foster the adoption of measures at the local, national, regional and international levels aimed at the promotion and protection of cultural rights through concrete proposals enhancing subregional, regional and international cooperation;
- Study the relationship between cultural rights and cultural diversity, with the aim of further promoting cultural rights;
- Integrate a gender and disabilities perspective into his or her work;
- Work in close coordination, while avoiding unnecessary duplication, with intergovernmental and non-governmental organizations, other special procedures of the Council, the Committee on Economic, Social and Cultural Rights and UNESCO.

The resolution creating the mechanism also recognizes that "cultural diversity and the pursuit of cultural development by all peoples and nations are a source of mutual enrichment for the cultural life of humankind"; that "no one may invoke cultural diversity to infringe upon human rights guaranteed by international law, nor to limit their scope"; and that "States have the responsibility to promote and protect cultural rights".

To contact the Independent Expert, e-mail ieculturalrights@ohchr.org.

Working Group of Experts on People of African Descent

Created in 2002 by the Commission on Human Rights pursuant to a recommendation contained in the Durban Programme of Action, the Working Group of Experts on People of African Descent addresses problems of racial discrimination faced by people of African descent and proposes measures to tackle those problems.[50] Since 2006, the Working Group has reported to its new parent body, the Human Rights Council.

The mandate of the Working Group, as first set out in Commission resolution 2002/68, has changed somewhat over time. The most recent extension of the mandate calls on the Working Group to, inter alia, study the problems of racial discrimination faced by people of African descent living in the diaspora; propose measures to ensure full and effective access to the justice system for people of African descent; submit recommendations on the design, implementation and enforcement of effective measures to eliminate racial profiling of people of African descent; and propose measures to eliminate racial discrimination against Africans and people of African descent in all parts of the world.[51] The Working Group submits an annual report to the Council on its activities.

In 2005, the Working Group began to solicit invitations from States so that it could conduct country visits and facilitate its own in-depth understanding of the issues. The Working Group's website underscores that "such missions are in no case designed to be inquisitorial; rather, they can enable the measures taken by a Government for the elimination of racial discrimination against people of African descent to be better known". So far, missions to Belgium, Ecuador, the United States of America and Portugal have been undertaken. Reports on these missions are presented to the Human Rights Council and posted on the Working Group's website.

The Working Group meets annually for one session of five working days, in both closed and public meetings. Each session is usually devoted to a particular theme, such as racial profiling, the administration of justice, racism and the media, access to education, racism and employment, racism and health, or racism and housing. NGOs in consultative status with the Economic and Social Council, as well as those organizations which were granted accreditation to the 2001 Durban Conference, may actively participate in the discussions during these sessions. Expert panellists are often drawn from civil society. In order to facilitate broader participation, Council resolution 9/28 recalled "the establishment of a voluntary fund to provide additional resources for, inter alia, the participation of people of African descent, representatives of developing countries, especially the least developed countries, non-governmental organizations and experts, in the open-ended sessions of the Working Group" and invited States to contribute to that fund.

To contact the Working Group, e-mail africandescent@ohchr.org.

[50] Commission on Human Rights resolution 2002/68. See www.ohchr.org/EN/Issues/Racism/WGAfricanDescent/Pages/WGEPADIndex.aspx (accessed 29 November 2012).

[51] Council resolution 9/28.

Contacts and further information

Specific contact information for the various procedures discussed in this chapter is given above. Information can also be sent to OHCHR (see address below), specifying the particular mechanism being addressed in the subject line of an e-mail or on the outside of an envelope.

Office of the United Nations High Commissioner for Human Rights (OHCHR)
Palais des Nations
8-14 Avenue de la Paix
CH-1211 Geneva 10
Switzerland

Telephone: 41 22 917 9220
E-mail: InfoDesk@ohchr.org

An important source of information on upcoming country visits by the special procedures and other related issues is the OHCHR Civil Society Section e-mail broadcast system.[52] A useful reference is *United Nations Special Procedures: Facts and Figures*, which is updated annually.[53]

52 To sign up to the system, click on "Subscribe to e-mail updates" at www.ohchr.org/EN/AboutUs/Pages/CivilSociety.aspx (accessed 29 November 2012).

53 The 2011 report is available from www.ohchr.org/Documents/HRBodies/SP/Facts_Figures2011.pdf (accessed 29 November 2012).

CHAPTER V

HUMAN RIGHTS TREATY BODIES

Summary: The United Nations treaty-based human rights system includes procedures through which members of minorities can seek protection of their rights. This chapter describes eight major international human rights treaties which deal respectively with civil and political rights; economic, social and cultural rights; racial discrimination; children's rights; women's rights; torture; the rights of persons with disabilities; and migrant workers' rights. The first section outlines the system of State reporting common to all human rights treaties and suggests ways in which minorities and their representatives can raise their concerns before international treaty bodies. The second section describes the complaint mechanisms available under six of the treaties to individuals who believe that their rights have been violated.

United Nations human rights treaties

There are nine core, legally binding international human rights treaties within the United Nations human rights system which deal with a broad range of human rights.[54] The most recent is the International Convention for the Protection of All Persons from Enforced Disappearance, which entered into force on 23 December 2010.

For each treaty there is a dedicated committee which monitors the way in which States are fulfilling their human rights obligations under the respective treaty (see fig. IV). The committees, generally known as treaty bodies, are composed of international human rights experts and vary in size from 10 to 25 members. Committee members serve four-year terms, and several treaties limit the number of terms a member can serve. Although they are elected by the States parties to the treaty, members serve in their personal capacity and not as representatives of their Governments. The committees meet for several weeks each year, usually in Geneva; the Committee on the Elimination of Discrimination against Women and the Human Rights Committee meet once in New York and twice in Geneva.

If a country is not a party to a relevant treaty, the treaty's procedures to redress violations cannot be invoked. In such situations, procedures based on the Charter of the United Nations, created by the United Nations Human Rights Council and other bodies (described in chapters III and IV), offer a way to address the human rights situation in the country.

OHCHR has an open consultation Treaty Body Strengthening Process under way aimed at streamlining and further strengthening the treaty body system.[55]

[54] The full text of each treaty and a list of the States which have ratified it are available from http://treaties.un.org.

[55] See www2.ohchr.org/english/bodies/HRTD/index.htm (accessed 30 November 2012).

Figure IV. United Nations human rights treaties and treaty bodies

Treaty	Treaty body	Number of members	Number and venue of sessions	General comments or recommendations adopted	Periodicity of obligation to report	Review of State party reports and issue of recommendations	Individual complaints procedure	Additional mechanisms
International Convention on the Elimination of All Forms of Racial Discrimination (175 parties)	Committee on the Elimination of Racial Discrimination	18	2/year, in Geneva	34	2 years	Under art. 9 Reports examined a year: 24 Reports pending examination: 16 (estimated backlog of less than 1 year)	Yes, through acceptance of art. 14 Registered communications pending examination: 3 Average time between registration and final decision on merits: 1 ½ years	
International Covenant on Economic, Social and Cultural Rights (160 parties)	Committee on Economic, Social and Cultural Rights	18	2/year, in Geneva	21	5 years	Under art. 16–17 Reports examined a year: 10 Reports pending examination: 44 (estimated backlog of over 4 years)	Yes, under the Optional Protocol (not yet in force)	Yes, under the Optional Protocol, art. 11 (not yet in force)
International Covenant on Civil and Political Rights (167 parties)	Human Rights Committee	18	3/year: 2 in Geneva, 1 in New York	34	At the Committee's discretion, but usually every 4 years	Under art. 40 Reports examined a year: 15 Reports pending examination: 25 (estimated backlog of nearly 2 years)	Yes, under the first Optional Protocol Registered communications pending examination: 340 Average time between registration and final decision on merits: 3 ½ years	
Convention on the Elimination of All Forms of Discrimination against Women (187 parties)	Committee on the Elimination of Discrimination against Women	23	3/year: 2 in Geneva, 1 in New York	28	4 years	Under art. 18 Reports examined a year: 24 Reports pending examination: 48 (estimated backlog of 2 years)	Yes, under the Optional Protocol Registered communications pending examination: 10 Average time between registration and final decision on merits: 2 years	Inquiries into grave or systematic violations, under the Optional Protocol, arts. 8–10
Convention against Torture and Other Cruel, Inhuman or Degrading Treatment or Punishment (149 parties)	Committee against Torture	10	2/year, in Geneva	2	4 years	Under arts. 19–20 Reports examined a year: 14 Reports pending examination: 20 (estimated backlog of nearly 2 years)	Yes, through acceptance of art. 22 Registered communications pending examination: 100 Average time between registration and final decision on merits: 2 ½ years	Inquiries into systematic practice of torture through acceptance of art. 20

(continued)

Figure IV. United Nations human rights treaties and treaty bodies *(continued)*

Treaty	Treaty body	Number of members	Number and venue of sessions	General comments or recommendations adopted	Periodicity of obligation to report	Review of State party reports and issue of recommendations	Individual complaints procedure	Additional mechanisms
Optional Protocol to the Convention against Torture and Other Cruel, Inhuman or Degrading Treatment or Punishment (61 parties)	Subcommittee on Prevention of Torture	25	3/year, in Geneva	0	n/a	n/a	n/a	Regular visits to places where people are deprived of their liberty, under arts. 11–16
Convention on the Rights of the Child (193 parties)	Committee on the Rights of the Child	18	3/year, in Geneva	13	5 years	Under art. 44 Reports examined a year: 30 (including reports on the first two Optional Protocols) Reports pending examination: 99 (estimated backlog of over 3 years)	Yes, under the Optional Protocol on a communications procedure (not yet in force)	Inquiries into grave or systematic violations, under the Optional Protocol, arts. 13–14 (not yet in force)
International Convention on the Protection of the Rights of All Migrant Workers and Members of Their Families (45 parties)	Committee on Migrant Workers	14	2/year, in Geneva	1	5 years	Under arts. 73–74 Reports examined a year: 4 Reports pending examination: 6 (estimated backlog of 1 ½ years)	Yes, through acceptance of art. 77 (not yet operative)	
Convention on the Rights of Persons with Disabilities (108 parties)	Committee on the Rights of Persons with Disabilities	18	2/year, in Geneva	0	4 years	Under arts. 35–36 Reports examined a year: 4 Reports pending examination: 23 (estimated backlog of nearly 6 years)	Yes, under the Optional Protocol Registered communications pending examination: 5 Average time between registration and final decision on merits: n/a (Committee has yet to adopt its first decision)	Inquiries into systematic violations, under the Optional Protocol, art. 6
International Convention for the Protection of All Persons from Enforced Disappearance (30 parties)	Committee on Enforced Disappearances	10	2/year, in Geneva	0	As requested by the Committee	Under art. 29 Reports examined a year: to be determined Reports pending examination: 0	Yes, through acceptance of art. 31	Visits, inquiries into grave or systematic violations, under arts. 33–34

The treaty bodies monitor a State's implementation of its treaty obligations in two main ways. The first is by considering reports submitted periodically by a State on its implementation of the relevant treaty. States parties are legally obliged to submit these reports, which inform the treaty body about actions a State has taken to fulfil its treaty obligations, both through legislation and by other means. This reporting requirement applies to all treaty bodies except the Subcommittee on Prevention of Torture established by the Optional Protocol to the Convention against Torture and Other Cruel, Inhuman or Degrading Treatment or Punishment.

They also monitor treaty compliance by considering complaints, generally called "communications", made by individuals that their rights under a particular treaty have been violated (see fig. IV above).

Some treaty bodies have additional powers and may, on their own initiative, initiate inquiries if they have received reliable information containing well-founded indications of serious or systematic violations of the relevant convention on the territory of a State party.

In addition, many of the treaty bodies adopt general comments or general recommendations which interpret or elaborate treaty provisions. Several of the treaty bodies also schedule thematic discussions during their sessions, which may contribute to the formulation and adoption of these. A compilation of all treaty bodies' general comments or recommendations is prepared and issued at regular intervals.

The rights protected

This section summarizes some of the articles in selected treaties which may be of particular relevance to minorities. It is important to note that each international human rights treaty applies to persons belonging to minorities via the non-discrimination clause included in the treaty. However, it is also important to remember that minorities are entitled to *all* of the rights accorded to those who live within the jurisdiction of the State. NGOs and others should use the mechanisms outlined in this chapter whenever they consider that a State could better guarantee human rights, whether the problems identified are specific to minorities or apply more generally. Further guidance on how NGOs may provide information to particular treaty bodies is given at the end of this chapter.

International Covenant on Civil and Political Rights

The International Covenant on Civil and Political Rights, which entered into force in 1976, protects a wide range of rights, many of which are often referred to as "civil rights" or "civil liberties" in domestic law. The Covenant is the only global treaty that includes a provision (art. 27) that specifically refers to minority rights (European mechanisms concerned with minorities are discussed in chaps. XII-XIV):

> *Article 27* In those States in which ethnic, religious or linguistic minorities exist, persons belonging to such minorities shall not be denied the right, in community with the other members of their group, to enjoy their own culture, to profess and practise their own religion, or to use their own language.

Article 27 technically applies only to "persons belonging to such minorities", not to minority groups or communities themselves, although the collective aspect of this right is underscored in the following phrase, "in community with the other members of their group". The wording "shall not be denied" may give the impression that the State merely has to refrain from certain actions rather than being obliged to adopt positive measures to promote or assist minorities in exercising their rights. However, the Human Rights Committee, in its general comment No. 23 (1994), has observed that States may be required to adopt "positive measures of protection" to protect rights from being violated, not only by the State party itself but also by other persons. The Committee has also stated that whether or not a minority exists is a question of fact, not dependent on formal recognition by a State. The Committee also suggested that a State may need to ensure the "effective participation of members of minority communities in decisions which affect them", in order to guarantee full enjoyment of the right to culture.

A number of other rights in the Covenant may be particularly relevant to minorities, including the following.

Article 1 sets forth the right of "all peoples" to self-determination, which includes the right to determine their political status and freely pursue their economic, social and cultural development. Peoples may freely dispose of their natural wealth and resources. However, according to the Human Rights Committee, this right does not belong to minorities per se, even though the distinction between "peoples" and "minorities" is not always easy to discern. In no event would this provision be considered to support demands by minorities for separation or secession from an existing State.

Article 2.1 guarantees that the rights protected by the Covenant apply to all individuals, "without distinction of any kind, such as race, colour, sex, language, religion, political or other opinion, national or social origin, property, birth or other status". This entitlement applies to all individuals within a State's territory or under its jurisdiction (see general comment No. 18 (1989)).

Article 3 provides for the equal enjoyment of all rights by men and women (see general comment No. 28 (2000)).

Article 12 guarantees free movement and choice of residence for everyone lawfully within the territory of a State, as well as the right to leave any country and to enter one's own country (see general comment No. 27 (1999)).

Article 17 protects against interference with a person's privacy, family, home or correspondence, as well as against attacks on honour and reputation (see general comments Nos. 16 (1988) and 23 (1994)).

Article 18 is essential to minorities and protects freedom of thought, conscience and religion. Minorities may manifest their religion in public or private through worship, observance, practice and teaching, and parents are free to ensure that the religious and moral education of their children conforms to their own convictions (see general comment No. 22 (1993)).

Article 19 protects freedom of opinion and expression. This is fundamental to the ability of minorities to communicate in their own language and includes "freedom to seek, receive and impart information and ideas of all kinds, regardless of frontiers, either orally, in writing or in print, in the form of art, or through any other media". As is true for many other rights, freedom of expression may be legitimately restricted by law, but only where such restrictions are necessary to protect the rights of others or to protect national security, public order, public health or public morality (see general comment No. 10 (1983)).

Article 20 requires Governments to prohibit any advocacy of national, racial or religious hatred that constitutes incitement to discrimination, hostility or violence (see general comment No. 11 (1983)).

Article 22 guarantees freedom of association. While most of its provisions concern trade unions, this article also protects the right to form and participate in minority educational, cultural, political and other organizations.

Article 25 sets forth the rights and opportunities of citizens to participate in the conduct of public affairs, to vote and be elected and to have access to public service (see general comment No. 25 (1996)).

Article 26 is a general non-discrimination clause that guarantees equality before the law and equal protection for all. As the Human Rights Committee stated in its general comment No. 18 (1989), "not every differentiation of treatment will constitute discrimination, if the criteria for such differentiation are reasonable and objective and if the aim is to achieve a purpose which is legitimate under the Covenant". Thus, this provision does not preclude the State from making reasonable distinctions among categories of people, such as the need to speak the official language under certain circumstances, but it prohibits any unreasonable distinction based on a person's status as a member of a minority group.

Jurisprudence arising from the consideration of individual cases also contributes to the Committee's understanding of the substantive rights guaranteed under the Covenant.[56]

International Covenant on Economic, Social and Cultural Rights

The International Covenant on Economic, Social and Cultural Rights entered into force in 1976. While it clearly sets out these particular rights, it allows States greater flexibility in how they implement them than does the International Covenant on Civil and Political Rights described above. In other words, States enjoy a wide degree of discretion in determining how best to protect these rights, given the different circumstances in each. Consequently, some have described the International Covenant on Economic, Social and Cultural Rights as creating obligations of result rather than obligations of conduct.

Article 2 of the Covenant recognizes that States have different capacities to provide services such as health care and higher education. At the same time, article 2 (1) establishes that each State party has committed itself "to take steps ... to the maximum of its available resources, with a view to achieving progressively the full realization of the rights recognized in the present Covenant, including particularly the adoption of legislative measures".

The Committee on Economic, Social and Cultural Rights has made it clear that concrete steps must be taken towards meeting the obligations of the Covenant. In particular, no State party may deliberately take retrogressive measures without providing acceptable justification for doing so. The Committee has also indicated that States are obliged, at a minimum, to ensure that essential levels of basic foodstuffs, primary health care, basic housing and at least the most basic forms of education are available, commensurate with the resources at the State's disposal. The Covenant also includes a non-discrimination clause (art. 2 (2)) to guarantee that rights will be exercised without discrimination of any kind. The content of this provision has been elaborated by the Committee in its general comment No. 20 (2009). For instance, in respect of the private sphere, the Committee states that "discrimination is frequently encountered in families, workplaces and other sectors of society. For example, actors in the private housing sector (e.g. private landlords, credit providers and public housing providers) may directly or indirectly deny access to housing or mortgages on the basis of ethnicity, marital status, disability or sexual orientation while some families may refuse to send girl children to school. States parties must therefore adopt measures, which should include legislation, to ensure that individuals and entities in the private sphere do not discriminate on prohibited grounds".

Other articles in the International Covenant on Economic, Social and Cultural Rights are of particular relevance to minorities, including the following.

---

56 The jurisprudence of the treaty bodies is available from: http://tb.ohchr.org/default.aspx (accessed 30 November 2012). (Under "Type", select "Jurisprudence".)

Article 3 requires States to ensure the equal enjoyment of all rights for men and women (see general comment No. 16 (2005)).

Articles 6 and 7 concern the right to work, including the opportunity to gain one's living by work freely chosen, as well as the right to enjoy just and favourable conditions of work (see general comment No. 18 (2005)).

Article 11 sets forth the right to an adequate standard of living, including adequate food, clothing and housing, and the continuous improvement of living conditions (see general comments Nos. 4 (1991) on adequate housing, 7 (1997) on forced evictions, 12 (1999) on food and 15 (2002) on water).

Article 12 requires States to ensure the highest attainable standard of physical and mental health, including an obligation to reduce infant mortality and to promote the healthy development of the child (see general comment No. 14 (2000)).

Articles 13 and 14 set forth the right of everyone to education, including a provision that primary education must be compulsory and free for all. Of particular interest to minorities is the liberty of "individuals and bodies" to establish and direct educational institutions, as long as these institutions conform to whatever minimum standards may be established by the State (see general comments Nos. 11 (1999) on primary education and 13 (1999) on education).

Article 15 states that everyone has the right to take part in cultural life and to have his or her intellectual property protected (see general comments Nos. 17 (2005) on intellectual property and 21 (2009) on cultural life); general comment No. 21 observes, inter alia, that "educational programmes of States parties should respect the cultural specificities of national or ethnic, linguistic and religious minorities" and that States should "respect free access by minorities to their own culture, heritage and other forms of expression, as well as the free exercise of their cultural identity and practices". Paragraphs 32 and 33 of the general comment are specifically devoted to minorities, and there are numerous other references to minorities throughout the text.

Like many of the other treaty bodies, the Committee on Economic, Social and Cultural Rights holds discussions on particular themes and issues, in which NGOs have participated regularly. Many are of direct interest to minority representatives, and they often lay the foundation for future general comments.

International Convention on the Elimination of All Forms of Racial Discrimination

The International Convention on the Elimination of All Forms of Racial Discrimination entered into force in 1969. It is sometimes assumed, mistakenly, that it can be invoked only to combat formal legal frameworks which discriminate on the basis of colour. In fact, application of the Convention is much more expansive: "racial discrimination" is defined as "any distinction, exclusion, restriction or preference based on race, colour, descent, *or national or ethnic origin* which has the purpose or effect of nullifying or impairing the recognition, enjoyment or exercise, on an equal footing, of human rights and fundamental freedoms in the political, economic, social, cultural or any other field of public life" (emphasis added). In fact, the Committee on the Elimination of Racial Discrimination has consistently considered discrimination against minorities in its examination of the periodic reports submitted to it by States. Therefore, the Convention should be a primary focus of minority representatives who wish to provide complementary or alternative information to a State's description of the situation of minorities in the country.

The Committee on the Elimination of Racial Discrimination has developed mechanisms, called early warning measures, which are designed to prevent existing problems from escalating into conflicts, and urgent action procedures, which are intended to address problems requiring immediate attention. Letters sent under these procedures are posted on the Committee's website.

Early warning measures may be utilized if one or more of the following indicators is present:

(a) A significant and persistent pattern of racial discrimination, as evidenced in social and economic indicators;

(b) A pattern of escalating racial hatred and violence, or racist propaganda or appeals to racial intolerance by persons, groups or organizations, notably by elected or other State officials;

(c) Adoption of new discriminatory legislation;

(d) Segregation policies or de facto exclusion of members of a group from political, economic, social and cultural life;

(e) Lack of an adequate legislative framework defining and criminalizing all forms of racial discrimination or lack of effective mechanisms, including lack of recourse procedures;

(f) Policies or practice of impunity regarding: (i) violence targeting members of a group identified on the basis of race, colour, descent or national or ethnic origin by State officials or private actors; (ii) grave statements by political leaders/prominent people that condone or justify violence against a group identified on the ground of race, colour, descent, national or ethnic origin; (iii) development and organization of militia groups and/or extreme political groups based on a racist platform;

(g) Significant flows of refugees or displaced persons, especially when those concerned belong to specific ethnic groups;

(h) Encroachment on the traditional lands of indigenous peoples or forced removal of these peoples from their lands, in particular for the purpose of exploitation of natural resources;

(i) Polluting or hazardous activities that reflect a pattern of racial discrimination with substantial harm to specific groups.[57]

The Convention specifically allows States to adopt "special measures" to ensure that certain racial or ethnic groups or individuals can enjoy equal rights in practice, provided that such measures do not lead to the permanent maintenance of separate rights for different racial groups. These measures are often known as "affirmative action" or "positive discrimination", and they may be adopted to correct historical injustices and to ensure that minorities are treated fairly. This issue is the subject of the Committee's general recommendation No. 32 (2009).

A State's obligation under the Convention extends not only to its own actions and those of other public authorities. It must also prohibit and bring to an end racial discrimination by any persons, group or organization (art. 2 (1)(d)). States must punish, by law, the dissemination of ideas based on racial superiority or hatred, and must prohibit organizations from promoting and inciting racial discrimination (art. 4 (a)). States must also adopt "immediate and effective measures, particularly in the fields of teaching, education, culture and information, with a view to combating prejudices which lead to racial discrimination and to promoting understanding, tolerance and friendship among nations and racial or ethnical groups" (art. 7).

The rights that must be guaranteed without racial discrimination are specified in article 5 and parallel those in other international human rights treaties. They include equal treatment before judicial bodies, the right to participate in public affairs and have equal access to public service, freedom of movement and residence, freedom of opinion and expression, and the right of access to any place or service intended for use by the general public. Among the issues which

[57] For further information about the early warning procedure, see www2.ohchr.org/english/bodies/cerd/early-warning.htm (accessed 2 December 2012).

the Committee has highlighted are non-citizens (general recommendations Nos. 11 (1993) and 30 (2004)), training of law enforcement officials (general recommendation No. 13 (1993)), self-determination (general recommendation No. 21 (1996)), indigenous peoples (general recommendation No. 23 (1997)), discrimination against Roma (general recommendation No. 27 (2000)), follow-up to the Durban Review Conference (general recommendations Nos. 28 (2002) and 33 (2009)) and descent-based discrimination (general recommendation No. 29 (2002)).

Convention on the Rights of the Child

With 193 States parties, this is the most widely ratified human rights treaty. It entered into force in 1990. It focuses on the promotion and protection of children's rights (with children defined as persons below 18 years of age). While children enjoy all of the human rights set out in the other treaties, the restatement of these rights in a single comprehensive document with emphasis on the particular circumstances of children provided an opportunity to develop additional provisions relevant to children. The Convention recognizes the child as a subject of rights capable of exercising its own rights in accordance with its evolving capacity, age and maturity. The problems of the involvement of children in armed conflict, and of sale of children, child prostitution and child pornography, are covered in more detail in the two optional protocols to the Convention, adopted in 2000. The following are among the articles in the Convention of particular relevance to minorities.

Article 2 provides that the rights in the Convention must be guaranteed without discrimination on the basis of, among other qualities, race, colour, language, religion, or national or ethnic origin. Non-discrimination is one of the four general principles enshrined in the Convention.

Article 3 sets forth another general principle, which is that the best interests of the child should be a primary consideration in all actions concerning children.

Article 7 requires that children be registered immediately after birth and have the right to a name and nationality.

Article 8 secures the right of the child "to preserve his or her identity".

Article 17 encourages the mass media to cooperate in producing and disseminating material from diverse cultural sources and "to have particular regard to the linguistic needs of the child who belongs to a minority group".

Article 20 provides that due regard should be paid to a child's ethnic, religious, cultural and linguistic background, when it is necessary to place a child deprived of his or her family environment in a home other than that of his or her family.

Article 29 reflects the fundamental purpose of education, and states, among other things, that a child's education shall be directed to developing respect for human rights and fundamental freedoms; his or her own cultural identity, language and values; the national values of the country in which he or she lives and from which he or she may have originated; and the values of other civilizations (see general comment No. 1 (2001)).

Article 30 is specifically dedicated to children belonging to ethnic, religious or linguistic minorities and essentially guarantees the right, contained also in the provisions of article 27 of the International Covenant on Civil and Political Rights, to enjoy one's culture, practise one's religion and use one's own language. When reporting to the Committee on the Rights of the Child, States parties are requested to provide information on measures to protect children belonging to minorities.

Article 31 calls upon States to respect and promote a child's right to participate in cultural and artistic life.

The Committee on the Rights of the Child has adopted a number of general comments and regularly holds discussions on relevant issues. While no general comment has been devoted to minority children per se, general comment No. 11 (2009) concerns indigenous children.

Convention on the Elimination of All Forms of Discrimination against Women

This Convention, which entered into force in 1981, deals with the rights of women, including the right to equal treatment under the law; equality in education, political participation, employment, health and the economy; freedom from sexual exploitation; and the possibility of temporary special measures to overcome inequality. In addition to agreeing to eliminate discrimination against women by "any person, organization or enterprise", States parties agree to take appropriate measures "to modify or abolish existing laws, regulations, *customs and practices*" which discriminate against women (emphasis added).

The Committee on the Elimination of Discrimination against Women has consistently spoken out about the situation of women during armed conflict and about gender-based violence. In 1992, the Committee adopted general recommendation No. 19 (1992) on violence against women, reflecting a major international concern that women continue to suffer multiple discrimination because of their gender. General recommendation No. 26 (2008) concerns the rights of women migrant workers, who are often members of a minority.

Certain articles of the Convention on the Elimination of All Forms of Discrimination against Women may be of particular relevance to minority women.

Article 5 obliges States parties to take "all appropriate measures ... [t]o modify the social and cultural patterns of conduct of men and women" in order to eliminate "prejudices and customary and all other practices which are based on the idea of the inferiority or the superiority of either of the sexes or on stereotyped roles for men and women".

Article 7 concerns the right of women to participate in public life and to hold public office (see general recommendation No. 23 (1997)).

Article 10 requires that educational programmes eliminate stereotyped concepts of the roles of men and women.

Article 14 concerns the particular problems faced by rural women, many of whom may be members of minorities (see general recommendation No. 16 (1991)).

Article 16 reiterates that women and men shall be equal in all matters related to marriage and family, including the right to marry freely and only with full and free consent. It also provides that no legal effect may be given to the betrothal or marriage of a child (see general recommendation No. 21 (1994)).

Convention against Torture and Other Cruel, Inhuman or Degrading Treatment or Punishment and its Optional Protocol

The Convention against Torture and Other Cruel, Inhuman or Degrading Treatment or Punishment entered into force in 1987 and its Optional Protocol in 2006. The principle of non-discrimination is a basic and general principle in the protection of human rights, and fundamental to the interpretation and application of the Convention. Non-discrimination is included within the Convention's definition of torture itself; article 1.1 explicitly prohibits specified acts when carried out for "any reason based on discrimination of any kind ...."

The protection of certain minority or marginalized persons or populations especially at risk of torture is a part of the obligation to prevent torture or ill-treatment. States parties must ensure that, insofar as the obligations arising under the Convention are concerned, their laws are in practice applied to all persons. States parties should, therefore, ensure the protection of members of groups especially at risk of being tortured, by fully prosecuting and punishing all acts of violence and abuse against them and ensuring implementation of other positive measures of prevention and protection. Also key to preventing such violations and building a culture of respect for minorities is the elimination of employment discrimination and provision of awareness training on an ongoing basis in contexts where torture or ill-treatment is likely to be committed. States parties are encouraged to promote the hiring of persons belonging to minority groups, particularly in the medical, educational, prison and detention, law enforcement, judicial and legal fields, within State institutions as well as the private sector.

Under the principle of non-discrimination as set out in the Convention, members of minorities have the same right as anyone else to be protected against torture and other cruel, inhuman, or degrading treatment or punishment. This is an absolute right that cannot be derogated from under any circumstances, including war.

Under *article 20*, if the Committee receives reliable information which appears to it to contain well-founded indications that torture is being systematically practised in the territory of a State party, the Committee may, after inviting the State to cooperate in the examination of the information, make a confidential inquiry, which might include a visit to the country. However, some States parties have not recognized this competence of the Committee.

Convention on the Rights of Persons with Disabilities

The Convention and its Optional Protocol entered into force in 2008. Their aim is to elaborate in detail the rights of persons with disabilities and set out a code of implementation.

Article 1 states that the Convention aims at promoting, protecting and ensuring "the full and equal enjoyment of all human rights and fundamental freedoms by all persons with disabilities, and to promote respect for their inherent dignity".

Article 4 requires that States which ratify the Convention undertake to develop and carry out policies, laws and administrative measures for securing the rights recognized in the Convention and abolish laws, regulations, customs and practices that constitute discrimination.

Article 24.3(b) specifically requires States parties to facilitate the learning of sign language and promote the linguistic identity of the deaf community.

Article 30.4 states that persons with disabilities shall be entitled, on an equal basis with others, to recognition and support of their specific cultural and linguistic identity, including sign languages and deaf culture.

The Convention is the first United Nations human rights treaty to contain certain important concepts which relate to non-discrimination. One is the concept of "reasonable accommodation", which concerns the modifications and adjustments needed to ensure to persons with disabilities the enjoyment or exercise of all human rights and fundamental freedoms on an equal basis with others.

International Convention on the Protection of the Rights of All Migrant Workers and Members of Their Families

The International Convention on the Protection of the Rights of All Migrant Workers and Members of Their Families entered into force in 2003. It does not create new rights for migrants but aims at guaranteeing equality of treatment and the same working conditions for migrants and nationals. Part III of the Convention enumerates rights for all migrant workers and members of their families, including those in undocumented situations. Part IV enumerates additional rights for those who are documented. The Convention applies to all migrant workers, not just those who may be ethnically distinct from the population of the receiving country, but many migrant workers are also members of minorities.

Article 1 states that the Convention applies, except as otherwise provided, to all migrant workers and members of their families "without distinction of any kind such as sex, race, colour, language, religion or conviction, political or other opinion, national, ethnic or social origin, nationality, age, economic position, property, marital status, birth or other status".

Article 12 states that migrant workers and members of their families have the right to freedom of thought, conscience and religion, in terms similar to those in the International Covenant on Civil and Political Rights. Paragraph 4 recognizes the liberty of parents, at least one of whom is a migrant worker, and, when applicable, legal guardians, to ensure the religious and moral education of their children in conformity with their own convictions.

Article 13 provides for freedom of expression, which includes "freedom to seek, receive and impart information and ideas of all kinds, regardless of frontiers". It also provides that expression may be limited in order to prevent "any advocacy of national, racial or religious hatred that constitutes incitement to discrimination, hostility or violence".

International Convention for the Protection of All Persons from Enforced Disappearance

The International Convention for the Protection of All Persons from Enforced Disappearance was adopted in December 2006 and entered into force in December 2010. Unlike many other human rights conventions, it contains no reference to non-discrimination, since forced disappearance is prohibited under all circumstances, even including war or other state of emergency. The Committee on Enforced Disappearances receives and reviews periodic reports from States and may bring to the urgent attention of the General Assembly any situation "which appears to it to contain well-founded indications that enforced disappearance is being practised on a widespread or systematic basis" in the territory of a State party (art. 34). Article 30 gives the Committee the authority to respond to a request that a disappeared person be sought and found and to recommend that the State concerned locate and protect the person, whether or not the State has accepted the optional system for individual complaints provided under article 31.

Using the reporting system

All major international human rights treaties, including those discussed in this chapter, require States parties to submit a report to the relevant treaty body every two to five years on how the State is fulfilling its treaty obligations. The International Covenant on Civil and Political Rights does not specify the frequency with which reports must be submitted to the Human Rights Committee, and the Committee sets the date for submission of a State's next report in its concluding observations. It may request that the next report be submitted within three, four or five years. Each report should contain detailed information on the efforts the State has made to realize the human rights contained in the treaty, including areas in which progress has been made and those in which the State has encountered obstacles or problems. *The Manual on Human Rights Reporting*[58] states that a submission which refers to article 27 of the International Covenant on Civil and Political Rights, for example, should identify the minority groups that exist in the country, describe the

[58] United Nations publication, Sales No. GV.E.97.0.16.

"positive measures" adopted by the State to preserve those minorities' identities, and describe any measures taken "to provide minorities with equal economic and political opportunities".

The respective treaty bodies review the reports with representatives of the State concerned, in two or three public sessions which generally last about three hours. After considering the State's report, the committee adopts public "concluding observations" which evaluate the State's performance by recognizing positive developments, highlighting areas of concern, and providing suggestions and recommendations on specific issues.

The reporting system encourages openness and constructive dialogue between the State and the committee. In practice, however, problems do arise. Many States have been extremely late in submitting their reports; not all reports are reviewed in a timely fashion; not all States give sufficient attention to the comments, suggestions and recommendations of the committees; and not enough publicity is given to the whole process. While the committees (and States) are aware of these issues and have attempted to consolidate and coordinate their activities, national NGOs have an important role to play in ensuring that this continues to be pursued at the national level.

The review process does offer an opportunity for an individual or group to help a treaty body better understand the situation of minorities in a particular country. There are various ways of making the best possible use of the reporting system, most of which are relevant to all the treaty bodies discussed above.

Encouraging the Government to draft a comprehensive and accurate report

A Government department or agency, or sometimes several of them, is responsible for preparing a State's reports for submission to the relevant treaty body. It is important to find out which agency is responsible and when a report is being prepared. The national foreign ministry often coordinates the preparation of a State's report and should be able to provide this information.

The reports become public United Nations documents after they are submitted to a committee, but there is no formal requirement that States discuss their reports with their own citizens or invite others to help prepare them. However, many Governments do allow or even encourage such participation and minorities are encouraged to take advantage of this, either as individuals or organizations. Whether or not it is possible to participate in drafting a report, NGOs may publicize the fact that a State report on human rights is being prepared. Once the report has been submitted to the relevant committee, minority-specific organizations or more mainstream human rights NGOs may wish to make their own submissions to the committee.

Preparing an alternative report

An alternative report is also called a parallel, NGO or shadow report. In some countries, alternative reports are coordinated by established human rights or community organizations which have a special interest in the subject that is the focus of a treaty. This enables various groups to contribute to the report and provides a more comprehensive view of the State's performance in respect of the treaty. Minority advocates should consider how they can contribute to discussion of minority human rights issues within the context of the State report. In some cases, it might be appropriate to prepare a specific alternative report wholly devoted to minority concerns. While this is likely to attract attention to specific minority issues, it also involves a great deal of work and resources, both financial and human.

In either case, an alternative report should address specific articles of the relevant treaty and specific sections of the State report. It should be concise, factually accurate and free of unnecessary political comment. Publication and submission of an alternative report can itself draw attention to the human rights issues discussed in the State report. For example, a media launch of an alternative report could be the first step in a continuing campaign to highlight omissions or errors in the State report and to publicize ongoing human rights issues. The report should generally be submitted after the State report, as it should take into account the information provided by the State, but well in advance of the session at which the State will be examined.

If a State report has not been submitted on time, this does not preclude NGO involvement in the reporting process. Some committees review the situation in non-reporting States in the absence of a report, precisely to encourage States to submit them. Whenever a State is scheduled for review, information from NGOs and other groups can be helpful to the committee.

Information for submission should be sent directly to the relevant committee in Geneva. The schedule for submission of reports and review sessions can be found on each committee's web page, accessible via the OHCHR website (under Human Rights Bodies). It is important that a committee receives supplementary information well before it meets to consider a State report. Contact OHCHR to ensure that the information provided is disseminated in time.

To allow the Committee to consider a comprehensive alternative view to the State report, rather than a large quantity of uncoordinated information, NGOs are encouraged to coordinate their submission with those of other organizations. It is best to organize the information according to the sequence in which the rights are set forth in the particular treaty. When available, reference should be made to relevant authorities and supporting material, such as statistical evidence, official reports, court decisions or materials from other bodies within the United Nations system. If possible, NGOs should send multiple copies of their materials to the committee, together with a written request that they be distributed to all committee members, where this is permitted. Supplying the materials in more than one language can be effective.

Participating in committee meetings

Although it may require considerable resources, NGOs might consider travelling to Geneva or New York to provide information directly to the committee when it meets to consider the State report. This can prove useful in clarifying and expounding on the written submission of NGOs or minority representatives.

Rules covering the participation of NGO representatives vary from committee to committee. All treaty bodies welcome written information submitted by NGOs and, apart from informal, so-called lunchtime briefings, most also allow time during their formal pre-session working groups or the plenary session for NGOs to interact with committee members.

During the consideration of a State report, the committee sets aside one hour for NGOs and national human rights institutions to present information directly and orally to the Committee, in addition to the written reports submitted in advance of the session. NGOs and national human rights institutions may also submit information for adoption in the list of issues produced by the committee and in the context of follow-up to the committee's concluding observations.

Further, NGOs may provide information for adoption in a list of issues prior to reporting. This optional reporting procedure consists of a list of issues which is transmitted to States parties before they submit their periodic reports; it is a mechanism to assist States parties to prepare and submit more focused reports. A list of issues prior to reporting thus guides the content and preparation of a State report, facilitates the reporting process and strengthens the capacity of States parties to fulfil their reporting obligation in a timely and effective manner.

Specific treaty bodies operate as follows.

- The Human Rights Committee allocates time during the morning of the first day of each session for oral NGO interventions. Members also interact with NGO representatives during informal meetings organized at lunchtime.

- The Committee on Economic, Social and Cultural Rights allocates the afternoon of the first day of each session to hearing NGOs. NGOs may also speak during part of the Committee's pre-session meetings. In 2000, the Committee adopted a paper on NGO participation which outlines how NGOs can best contribute to the Committee's work.[59]
- The Committee on the Rights of the Child accepts written information and may invite NGOs to participate in its pre-session working group. NGOs may attend but not participate in the Committee's formal sessions in which public discussion with State representatives occurs. An informal NGO Group for the Convention on the Rights of the Child helps coordinate NGO participation in Committee sessions and has prepared a useful guide for participants.[60]
- The Committee on the Elimination of Discrimination against Women schedules an informal meeting with NGOs on the first two Mondays of each session, for the purpose of receiving country-specific information on States parties whose reports will be before the Committee at that session.[61]
- Although practice of its oversight Committee is not yet fully developed, the Convention on the Rights of Persons with Disabilities (art. 33) states that civil society is to be involved and participate fully in the monitoring process, thus giving civil society a meaningful role in promoting the implementation of the Convention.

Even if a committee does not provide for formal participation in its meetings, NGOs can seek out individual committee members outside the formal sessions to discuss their concerns and present them with information.

It may be helpful to seek the advice of experienced Geneva-based NGOs and organizations which facilitate participation in United Nations human rights meetings. There are also a number of publications designed to help NGOs effectively navigate the United Nations system (listed at the end of this chapter).

Formal accreditation as an NGO in consultative status with the Economic and Social Council is not required in order to work with the treaty bodies, but it is helpful in gaining access to the committees. When planning to attend a committee session, NGOs should contact OHCHR well in advance, to ensure they are aware of current practices.

Publicizing the committee's review and monitoring the Government's response to recommendations

The work of the treaty bodies has little meaning if knowledge of it remains in Geneva. NGOs should ensure that a committee's conclusions and recommendations are made known to the national media and general public in the country concerned, as soon as possible after they are issued at the end of each session. NGOs can obtain any committee's conclusions regarding any country via the OHCHR website.[62]

Committee conclusions on a State's performance in protecting minority rights can be used to generate media and public awareness. If domestic NGOs and media outlets have been contacted prior to the committee's review, they will more likely be interested in the outcome. NGOs may also wish to issue a press release once the committee's concerns and recommendations have been issued, highlighting both the positive and negative conclusions reached by the committee.

59 E/C.12/2000/6.

60 Available from www.childrightsnet.org.

61 Further information on NGO participation is available from www2.ohchr.org/english/bodies/cedaw/docs/NGO_Participation.final.pdf (accessed 2 December 2012).

62 See www.ohchr.org/EN/Countries/Pages/HumanRightsintheWorld.aspx (accessed 2 December 2012).

Some States are responsive to the recommendations of the treaty bodies, but others may need to be encouraged by NGOs and public opinion to implement a committee's conclusions. Although most committees now have a follow-up mechanism with respect to their recommendations, it is nonetheless useful in almost every situation to publicize the State's report, the committee's observations and the State's response to the committee. The United Nations treaty-monitoring system can only work if it is actively supported by minority groups and organizations; it is they who have the greatest interest in its being effective.

Making complaints about human rights violations

The International Covenant on Civil and Political Rights; the International Convention on the Elimination of All Forms of Racial Discrimination; the Convention against Torture and Other Cruel, Inhuman or Degrading Treatment or Punishment; the Convention on the Elimination of All Forms of Discrimination against Women; and the Convention on the Rights of Persons with Disabilities have mechanisms that enable individuals to send an individual complaint, generally called a "communication", to the corresponding committee, alleging that their rights set forth in the respective human rights treaty have been violated.[63] However, the acceptance of such mechanisms is optional. The author of a communication should also be aware that the State concerned may have filed a reservation to any of the treaty's provisions, which limits the substantive scope of the State's obligations.

The provisions for individual complaints are set out in the first Optional Protocol to the International Covenant on Civil and Political Rights, article 14 of the International Convention on the Elimination of All Forms of Racial Discrimination, article 22 of the Convention against Torture and Other Cruel, Inhuman or Degrading Treatment or Punishment, the Optional Protocol to the Convention on the Elimination of All Forms of Discrimination against Women and the Optional Protocol to the Convention on the Rights of Persons with Disabilities. The procedure for handling complaints is similar under all five treaties. It is imperative, however, to consult the exact language of the respective treaty before filing a communication.[64]

Several of the committees have developed forms to facilitate the submission of a communication.[65] It is not mandatory to use these forms, but they do offer guidance on the type of information which should be included in a communication. Each communication should be sent to OHCHR in Geneva, clearly indicating the name of the committee to which it is addressed.

Upon receipt of an individual complaint, the secretariat of the committees makes an initial assessment as to whether certain preliminary criteria for a prima facie case have been met. If

[63] The complaints procedure differs in respect of the International Covenant on Economic, Social and Cultural Rights; the International Convention on the Protection of the Rights of All Migrant Workers and Members of their Families; and the International Convention for the Protection of All Persons from Enforced Disappearance, as follows. An optional protocol authorizing communications to the International Covenant on Economic, Social and Cultural Rights was opened for signature in September 2009 and will enter into force three months after 10 States parties have ratified it. It also provides for an optional procedure under which an inquiry may be initiated by the Committee on Economic, Social and Cultural Rights itself, if it receives information that indicates "grave or systematic" violations of the Covenant. The International Convention on the Protection of the Rights of All Migrant Workers and Members of their Families has an individual complaints procedure that will come into force once 10 States parties have accepted this procedure in accordance with article 77 of the Convention. In accordance with article 31 of the International Convention for the Protection of All Persons from Enforced Disappearance, a State party may at the time of ratification of this Convention or at any time afterwards declare that it recognizes the competence of the Committee on Enforced Disappearances to receive and consider individual communications.

[64] Further information on complaints procedures under specific human rights treaties is available from OHCHR Fact Sheet No. 7/Rev. 2 (forthcoming).

[65] Ibid., annexes.

so, a summary of the communication is sent to the special rapporteur/working group, who acts on behalf of the respective committee. The special rapporteur/working group also assesses the registration criteria and, on behalf of the committee, instructs as to whether or not the communication will be registered.

Once a communication is registered, it is communicated to the State party concerned so that the State may comment on the allegation(s). The State's response, if any, is forwarded to the author of the communication, who may in turn comment on the State's observations. The committee sets a time limit on this exchange. The failure of a State to respond does not prevent the committee from proceeding with examination of a case.

The first step a committee takes in considering a complaint is to determine whether the complaint is admissible. Conditions for admissibility are normally specified in the treaty itself and in the committee's rules of procedure and include that:

- The communication is not anonymous and that it stems from an individual or a group of individuals[66] subject to the jurisdiction of a State party recognizing the competence of the committee concerned to receive and consider individual communications;
- The individual claims to be a victim of a violation by the State party concerned of any of the rights set forth in the covenant or convention. No general complaints about the human rights situation in a country are admissable. As a general rule, the communication should be submitted by the individual themselves or by his or her relatives or designated representatives. Although it is not mandatory to have a lawyer prepare the case, legal advice usually improves the quality of the submissions;
- The communication is compatible with the provisions of the treaty invoked;
- The communication is not an abuse of the right to submit a communication;
- The complainant has exhausted all available domestic remedies. This usually includes pursuing legal claims through the national judicial system; mere doubt about the effectiveness of such action does not dispense with this requirement. However, this shall not be the rule where the exhaustion of remedies would be unreasonably prolonged, or if they would be ineffective or otherwise unavailable;
- The same matter is not being examined under another procedure of international investigation or settlement;[67]
- The complaint is sufficiently substantiated. The alleged victim should provide as much relevant information as possible in support of the allegation(s) made, and enclose copies of all relevant documents, in particular administrative and judicial decisions by national authorities concerning the claims. If the situation does not obviously constitute a human rights violation, the complainant may consider consulting relevant international jurisprudence, both within and outside the United Nations system.

[66] The treaty bodies of the International Covenant on Civil and Political Rights and the Convention against Torture and Other Cruel, Inhuman or Degrading Treatment or Punishment allow only individuals to submit complaints. If a group of individuals submits a complaint to the Human Rights Committee or the Committee against Torture, each member of the group must provide a power of attorney. The Committee on the Elimination of Racial Discrimination, the Committee on the Elimination of Discrimination against Women and the Committee on the Rights of Persons with Disabilities allow groups of individuals to submit a complaint.

[67] Article 5, paragraph 2 (a), of the Optional Protocol to the International Covenant on Civil and Political Rights. Please note that this provision is expressed differently in the Convention on the Elimination of All Forms of Discrimination against Women (art. 4 (2) (a) of the Optional Protocol); the Convention against Torture and Other Cruel, Inhuman or Degrading Treatment or Punishment (art. 22 (4) (a) of the Convention); and the Convention on the Rights of Persons with Disabilities (art. 2 (c) of the Optional Protocol).

As a rule, committees consider the admissibility and merits of a communication jointly with its author. However, a committee may decide either at its own initiative or having received information from the State party concerned, pursuant to its rules of procedure, to separate consideration of the admissibility and merits of a case. The committee examines the communication in the light of all available information. Committee deliberations are confidential, and there is no opportunity to call witnesses or to engage the State concerned in oral debate, as there would be in a domestic court. The committee then forms its conclusion (depending on the committee, this may be called a "view", "decision" or "opinion"), which is transmitted to the author of the communication and the State party, together with any suggestions and recommendations the committee may wish to make. In the event that a violation is found, the State party is invited to inform the committee in due course of the action it has taken in conformity with the committee's suggestions and recommendations. All decisions of the committee are made public and reproduced in the committee's annual report.

Committee conclusions are not legally binding judgements or decisions.[68] However, each one represents an authoritative determination by the organ, established under the treaty itself, charged with the interpretation of that treaty. Ignoring a committee's conclusions exposes a State to domestic and international criticism for not complying with its international obligations.

Most committees have established a follow-up procedure in order to monitor the implementation of its conclusions where it has found a violation of the relevant treaty by the State party. This procedure can facilitate compliance with the committee's recommendations, which has sometimes been weak. Indeed, the mere fact that a well-founded case is brought to a committee may encourage a State to re-examine its policies or begin dialogue with minority representatives.

For minority rights activists it would be instructive to examine procedures related to the following communications: Complaint No. 161/2000 submitted under the Convention against Torture and Other Cruel, Inhuman or Degrading Treatment or Punishment by Hajrizi Dzemajl and 64 other Yugoslav citizens of Roma ethnicity; Communication No. 31/2003 submitted under the International Convention on the Elimination of All Forms of Racial Discrimination by Ms. L. R. and 26 other Slovak citizens of Roma ethnicity; and Communication No. 4/2004 submitted under the Convention on the Elimination of All Forms of Discrimination against Women by Ms A. S. of Hungary.

Urgent cases (Request for interim measures)

Each committee is competent to take urgent action where there is an imminent risk of serious and irreparable harm to the alleged victim before the case is considered by the committee. The alleged victim may ask that the committee adopt interim measures and immediately request the State party to take such appropriate and concrete measures of protection as may be required to avoid irreparable damage to the alleged victim while the communication is under consideration by the committee. Such a course will be adopted only when there is specific information about an imminent risk, for example, a pending execution or deportation. (Reporting urgent cases under the special procedures mechanisms is discussed in chapter IV.)

[68] The Human Rights Committee has stated, "The character of the views of the Committee is further determined by the obligation of States parties to act in good faith, both in their participation in the procedures under the Optional Protocol and in relation to the Covenant itself. A duty to cooperate with the Committee arises from an application of the principle of good faith to the observance of all treaty obligations." See general comment No. 33 (2008) on the obligations of States Parties under the Optional Protocol to the International Covenant on Civil and Political Rights, para. 15.

Contacts and further information

All the treaty bodies discussed in this chapter may be contacted via:

Office of the United Nations High Commissioner for Human Rights (OHCHR)
Palais des Nations
8-14 Avenue de la Paix
CH-1211 Geneva 10
Switzerland

Fax: 41 22 917 90 22

The specific committee being addressed should be specified in both the address and correspondence.

Information on the treaty system may be found in *The United Nations Human Rights Treaty System* (OHCHR Fact Sheet No. 30/Rev.1).[69] Detailed guidance on working with the treaty bodies is given in: *Working with the United Nations Human Rights Programme: A Handbook for Civil Society*.

A number of works describe the practical aspects of using the treaty-based procedures described above. These include: G. Alfredsson and E. Ferrer, *Minority Rights: A Guide to United Nations Procedures and Institutions* (Minority Rights Group and Raoul Wallenberg Institute, 1998); S. Lewis-Anthony and M. Scheinin, "Treaty-based Procedures for Making Human Rights Complaints Within the UN System", in H. Hannum, *Guide to International Human Rights Practice*, 4th ed., (Transnational/Nijhoff, 2004); S. Farrior, "International Reporting Procedures", in H. Hannum, *Guide to International Human Rights Practice*, 4th ed. (Transnational/Nijhoff, 2004).

Other useful guides to the work of particular treaty bodies include: A. Tanaka and Y. Nagamine, *The International Convention on the Elimination of All Forms of Racial Discrimination: A Guide for NGOs* (International Movement Against All Forms of Discrimination and Racism and Minority Rights Group International, 2001); M. Banton, *Combating Racial Discrimination: The UN and its Member States* (Minority Rights Group International, 2000); Division for the Advancement of Women, *Assessing the Status of Women: A Guide to Reporting under the Convention on the Elimination of All Forms of Discrimination against Women* (Commonwealth Secretariat, United Nations and International Women's Rights Action Watch, 2000); P. R. Ghandhi, *The Human Rights Committee and the Right of Individual Communication: Law and Practice* (Ashgate, 1999); and K. A. Young, *The Law and Process of the U.N. Human Rights Committee* (Transnational, 2002).

69 Available from www.ohchr.org/Documents/Publications/FactSheet30en.pdf (accessed 2 December 2012).

PART TWO
OTHER RELEVANT BODIES IN THE UNITED NATIONS SYSTEM

In addition to OHCHR, virtually all other entities of the United Nations pursue activities that relate, directly or indirectly, to minority issues. The Department of Political Affairs, for example, touches upon minority issues as it provides support to electoral processes, pursues mediation and tackles power-sharing and other issues; the Office of the Special Adviser on the Prevention of Genocide has included minority rights as a key component of its framework of analysis; and UN-Women has addressed the intersection of gender inequality with discrimination based on descent, race or ethnicity. Minority issues are also regularly present in the work of the associated programmes, funds and agencies which form part of the United Nations system.

Pursuant to article 9 of the Minorities Declaration, all specialized agencies and other organizations of the United Nations system are to contribute to the full realization of the rights and principles set forth in the Declaration, within their respective fields of competence. The Inter-Agency Group on Minorities met between 2004 and 2011 to cooperate and advance the implementation of this article. To further enhance the scope and depth of such work, the Secretary-General's Policy Committee decided in March 2012 to establish a United Nations network on racial discrimination and protection of minorities, to be coordinated by OHCHR.

Within the United Nations system, the United Nations High Commissioner for Refugees and the United Nations Children's Fund are specifically concerned with the groups identified in their names, and many of those who fall within their mandates are also members of minorities. The United Nations Development Programme has one of the broadest mandates within the United Nations system and is present in over 160 countries. Dedicated to promoting human development, it undertakes various activities related to minorities and is therefore often of great importance to minorities, both directly and indirectly.

Specialized agencies have their own constitutions and membership rules, and the relationship of each with the United Nations is set out in agreements between them. There are many such agencies, two of which are regularly concerned with minority issues – the International Labour Organization and the United Nations Educational, Scientific and Cultural Organization. Both have formal procedures under which allegations of human rights violations can be submitted to them and both pay specific attention to minority issues in some aspects of their work.

CHAPTER VI

THE UNITED NATIONS DEVELOPMENT PROGRAMME

Summary: The United Nations Development Programme (UNDP) is the global development network of the United Nations, whose goal it is to assist countries in acquiring knowledge, experience and resources to help people build a better life. UNDP works on the ground in 177 countries and territories, collaborating with Governments and people to find their own solutions to global and national development challenges. This chapter describes how the work of UNDP affects members of minorities and suggests several ways in which minorities might increase their participation in and better influence development processes and outcomes.

The United Nations Development Programme (UNDP) supports States Members of the United Nations in developing national and local capacities for human development and in achieving the Millennium Development Goals, which world leaders have pledged to do by 2015.[70] Capacity development cuts across its four key focus areas: democratic governance; poverty reduction and achievement of the Millennium Development Goals; crisis prevention and recovery; and environment and energy for sustainable development. In each of these areas, UNDP advocates for the advancement of human rights and the empowerment of women. It also promotes the efficiency and effectiveness of the United Nations system as a whole at the country level.

Minorities in development programming

There are ethnic, religious or linguistic minorities in all UNDP countries of operation and a strong link between minority issues and each of its key focus areas. Minorities are often poorer than other segments of a country's population, are regularly affected by conflict, have less access to governance mechanisms, have higher HIV prevalence, and may suffer from higher levels of environmental degradation than exist elsewhere in the country. Increased attention to minority rights can help overcome obstacles to achieving the Millennium Development Goals. UNDP strives to strengthen national development plans by drawing attention to the negative impact of excluding minorities and the benefits of working to include minorities.

UNDP recognizes that minority-based civil society organizations and its own employees who belong to minority groups bring valuable experiences, skills and knowledge to its work. UNDP thus strives to build diversity among its employees and invites minorities to become strategic partners and support it in achieving its development goals.

Minorities and the UNDP focus areas

Poverty reduction and achievement of the Millennium Development Goals

UNDP supports Governments to ensure that minorities overcome poverty. It does this through improving capacity to monitor poverty reduction among minorities, facilitating the participation of minorities in designing poverty reduction strategies and advocating for improved human development among minority groups. It assists Governments to understand the particular challenges faced by minorities in reaching the Millennium Development Goals, and to put in place sound strategies – linked to minority rights protection – for overcoming such challenges.[71]

Democratic governance

Mainstreaming minority issues strengthens the work of UNDP on democratic governance, since democratic institutions are less effective at ensuring equality in the absence of special protection

70 See www.undp.org/mdg.

71 In the Republic of Moldova, for example, UNDP is working on human rights issues within the Millennium Development Goals through supporting Roma inclusion, reflected in the adoption of the 2012 Roma Inclusion Strategy.

for minorities. Programmes to support democratic governance therefore consider barriers to access and participation which minorities may face, and work to overcome them. Two key issues are minority access to justice and participation in governance.

Crisis prevention and recovery

Attention to minority issues is crucial for the long-term sustainability of peace and development, because minority identities can become a continuing focus of conflict. Historical patterns of minority exclusion that causes conflict may re-emerge if they are not adequately addressed, and minority inclusion helps create national stability. *Practical Guide to Multilateral Needs Assessments in Post-Conflict Situations* (United Nations Development Programme, World Bank, United Nations Development Group, 2004) identifies conflict factors which have roots in minority rights violations, such as unequal access to land and education, weak political participation and discrimination.[72]

Environment and energy for sustainable development

The special relationship between indigenous peoples and the environment has been well documented. Often overlooked, however, is the impact of environmental and energy issues on minority groups and how the exclusion of minorities affects these sectors. The poor, who often correlate with minority groups, are disproportionately affected by environmental degradation and lack of access to clean, affordable energy services. Minority regions may be disproportionately affected by environmental change and minority groups may find it more difficult to obtain relief during environmental disasters, due to discrimination or to their location in disproportionately underserviced areas.

HIV/AIDS

Minority groups are one of the key populations at higher risk of HIV/AIDS. Interventions for addressing the prevalence of HIV/AIDS in minority groups must take a "social determinants of health" approach. Public policy responses may not be effective for minority populations if strategies are based on addressing risk factors characteristic only of majority populations and not adapted to minority cultural and social realities. Minorities living with HIV/AIDS may not enjoy equal access to health care because of discrimination in health-care services, lack of culturally appropriate health care or higher poverty levels that render retroviral treatment unaffordable. Infrastructure for medical services may be more limited in remote or impoverished areas where minorities are settled.

Advocacy and partnership

UNDP has an important role in the promotion of human development and human rights. UNDP publications such as national human development reports[73] or MDG progress reports[74] can raise awareness of gaps in human development for minorities and highlight good practices. Where national human development reports include disaggregated statistics it may encourage other actors to collect such data, which would enable minority groups to utilize them in their advocacy efforts. The launch of a human development report can provide the opportunity to begin dialogue with stakeholders on human development and governance issues of concern to minorities. For example, the regional report, At Risk: Roma and the Displaced in Southeast Europe,[75] has been

72 Available from www.conflictsensitivity.org/publications/practical-guide-multilateral-needs-assessments-post-conflict-situations (accessed 2 December 2012).

73 Available from http://hdr.undp.org/en/reports/ (accessed 2 December 2012).

74 Available from www.undp.org/content/undp/en/home/librarypage/mdg/mdg-reports/ (accessed 2 December 2012).

75 Available from http://europeandcis.undp.org/uploads/public/File/rbec_web/vgr/vuln_rep_all.pdf (accessed 2 December 2012).

helpful in advancing dialogue between national Governments and Roma. Further, such reports focused on minority groups could highlight critical issues affecting these populations.

There is immense capacity within minority communities to support UNDP in achieving its goals. Many minority NGOs are already working towards these goals, and strategic partnerships may be forged between them and UNDP for greater impact. Moreover, many minority NGOs are working in these and other UNDP focus areas, taking the lead in providing HIV care and education or providing access to information and communication technologies for communities. NGOs may also work on contract to UNDP to deliver specific inputs to projects, such as consultancy services or equipment.

UNDP has experience in working with a wide range of civil society organizations to strengthen networks, encourage dialogue and build capacity. In Nepal, for example, the United Nations country team involved minority civil society organizations representing various ethnic and women's groups in the development of the United Nations Development Assistance Framework (UNDAF) and in country programming processes.

Resource guide on marginalized minorities in development programming

In partnership with the Independent Expert on minority issues and OHCHR, UNDP has published *Marginalised Minorities in Development Programming: A UNDP Resource Guide and Toolkit.*[76] It aims to:

- Introduce and enhance understanding of the rights and interests of minorities;
- Identify institutions and mechanisms at international, regional and national levels for the protection, promotion and fulfilment of minority rights;
- Raise awareness of the importance of addressing marginalized minorities' issues in development programming and provide guidance in applying the relevant normative frameworks in programme and project planning, design, implementation and evaluation;
- Facilitate capacity development and identify strategies to strengthen partnerships with Government counterparts, the donor community and civil society organizations and NGOs.

The primary audience for this resource is UNDP country office staff and those with policy responsibilities. However, it may also serve as a reference document for other United Nations agencies, Government counterparts and other partners. It is also intended to enable minority group(s) to understand conceptual issues and fundamental principles on the promotion and protection of minorities, and increase their opportunities for participation and representation in development processes.

Contacts and further information

UNDP is based in New York and has offices in most countries. The main entry point to UNDP for minority advocates is:

United Nations Development Programme
Democratic Governance Group/Bureau for Development Policy
304 East 45th Street
New York, NY 10017
United States of America

Fax: 1 212 906 6471
E-mail: dgg@undp.org
Website: www.undp.org/governance
www.undp.org/countries

[76] Available from www.ohchr.org/Documents/Issues/Minorities/UNDPMarginalisedMinorities.pdf (accessed 2 December 2012).

CHAPTER VII

THE UNITED NATIONS HIGH COMMISSIONER FOR REFUGEES

Summary: Many of the world's refugees, asylum seekers, internally displaced persons and stateless persons are members of minority groups who have specific protection needs and often cannot rely on their own State for protection. The United Nations High Commissioner for Refugees is mandated by the United Nations to lead and coordinate international action for the worldwide protection of refugees and to find durable solutions which protect them. The United Nations General Assembly has also requested UNHCR to work for the prevention and reduction of statelessness and the protection of stateless persons. In all its activities, UNHCR promotes an age-, gender- and diversity-sensitive approach and pays particular attention to groups with specific needs, seeking to promote the equal rights of disenfranchised groups, among others.

The mandate of the United Nations High Commissioner for Refugees

The Office of the United Nations High Commissioner for Refugees (UNHCR), the agency mandated to oversee the application of the 1951 Convention relating to the Status of Refugees and its 1967 Protocol, provides international protection and assistance to almost 40 million people, including asylum seekers, refugees, returnees (former refugees), internally displaced persons and stateless persons around the world.

In the 21st century, UNHCR has assisted with major refugee crises in Africa (e.g., in the Democratic Republic of the Congo and Somalia) and Asia (especially regarding Afghan refugees). UNHCR has also been asked to use its expertise to help people internally displaced by conflict, in particular in the Sudan, Colombia and Iraq. UNHCR actively contributes to the protection of minorities in the context of its major operations in support of internally displaced persons. However, failure to protect the rights of minorities has itself often been at the heart of the causes of displacement and may present an obstacle to the identification of durable solutions. The operational context in the Balkans, the Sudan, Sri Lanka, Georgia and Afghanistan, among other places, presents particularly complex realities in this regard.

Since it began operations, UNHCR has also been involved with statelessness, first with stateless refugees, then with all stateless persons. Members of national minorities are often exposed to greater risks of becoming stateless; risks which tend to be heightened by the impact of displacement. Statelessness is a massive problem that affects an estimated 12 million people worldwide. Possession of nationality is essential for full participation in society and is a prerequisite for the enjoyment of the full range of human rights. The work of UNHCR on statelessness relies on the international human rights framework, in particular on the 1954 Convention relating to the Status of Stateless Persons and the 1961 Convention on the Reduction of Statelessness.

Today, inter-ethnic and interracial tensions and conflict exist in nearly every region of the world. These conflicts are often rooted in power struggles and are aggravated by socioeconomic inequalities and competition for scarce resources. National, ethnic and religious minorities are often vulnerable in these conflicts; many of those who flee their countries for fear of persecution are members of minority groups. The 1951 Convention relating to the Status of Refugees recognizes this link in its definition of a refugee, which includes persons who flee persecution not only because of their political opinion but also because of their race, religion, nationality, or membership of a particular social group.

Refugees fleeing conflicts and persecution are often in a very vulnerable situation. They have no protection from their own State – indeed, it is often their own Government that is threatening to persecute them. Refugees seeking asylum in another country usually constitute minorities in those societies and often face rejection, discrimination and sometimes even xenophobic attacks. Stateless persons and internally displaced persons are also often exposed to stigmatization and harassment. *Guiding Principles on Internal Displacement* (United Nations Office for the Coordination of Humanitarian Affairs, 2004)[77] refers directly to the specific protection needs of minorities: principle 9 declares that "States are under a particular obligation to protect against the displacement of indigenous peoples, minorities, peasants, pastoralists and other groups with a special dependency on and attachment to their lands".

Protection activities

The principal role of UNHCR is to provide international protection for persons who have been forced to flee their country of origin. The organization ensures that the international standards of refugee protection guaranteed in the 1951 Convention, its 1967 Protocol, and various regional instruments and declarations, including the 1969 Convention Governing the Specific Aspects of Refugee Problems in Africa, of the Organization of African Unity, and the 1984 Cartagena Declaration on Refugees, Colloquium on the International Protection of Refugees in Central America, Mexico and Panama, are respected. Among the rights UNHCR works to protect is the fundamental right not to be forcibly returned, or refouled, to a territory where the refugee's life, liberty or physical security may be threatened. The 1951 Convention also requires non-discrimination in the application of its provisions and guarantees a certain standard of treatment in relation to education, housing and employment.

UNHCR regularly issues notes and guidelines on a variety of matters related to the protection of persons of concern. Many such notes and guidelines relate specifically to national, ethnic, linguistic and religious minorities, including *Guidelines Relating to the Eligibility of Slovak Roma Asylum Seekers, Note on the nationality status of the Urdu-speaking community in Bangladesh and UNHCR's Eligibility Guidelines for Assessing the International Protection Needs of Individuals from Kosovo.*

According to the Statute of UNHCR (art. 8(a)), the High Commissioner for Refugees shall provide for the protection of refugees falling under the competence of his (or her) Office by "promoting the conclusion and ratification of international conventions for the protection of refugees, supervising their application and proposing amendments thereto". The governing Executive Committee of UNHCR has adopted conclusions on international protection which relate to minority issues. In conclusions No. 68 and No. 71, the Executive Committee acknowledges that ethnic intolerance causes forced migration, and conclusion No. 80 states that upholding human rights for minorities is one way to combat displacement. Conclusion No. 102 stresses the importance of identifying the particular protection risks of minority refugees in order to protect all refugees. Although not formally binding, the Executive Committee's conclusions constitute "soft law" which is relevant to the international protection regime, as they express opinions that are broadly representative of the views of the international community.

When UNHCR is active in a minority group's country of origin, whether to assist returnees or protect internally displaced persons, it has often been engaged in specific activities to protect and assist minority groups. With the dissolution of the Soviet Union, for example, UNHCR facilitated durable solutions not only for refugees but also for minority groups whose members had been deported to other parts of the Soviet Union decades earlier. UNHCR was directly

[77] Available from www.unhcr.org/43ce1cff2.pdf (accessed 2 December 2012).

involved in the return of Crimean Tatars to Ukraine and still assumes a limited role with regard to a programme for the return of Meskhetian Turks to Georgia.

Minorities and statelessness

Minorities are often disproportionately affected by problems of statelessness, sometimes as a result of discriminatory legislation on nationality, or discriminatory practices, or because of differences in nationality laws among the various States to which a minority group may have ties. To address this issue, UNHCR conducts a number of activities in the field under the four broad categories of identification, prevention and reduction of statelessness and protection of stateless persons.

The *identification* of stateless persons is the first step in combating statelessness, and UNHCR works actively to gather information regarding stateless populations. Statistics alone, however, are not effective in eradicating statelessness. Identifying the causes of statelessness and the characteristics of stateless populations is essential for the formulation of responses. Identification activities include surveys, studies on legislation and administrative gaps, population censuses and discussions with the people affected. Once a population or person is identified as stateless, UNHCR coordinates efforts with the Government and civil society partners to address the issue.

Prevention is the easiest and most effective way to address statelessness. UNHCR works in a variety of ways to change conditions which could lead to statelessness. Where legislative or administrative gaps exist, UNHCR, in partnership with other organizations, provides technical and advisory services to States on amending their legislation and practice to align with the 1961 Convention and other international standards.

In many situations, people risk not being recognized as nationals, because they cannot prove their identity or links with any country. For this reason, with NGO and United Nations partners, UNHCR promotes birth registration. It also provides practical advice and legal assistance to help persons obtain identity and nationality documentation, which eliminates many risks of statelessness. In the Balkans, for example, some 50,000 members of the Roma, Ashkali and Egyptian minorities lack personal documentation. Many are refugees or have been internally displaced and socially excluded. UNHCR is engaging in a comprehensive project facilitating their civil registration and documentation, which has thus far addressed the needs of almost 8,000 persons.

Through similar projects, UNHCR and its partners enable persons to avail themselves of naturalization procedures and thus to *reduce statelessness*. On a large scale, UNHCR engages in citizenship campaigns, supporting Governments which have taken steps to resolve a stateless situation. In these campaigns, stateless persons are made aware of the importance of nationality and relevant procedures, for example through radio shows or posters.

As is the case for refugees, special measures of protection are often necessary to *protect* stateless people. UNHCR encourages the ratification of the 1954 Convention relating to the Status of Stateless Persons, which guarantees those persons specific rights. UNHCR also assists States in implementing their obligations and intervenes in specific cases.

Forced displacement of minorities

While ethnicity sometimes lies at the centre of conflict or persecution, ethnic or religious minorities may also become the unintended victims of forced displacement, especially where their security is at risk as a consequence of where they live or for other reasons unrelated to their ethnic background. In either case, forced displacement may have an additional impact on the preservation of minority identity and culture.

In many situations, minorities and indigenous peoples who have specific ties to land are disproportionately affected by conflict, and their forced displacement may even lead to the extinction of entire groups. At the same time, their presence in remote or border areas poses challenges for their effective registration and access to the refugee protection regime. Minorities affected by forced displacement are commonly not aware of their right to seek asylum, and frequently seek protection within their kin communities across the border. In consequence, they often do not have access to effective protection due to their geographic location and/or language barriers. The farther indigenous peoples move from their ancestral lands, the more obstacles they encounter to exercising their fundamental individual and collective rights, a situation that sometimes threatens their survival as a people.

Partnership with civil society

UNHCR believes that partnerships are the best means of ensuring that persons of concern, especially minorities, are protected. One of its main priorities is working with civil society partners around the world. More than 75 per cent of the civil society organizations with which UNHCR works are local organizations which provide expertise and are able to become operational immediately in an emergency situation.[78]

UNHCR will generally formalize a partnership through a project agreement and memorandum of understanding (MOU). UNHCR works with both implementing and operational partners. An *implementing partner* is an entity with which UNHCR enters into a subagreement to implement a project on a contractual basis for the benefit of persons of concern. An *operational partner* is an entity whose work is complementary to that of UNHCR and which may be assisting the same populations of concern or working towards the same goals; however, it does not receive funds from UNHCR for that purpose. An example of an operational partner is the World Food Programme, which distributes food to persons of concern in certain locations.

Contacts and further information

UNHCR is based in Geneva and has offices in most countries.

For further information, contact:

United Nations High Commissioner for Refugees
Case Postale 2500
CH-1211 Geneva 2
Switzerland

Tel. 41 22) 739 81 11
Fax: 41 22) 739 73 77
E-mail: webmaster@unhcr.org
Website: www.unhcr.org

Another leading source of information is the extensive Refworld database (see annex II), selected and compiled from the global network of UNHCR.

UNHCR has developed resource materials to guide Governments and civil society on addressing statelessness.[79] A useful resource is: L. van Waas, *Nationality Matters: Statelessness under International Law* (Intersentia, 2009).

78 Further information and resources on forming civil society partnerships are available from www.unhcr.org/pages/49c3646c296.html (accessed 2 December 2012).

79 See www.unhcr.org/statelessness.

There are a great many works on national and international refugee law. Among those recommended are: E. Feller, V. Turk, and F. Nicholson (eds.), *Refugee Protection in International Law, UNHCR's Global Consultations on International Protection* (Cambridge University Press and UNHCR, 2003); M. Foster, *International Refugee Law and Socio-Economic Rights: Refuge from Deprivation* (Cambridge University Press, 2007); G. S. Goodwin-Gill and J. McAdam, *The Refugee in International Law,* 3rd ed. (Oxford University Press, 2007); J. C. Hathaway, *The Rights of Refugees under International Law* (Cambridge University Press, 2005); K. Wouters, *International Legal Standards for the Protection of Refoulement* (Intersentia, 2009).

CHAPTER VIII

THE UNITED NATIONS CHILDREN'S FUND

Summary: The United Nations Children's Fund (UNICEF) works to secure the rights of minority children and women by undertaking a wide range of activities in five focus areas: young child survival and development; basic education and gender equality; children and HIV/AIDS; child protection from violence, exploitation and abuse; and policy advocacy and partnerships for children's rights.

The United Nations Children's Fund (UNICEF) is a specialized agency of the United Nations. It was established in 1946, initially to provide short-term relief to children after the Second World War in Europe. Its mission is to advocate for the protection of children's rights, to help meet their basic needs and to expand their opportunities to reach their full potential. Its work, carried out in 190 countries, helps children survive and thrive from early childhood through adolescence. UNICEF supports child health (it is the world's largest provider of vaccines in developing countries) and nutrition, good water and sanitation, quality basic education for all boys and girls, and the protection of children from violence, exploitation and AIDS. UNICEF is funded entirely by the voluntary contributions of individuals, businesses, foundations and Governments.

UNICEF carries out its work primarily in the field, integrating with other United Nations activities within a country. Each UNICEF country office pursues the agency's mission through a unique programme of cooperation developed with the host Government and with input from a range of stakeholders. This programme focuses on practical ways to realize the rights of children and women within the country. Needs are analysed in a situation report produced during the five-year programme cycle. Regional offices guide this work and provide technical assistance to country offices as needed.[80]

Many people in industrialized countries first hear about the work of UNICEF through the activities of its 36 national committees. These NGOs promote children's rights, raise funds, sell UNICEF greeting cards and other products, create key partnerships and provide other invaluable support. They raise one third of the agency's resources.

A 36-member Executive Board made up of Government representatives guides and monitors all of the agency's work. Overall management and administration is determined at the New York headquarters where global policy on children is shaped. Specialized offices include the Supply Division, based in Copenhagen, which provides such essential items as life-saving vaccines for children in developing countries. UNICEF also operates the Innocenti Research Centre in Florence, Italy, and has offices in Japan and Brussels which assist in fundraising and liaison with policymakers.

The work of UNICEF is guided by the provisions and principles of the 1989 Convention on the Rights of the Child, the most widely ratified international human rights instrument in history. Because it is in force in virtually the entire community of nations, the Convention provides a common ethical and legal framework to develop an agenda for children and, in addition, constitutes a common reference against which progress may be assessed. The Convention and the Committee on the Rights of the Child are discussed in chapter V.

80 See www.unicef.org/about/structure/index_worldcontact.html (accessed 2 December 2012).

UNICEF and minorities

Because UNICEF is a human rights-based organization, its involvement in the promotion and protection of the rights of minority children and women is not a choice but an obligation. Its mission statement provides that "UNICEF is non-partisan and its cooperation is free of discrimination. In everything it does, the most disadvantaged children and the countries in greatest need have priority". Given that minority children are often the most disadvantaged in the societies in which they live, this founding principle offers a sound basis for the agency's engagement in minority issues.

With a wide network of offices in both the developing and industrialized worlds, UNICEF is in a unique position to encourage the introduction of minority issues into public policy agendas and thus to make a difference in the lives of minority children and women. In the most disadvantaged regions and countries, UNICEF is capable not only of influencing policies but also of supporting Governments' efforts and directly delivering assistance to minority children and women.

The work of UNICEF

The agency's medium-term strategic plan covering the period 2006-2013 is entitled *Investing in Children: The UNICEF Contribution to Poverty Reduction and the Millennium Summit Agenda*. It covers five focus areas: young child survival and development; basic education and gender equality; children and HIV/AIDS; child protection from violence, exploitation and abuse; and policy advocacy and partnerships for children's rights. In each of these focus areas UNICEF works to secure minority rights.

Young child survival and development

This focus area covers UNICEF activities related to, for example, immunization services and prevention and control of malaria, diarrhoea and pneumonia; eradication of polio and guinea worm disease; care of pregnant women and newborn babies; food fortification; improvement of family and community care practices for young children; and access to water and sanitation, including in emergency situations. Most commonly, work regarding minorities relates to capacity-building for improved family care practices, for example, by improving minority participation in health projects, particularly through social workers or health mediators. UNICEF Romania works with its partners to strengthen the network of social workers, community nurses and Roma health mediators to increase the accessibility and quality of community-level health and social services, mainly for vulnerable groups.

Basic education and gender equality

Within this focus area UNICEF seeks to implement the right to education of every boy and girl, as stipulated under the Convention (arts. 28 and 29). It also contributes to the achievement of two of the Millennium Development Goals, the achievement of universal primary education, and the promotion of gender equality and the empowerment of women. Most commonly, working for minorities in this area involves improving educational quality and increasing school retention, completion and achievement rates, and improving children's developmental readiness to start primary school on time. Particular focus has been given to marginalized children in Thailand, where Muslim minority children affected by conflict benefited from the training of Islamic teachers through the Child-Friendly School quality standards approach. In the conflict-affected Northern Province of Sri Lanka, the primary home of the Tamil minority, education officers were trained in emergency preparedness and response planning. They carried out rapid assessments and reopened schools near areas with internally displaced children to ensure minimal disruption to education. In addition, 1,260 teachers and principals from more than 300 schools were trained in developing school-level plans.

Children and HIV/AIDS

This focus area relates to reducing and preventing HIV infections, improving treatment for HIV-positive women and children, expanding care and services for children orphaned and made vulnerable by HIV/AIDS, and increasing HIV/AIDS awareness through the use of gender-sensitive information, skills and services. In Ethiopia, for example, UNICEF seeks to enhance the participation of girls in HIV/AIDS-related development programmes through a Girls' Forum Initiative which extends coverage to students, including minority girls from the Oromia region. In Brazil, UNICEF supports a network of Afro-descendent adolescent girls, residents and community leaders. Adolescent girls engaged their communities in the planning, implementation and monitoring of HIV-related initiatives, including initiatives related to issues of gender and race.

Child protection from violence, exploitation and abuse

Within this focus area, UNICEF seeks to strengthen country environments, capacities and responses to prevent and protect children from violence, exploitation, abuse, neglect and the effects of conflict. Most commonly, UNICEF is involved in increasing Governments' awareness of child protection rights and encouraging improved data on and analysis of child protection. In the Philippines, for example, UNICEF assessed the effectiveness of monitoring and reporting mechanisms of human rights violations against children in Mindanao, where many conflict-affected Muslim minorities reside. UNICEF also works to better protect children from the impact of armed conflict and natural disasters. In the Sudan, for example, a gender-inclusive National Reintegration Strategy for Children Associated with the Armed Forces and Groups was developed by UNICEF and Government authorities, facilitating more appropriate support to girls released from conflict, including those from minority communities.

Policy advocacy and partnerships for children's rights

Within this focus area, UNICEF promotes effective participation of minorities in mapping, planning, implementation, monitoring and evaluation. This, coupled with relevant advocacy initiatives within and for minority communities, facilitates the development of tailored initiatives to meet their needs. In Nepal, the Decentralized Action for Children and Women programme employs an evidence-based framework informed by data disaggregated by ethnicity and engages participatory approaches with marginalized groups such as Dalits. UNICEF is also active in the development and dissemination of high-quality research and policy analysis on children and women, in collaboration with partners. UNICEF has also generated socioanthropological research through an agreement with the University of the Autonomous Regions of the Caribbean Coast of Nicaragua, a community university focusing on Afro-descendant communities.

Collaboration with civil society organizations

Civil society organizations are closely involved in the work of UNICEF in the 190 countries where it is active. UNICEF has formal agreements with hundreds of NGOs and individual leaders in 160 countries, ranging from large networks such as Save the Children to village water committees.

NGOs working in a specific country should approach the UNICEF country office to discuss potential partnership. Partnership can be informal (e.g., information sharing, coordination of efforts) or more formalized, which can include the provision of UNICEF funds to an NGO to implement activities for minority children.

NGOs may wish to partner with UNICEF through the agency's NGO Committee. Established in 1952, this is now a worldwide network of over 80 international NGOs working on behalf of children. The Committee:

- Facilitates a two-way exchange of information and experience between UNICEF and NGOs at international and national levels;
- Encourages cooperative efforts among NGOs and between NGOs and UNICEF;
- Encourages member organizations and their national affiliates to document and make known to UNICEF special needs of children which remain unmet;
- Shares with UNICEF innovative and successful programmes undertaken by NGOs at local, national and international levels, and lessons learned;
- Provides input to UNICEF Executive Board meetings.

The main office of the NGO Committee is in New York. Its governing body, the Global Forum, is an elected board consisting of six international NGO member organizations and seven regional representatives.

Contacts and further information

All communications to UNICEF headquarters regarding minority rights should be addressed to:

United Nations Children's Fund
Gender and Rights Unit
Division of Policy and Practice
3 United Nations Plaza
New York, New York 10017
United States of America

Fax: 1 212 735 44 20
Website: www.unicef.org

For further information on the NGO Committee, contact:

NGO Committee on UNICEF
UNICEF House, 526-1
3 United Nations Plaza,
New York, NY 10017
United States of America

Phone: 1 212 326 77 13
E-mail: ngocommittee@unicef.org
Website: www.ngocomunicef.org

A useful resource is *Promoting the Rights of Minority Children and Women: A Review of UNICEF's Policies and Practices* (Minority Rights Group International, 2010).[81]

[81] Available from www.minorityrights.org/download.php?id=920 (accessed 2 December 2012).

CHAPTER IX

THE INTERNATIONAL LABOUR ORGANIZATION

Summary: The complaints procedures developed by the International Labour Organization (ILO) for the protection of human rights may be used directly only by a Government, workers' or employers' association, or by a delegate to the International Labour Conference. However, many of the ILO non-discrimination norms and its promotional, oversight and technical assistance activities may be of interest to minorities. This chapter outlines some of the relevant ILO standards and initiatives.

The International Labour Organization (ILO) was established in 1919 by the Treaty of Versailles. It was the only element of the League of Nations to survive the Second World War and in 1945 it became the first specialized agency of the United Nations system. The tripartite structure of ILO (consisting of representatives of Governments, employers and workers) is unique among intergovernmental organizations; ILO is the only organization in which Governments do not control all the votes.

ILO is composed of three organs: the General Conference of representatives of member States (the International Labour Conference), the Governing Body and the International Labour Office. The General Conference and the Governing Body are both composed of 50 per cent Government representatives and 50 per cent representatives of employers and workers in member States. The presence and voting power of these non-governmental elements give ILO a unique perspective on the issues before it and expand the possibilities for dealing with practical problems facing ILO members.

One of the principal activities of ILO is adopting and implementing international labour standards. ILO adopts conventions and recommendations at the annual International Labour Conference, requires Governments to examine whether conventions should be ratified, and closely supervises and comments on how member States apply the conventions they choose to ratify. There are now approximately 7,714 ratifications of the nearly 200 conventions adopted under the auspices of ILO.

ILO standards

While ILO has specific standards for indigenous peoples and migrants, there are no specific standards for ethnic, linguistic and religious minorities. Nevertheless, several of the main ILO standards are highly relevant to the protection of minorities, since they must be applied in a context of non-discrimination and equal protection for all.

Non-discrimination

ILO action for the elimination of discrimination in employment and occupation is based on the ILO Constitution, which commits ILO to fighting against discrimination based on race, creed or sex. Its principal convention in this area is the Discrimination (Employment and Occupation) Convention, 1958 (No. 111), which is supplemented by a number of other ILO standards and which prohibits discrimination in employment and occupation on the grounds of race, colour, religion and national extraction, among others. Convention No. 111 (ratified by 169 countries) is one of the eight fundamental conventions of ILO, and, as such, it is among the targets of a ratification campaign instituted by the Director-General in 1995.

ILO carries out intense supervisory activities related to this Convention, as it does with all other conventions for which it is responsible, and the ILO Committee of Experts on the Application of Conventions and Recommendations draws attention to problems in the implementation of conventions in its annual report. Many of these comments concern discrimination on the basis of race, religion and national extraction, and raise issues such as underrepresentation of ethnic minorities in private and public sector employment, the lack of positive measures to promote the employment of members of minorities, or the lack of appropriate means to assess existing policies, strategies and programmes to promote equal opportunities for members of minority groups. They consistently highlight the need to take proactive measures to address persistent inequalities faced by minorities and to establish appropriate data on their situation in employment and occupation.

Forced labour

Another convention that can have direct impact on the situation of minorities is the Forced Labour Convention, 1930 (No. 29), which prohibits all forms of forced or compulsory labour. The Abolition of Forced Labour Convention, 1957 (No. 105) is even more precise, providing that forced labour may not be used for the purposes of racial discrimination. In addition, minority children are specially protected under the Worst Forms of Child Labour Convention, 1999 (No. 182). For instance, in a 2006 comment regarding Thailand, the Committee of Experts addressed the problem of children of ethnic minorities being victims of trafficking for labour or sexual exploitation.

Declaration on Fundamental Principles and Rights at Work

Adopted in 1998, the ILO Declaration on Fundamental Principles and Rights at Work declares that "all Members [of ILO], even if they have not ratified the Conventions in question, have an obligation arising from the very fact of membership in the Organization, to respect, to promote and to realize, in good faith and in accordance with the Constitution, the principles concerning the fundamental rights which are the subject of those Conventions … [including] the elimination of discrimination in respect of employment and occupation". In addition to discrimination, the Declaration covers freedom of association, elimination of forced labour and abolition of child labour. Member States which have not ratified the relevant conventions nevertheless have to report to ILO annually on how they are attempting to realize the principles in the Declaration.

Each year, ILO issues a global report on one of the four rights covered in the Declaration.[82] The global reports on discrimination published in 2003 and 2007 paid close attention to discrimination faced by minorities. The 2007 report, for example, noted an increase in complaints about religious discrimination against Muslims in Europe and the United States of America; Pasmanda and Dalits in India; Hindus in Afghanistan, Bangladesh and Pakistan; and non-Muslims (particularly Christians) in Saudi Arabia, the Islamic Republic of Iran, Senegal, Egypt and the Sudan. Similarly, the global reports on forced labour and child labour have examined how these practices affect minorities. The 2005 report on forced labour noted that "[i]n some cases, the persistence of forced labour today can be the result of very longstanding patterns of discrimination against certain ethnic and caste minorities", particularly in some countries in Asia. Following each global report, a programme of action is drawn up to focus ILO and other technical assistance on these problems (see below).

Domestic labour

The Domestic Workers Convention, 2011 (No. 189) is the latest ILO convention which can have a direct impact on persons belonging to minorities. Domestic workers, often subject to exploitation and denial of human rights, also often belong to minorities. The Convention does

82 Available from www.ilo.org/declaration/follow-up/globalreports/lang--en/index.htm (accessed 2 December 2012).

not mention persons belonging to minorities per se but sets out standards for the treatment of domestic workers. Supplemented by the Domestic Workers Recommendation, 2011 (No. 201), the Convention aims at protecting and improving the working and living conditions of domestic workers worldwide, estimated to number between 53 million and 100 million.

Supervision, reporting and complaints procedures

Supervision of ILO standards is mainly carried out by the Committee of Experts on the Application of Conventions and Recommendations and the Conference Committee on the Application of Conventions and Recommendations.

The Committee of Experts is composed of 20 independent legal experts from all the major social and economic systems and all parts of the world. It meets annually to examine reports received from Governments, which are obligated to report periodically on how they are applying the conventions they have ratified. Under article 23 of the ILO Constitution, the workers' and employers' representatives of a State member that has ratified conventions may also submit comments on how the conventions are applied in practice, thus offering a valuable supplement to their Government's reports. The Committee of Experts reports publicly on its comments and observations concerning specific conventions and specific countries.

The Conference Committee on the Application of Conventions and Recommendations represents the next level of supervision. Established each year by the International Labour Conference, it reflects the tripartite structure of ILO. On the basis of the report of the Committee of Experts, the Conference Committee selects a number of especially important or persistent cases and asks the Governments concerned to appear before it and explain the situations on which the Committee of Experts has commented. At the end of each session, the Conference Committee reports to the full Conference on the problems encountered by Governments in fulfilling their obligations under the ILO Constitution or in complying with conventions they have ratified. The Conference Committee's report is published in the *Proceedings of the International Labour Conference* each year, along with the Conference's discussion of that report.

Most of the supervisory work of ILO takes place through an ongoing dialogue between the Committee of Experts and ILO member States, on the basis of State reports supplemented by comments submitted by the workers' and employers' representatives under article 23 of the ILO Constitution. Members of minority groups or NGOs promoting minority rights may wish to investigate the possibility of submitting information to the Committee of Experts through a workers' or employers' organization. Minority groups and NGOs can send documentation on the situation of minorities directly to ILO. Such information cannot be formally submitted to the supervisory bodies, but it is useful in expanding the ILO knowledge base.

In addition to report-based supervision, ILO has complaints procedures which can address problems of discrimination on the basis of ethnicity which affect working life. Of the various mechanisms established by ILO, the most relevant to discrimination against minorities is the possibility of filing a "representation" against a State member under article 24 of the ILO Constitution. A representation will be considered if it originates from "an industrial association of employers or of workers"; it concerns a member State of ILO; it refers to a convention ratified by the State against which it is made; and it alleges that the State "has failed to secure in some respect the effective observance within its jurisdiction of any Convention to which it is a party".

After a representation has been received, the substance of the allegation(s) is examined by a special tripartite committee appointed by the Governing Body. The committee submits its report to the Governing Body for consideration and adoption, and questions raised in the representation are normally followed up by the regular supervisory machinery, that is, the Committee of Experts and the Conference Committee on the Application of Conventions and Recommendations.

A different complaints procedure is available under article 26 of the ILO Constitution. Such complaints alleging non-observance by an ILO member State of a ratified convention can be filed by any other member State or delegate to the International Labour Conference.

Technical assistance

The International Labour Office (the ILO Secretariat) provides technical assistance and advisory services to member States that wish to ratify conventions or to apply them more fully. ILO frequently provides advice in the form of convening national, regional and subregional tripartite seminars on the ratification and application of all the conventions referred to above. Recent technical assistance activities with regard to non-discrimination have focused on strengthening non-discrimination legislation and its enforcement. ILO also organizes training programmes on non-discrimination and equality at work, including through its International Training Centre in Turin, Italy. In 2008, in cooperation with the International Trade Union Confederation, ILO supported the development and implementation of action plans aimed at combating racial discrimination and xenophobia in the workplace by trade unions in Brazil, Nepal, Romania and South Africa.

The role of NGOs

Direct access to ILO and its supervisory machinery occurs through trade unions, employers' organizations or Governments. Where minority workers are discriminated against or otherwise subject to human rights violations in the context of employment, they should seek to interest either a national or international organization to take up their cause with ILO.

Contacts and further information

All communications to ILO should be addressed to:

International Labour Office
International Labour Standards Department
4 route des Morillons
CH-1211 Geneva 22
Switzerland

Tel.: 41 22 799 62 51
Fax: 41 22 799 63 44
E-mail: normes@ilo.org
Website: www.ilo.org

The ILOLEX database, on the ILO website, contains the complete texts of all the ILO conventions, in English, French and Spanish, as well as the comments and reports issued by the ILO supervisory bodies. It also contains the ratification status of the eight fundamental ILO conventions.[83]

L. Swepston, "Labour rights", in *Economic, Social and Cultural Rights: A Guide for Minorities and Indigenous Peoples*, Margot E. Salomon, ed. (Minority Rights Group International, 2005) elaborates on the protection of minority rights through ILO standards.[84]

L. Swepston, "Human rights complaint procedures of the International Labor Organization", in H. Hannum, *Guide to International Human Rights Practice*, 4th ed. (Transnational/Nijhoff, 2004) provides a detailed description of the ILO complaint procedures (also available from www.ilo.org under "Labour standards").

[83] See www.ilo.org/ilolex/english/index.htm; ratification status is available from www.ilo.org/ilolex/english/docs/declworld.htm (both accessed 2 December 2012).

[84] Available from www.minorityrights.org/?lid=874 (accessed 2 December 2012).

CHAPTER X

THE UNITED NATIONS EDUCATIONAL, SCIENTIFIC AND CULTURAL ORGANIZATION

Summary: The United Nations Educational, Scientific and Cultural Organization (UNESCO) undertakes a wide range of studies, projects, technical assistance activities and other initiatives that may be relevant to minorities in protecting their culture, religion and education and preventing discrimination. Of particular significance is the work of UNESCO in promoting education, protecting tangible and intangible cultural heritage, and combating racism and all forms of discrimination and intolerance. Members of minorities are able to submit complaints under a confidential UNESCO procedure, alleging that rights falling within the mandate of UNESCO on education, science, culture and communication have been violated.

The United Nations Educational, Scientific and Cultural Organization (UNESCO) is a specialized agency of the United Nations, founded in 1945. It now has 195 member States and eight associate members; the General Conference of member States is its supreme governing body. Much of its work is accomplished in cooperation with various national institutions which assist in implementing its programme. Member States create national commissions composed of representatives of national educational, scientific and cultural communities; over 9,000 "associated schools" help young people form attitudes of tolerance and international understanding; and close to 4,000 UNESCO clubs, associations and centres promote the organization's ideals and activities at the grass-roots level. Hundreds of NGOs maintain official relations with UNESCO and over 1,000 cooperate with it on an occasional basis.

The main objective of UNESCO is to contribute to peace and security in the world by promoting collaboration among nations through education, science, culture and communication.

UNESCO and minorities

The major programmes of UNESCO focus on minorities and respect for their rights as set forth in the International Covenant on Economic, Social and Cultural Rights; article 27 of the International Covenant on Civil and Political Rights; the Declaration on the Rights of Persons Belonging to National or Ethnic, Religious and Linguistic Minorities and other relevant international instruments. There are also provisions regarding the rights of minorities in other major UNESCO standard-setting instruments, some of which are discussed below.[85] In addition, UNESCO has undertaken activities which address minority issues in its education, social science, culture, communication and information programmes.

The fight against racism, discrimination, xenophobia and intolerance has been central to the mandate of UNESCO since its creation. Article 1 of the Constitution of UNESCO stipulates its purpose as being "to contribute to peace and security by promoting collaboration among the nations through education, science and culture in order to further universal respect for justice, for the rule of law and for the human rights and fundamental freedoms which are affirmed for the peoples of the world, without distinction of race, sex, language or religion by the Charter of the United Nations".

[85] See http://portal.unesco.org/en/ev.php-URL_ID=23772&URL_DO=DO_TOPIC&URL_SECTION=201.html (accessed 3 December 2012).

UNESCO has upheld its commitment to this mandate by, among other actions, mobilizing the scientific community to refute the concept of "race". UNESCO has drafted international instruments that outline standard principles, concepts and universal criteria to support the fight against racism and discrimination, which serve as key standards to thwart threats to peace and social stability. By far the most important instrument elaborated by UNESCO in this domain is its 1978 Declaration on Race and Racial Prejudice,[86] which represents a milestone in the development of international normative instruments in this area and remains a key reference point for UNESCO in its struggle against racism and intolerance.

UNESCO participated actively in the Durban Conference. Many of the recommendations of the Durban Declaration and Programme of Action relate to its mandate, such as those on education and awareness-raising, information, communication and the media, and data collection and research. In addition, UNESCO was expressly called upon to act in specific areas linked to its constitutional mandate.

Its work against racism and all forms of discrimination was further entrenched by its adoption in 2003 of an Integrated Strategy to Combat Racism, Discrimination, Xenophobia and Related Intolerance.[87]

Education and minorities

The right to education is at the heart of the mission of UNESCO and is an integral part of its constitutional mandate. In 1960, UNESCO adopted the Convention against Discrimination in Education, which acknowledges the crucial role of education in ensuring equality of opportunity for members of all racial, national or ethnic groups. It was the first time that a binding instrument in the United Nations system contained a detailed definition of the term "discrimination", which is defined as "any distinction, exclusion, limitation or preference which, being based on race, colour, sex, language, religion, political or other opinion, national or social origin, economic condition or birth, has the purpose or effect of nullifying or impairing equality of treatment in education ...". The Convention calls on States to adopt immediate measures in favour of equality in education and it links the concept of education directly to human rights.

Minority communities are among the world's most educationally disadvantaged and UNESCO gives them special focus in its education programme. The Education for All (EFA) 2000 Assessment suggested many ways in which schools can respond to the needs of their pupils, including through affirmative action programmes for girls to remove obstacles to their enrolment, bilingual education for the children of ethnic minorities, and imaginative and diverse approaches to engage children who are not enrolled in school.[88]

UNESCO has also been actively involved in the implementation of the World Programme for Human Rights Education, adopted by the United Nations General Assembly in 2004. UNESCO advocates the inclusion of human rights principles and values within education systems and encourages States to develop and implement national plans of action for inclusive human rights education.

UNESCO has produced Guidelines on Intercultural Education to help policymakers understand the key issues concerning intercultural education with emphasis on minorities. Drawing from the key standard-setting instruments and numerous conferences, they present concepts and principles to guide future activities and policymaking.

---

[86] E/CN.4/Sub.2/1982/2/Add.1, annex V.

[87] Available from http://unesdoc.unesco.org/images/0013/001312/131202e.pdf (accessed 3 December 2012).

[88] See www.unesco.org/education/efa/efa_2000_assess/index.shtml (accessed 3 December 2012).

In collaboration with the Council of Europe, UNESCO is promoting basic education for Roma children, who suffer from discrimination in terms of not only their access to basic education but also the nature of education they receive in school.

UNESCO has mobilized a number of its partners through its Associated Schools Programme (ASPnet). Many ASPnet schools have been involved in school-based projects against discrimination such as the ASPnet All Equal in Diversity International Campaign.

Social sciences, human rights and the struggle against discrimination and intolerance

In order to contribute to the fight against racism and discrimination, UNESCO is strengthening its research on the link between current forms of racism and discrimination and certain traditional prejudices and forms of discrimination. It is researching the construction of identities in multicultural and multi-ethnic societies, analysing the discrimination and exclusion to which it may give rise and searching for responses which respect the diversity of identity. It is launching studies and mobilizing the scientific community and the public to raise awareness about the emergence of potential new forms of discrimination. As part of this initiative, special attention is being paid to the stigmatization and discrimination associated with HIV/AIDS and new epidemics.

International Coalition of Cities against Racism, Discrimination, Xenophobia and Intolerance

Cities are places where people from different backgrounds, origins, religions, social classes, ethnic groups and nationalities live and work together. The city can be a place where fear, hatred and discrimination prevail or a place of inclusiveness, harmony and mutual respect. Even though Governments have responsibilities and legal obligations, cities can play a major role in building inclusive societies.

It is in this context that the creation of an International Coalition of Cities against Racism, Discrimination, Xenophobia and Intolerance was first conceived. The project aims at assisting municipalities to develop and strengthen their policies for greater social inclusion. It encourages partnership-building in the struggle against discrimination and exclusion in cities around the world. Following the establishment of six regional coalitions, the International Coalition was launched in June 2008. It allows cities to exchange experiences and information, to learn from one another, to jointly evaluate policy impacts and to commit to undertaking certain actions collectively.

Youth

UNESCO considers the energy and motivation of young people to be outstanding assets for launching positive change, particularly with respect to the action needed to counter all forms of discrimination. Its strategy for acting with and for young people was based on the World Programme of Action for Youth to the Year 2000 and Beyond, adopted by the United Nations General Assembly in 1995. To promote the participation of young people in policymaking at different levels, every two years UNESCO organizes the UNESCO Youth Forum, bringing together youth representatives from across the globe. The seventh UNESCO Youth Forum in 2011 discussed "How Youth Drive Change".

The MOST programme

MOST (Management of Social Transformation) is a UNESCO research programme designed and managed by the Sector of Social Science which promotes international comparative social science research. MOST focuses on the nature of change in multicultural and multi-ethnic societies in which issues of education, culture and religion, identity and human needs, democratic governance, conflict and cohesion interact in complex patterns. This research should help in designing policies which contribute to achieving equal citizenship rights among ethnic groups and avoid and resolve ethnic conflict. Numerous MOST projects, either completed or ongoing, deal with the social and political aspects of international migration and growing ethnocultural diversity.[89]

Culture and minorities

Cultural heritage

According to the 1972 World Heritage Convention, "cultural heritage" refers to a monument, group of buildings or site of historical, aesthetic, archaeological, scientific, ethnological or anthropological value. "Natural heritage" designates outstanding physical, biological and geological features, such as habitats of threatened plants or animal species and areas that have scientific or aesthetic value or are important from the point of view of conservation. Each country that ratifies the Convention pledges to conserve the sites situated on its territory, some of which may be recognized as World Heritage Sites. Their preservation for future generations then becomes a responsibility shared by the international community as a whole.

The Convention is overseen by the World Heritage Committee, which meets annually to discuss all matters related to its implementation. It also decides on the inscription of new sites on the World Heritage List. Some of the cultural or natural sites included in the World Heritage List are located in regions where minority communities live, such as the Asian Rice Culture and its Terraced Landscapes of the Ifugao in the Philippines and the Old Town of Lijiang of the Naxi in China. UNESCO encourages minority communities to participate in identifying sites which might be nominated by their Government for inscription on the World Heritage List.[90]

For further information, contact:

World Heritage Centre
UNESCO
7, place de Fontenoy
75352 Paris 07SP
France

E-mail: whc-info@unesco.org
Website: whc.unesco.org

Intangible cultural heritage

UNESCO has protected "intangible cultural heritage" since 1989, pursuant to the UNESCO Recommendation on the Safeguarding of Traditional Culture and Folklore. Intangible cultural heritage includes oral cultural heritage, languages, performing arts and festive events, social rituals and practices, knowledge systems and beliefs and practices about nature. In many cultures, and for minority and indigenous populations in particular, intangible cultural heritage is an essential source of identity.

Since UNESCO launched the Safeguarding and Promotion of Intangible Heritage programme in 1993, it has undertaken many activities covering different aspects of the intangible cultural heritage of minorities in Asia, Africa and the Pacific; some are still in progress. UNESCO is also conducting a feasibility study on the elaboration of a new standard-setting instrument to protect intangible cultural heritage.

---

[89] See www.unesco.org/new/en/social-and-human-sciences/themes/social-transformations/most-programme (accessed 3 December 2012).

[90] See http://whc.unesco.org/en/committee (accessed 3 December 2012).

In recent years, UNESCO has adopted two important conventions related to the promotion of the cultural rights of minorities. The 2003 UNESCO Convention for the Safeguarding of the Intangible Cultural Heritage provides safeguards and promotes the practices, representations, expressions, knowledge and skills – as well as the associated instruments, objects, artefacts and cultural spaces – which communities, groups and, in some cases, individuals recognize as part of their cultural heritage. The Convention establishes a fund and a system of listing representative and endangered heritage. Article 15 calls for the full participation of communities and others who create and maintain such heritage and their involvement in its active management.

The 2005 UNESCO Convention on the Protection and Promotion of the Diversity of Cultural Expressions encourages States to incorporate culture as a strategic element in national and international development policies and adopt measures aimed at protecting and promoting the diversity of cultural expressions within their territory. It emphasizes the importance of recognizing equal dignity and respect for all cultures, including those of persons belonging to minorities, and the freedom to create, produce, disseminate, distribute and have access to traditional cultural expressions, and asks States to create environments conducive to this. The preamble to the Convention recognizes the importance of the vitality of cultures, including for persons belonging to minorities and indigenous peoples. Similarly, article 2 (3) reiterates the equal dignity of cultures, with specific reference to the cultures of minorities and indigenous peoples.

Promotion of intercultural dialogue

As lead agency for the 2001 United Nations Global Agenda for Dialogue among Civilizations,[91] UNESCO attempts to relate more closely the principles of cultural diversity and intercultural dialogue. Through its programmes on intercultural and interfaith dialogue, UNESCO fosters reflection on the conditions for mainstreaming principles of cultural diversity and intercultural dialogue in policies for sustainable development, and on the search for transversal values, in the face of the new challenges of cultural diversity in the context of globalization.

Celebration of the World Day for Cultural Diversity for Dialogue and Development, which was proclaimed by the General Assembly and is marked on 21 May each year, is of increasing importance. Under the auspices of UNESCO, it offers an opportunity to amplify reflection on the values of cultural diversity in order to learn to "live together" better.

The media and communications

Given their impact and reach, communications media can play a major role in protecting human rights and fighting discrimination. To be effective, journalism must be inclusive, reflect the composition, concerns and views of the whole community, and be accountable. Hence, journalists should develop sources who represent the diversity of thought, feeling and experience of the people they serve. UNESCO supports diversity inside the newsroom, and has supported both training initiatives (e.g., on investigative journalism on human rights and diversity) and the production of relevant handbooks for journalists (e.g., *Reporting on Diversity*).

The Power of Peace Network is a stand-alone multimedia and ICT platform created by UNESCO. It has a sustainable, not-for-profit business structure and is designed to produce and distribute locally generated content through a network of collaborating television and radio services, satellite distributors, mobile phone companies and Internet providers.[92]

[91] General Assembly resolution 56/6.

[92] See http://portal.unesco.org/ci/en/ev.php-URL_ID=28488&URL_DO=DO_TOPIC&URL_SECTION=201.html (accessed 3 December 2012).

Human rights complaints procedure

Most of the work of UNESCO in the field of human rights is promotional rather than protective, but since 1978 it has had a procedure for the examination of communications (complaints) concerning alleged violations of human rights.[93] The procedure is confidential and extends only to human rights violations within its fields of competence, namely education, science, culture and information. Many minority concerns are directly related to issues of language, culture and education, and it should be relatively easy to demonstrate that such issues fall within the jurisdiction of UNESCO.

Individuals, groups of individuals and NGOs may submit communications to UNESCO concerning violations of human rights, whether they are themselves victims or whether they only have "reliable knowledge" of such violations. In theory, a communication may be filed against any State; in practice, communications will be considered against any State that is a member of UNESCO.

Communications should be sent to:

Director of the Office of International Standards and Legal Affairs
UNESCO
7, place de Fontenoy
75352 Paris 07
France

An initial letter (which must be drafted in one of the working languages of UNESCO, English or French) should contain a concise statement of the allegations. On its receipt, the UNESCO Secretariat will send the author of the letter a form to be filled in, which constitutes the formal communication and will be transmitted to the State concerned. A copy of the form may be completed and attached to the initial letter.

Communications are examined in private by the Committee on Conventions and Recommendations of the Executive Board, which is composed of Government representatives and generally meets twice each year. In examining the communication, the Committee invites the State concerned to provide information or answer questions on either the admissibility or the merits of the communication.

Since the Committee is not an international tribunal, it tries to resolve the problem in a spirit of cooperation, dialogue and mutual understanding. Its goal is to achieve a mutually satisfactory settlement, not simply to decide whether or not a violation has occurred. The Committee submits a confidential report to the Executive Board on each communication considered, including any decisions or recommendations it may make; the author of the communication and the State concerned are also informed of the Committee's decisions.

The Director-General of UNESCO has long enjoyed a right of intercession vested in him or her by the General Conference.[94] It is thus possible for the Director-General personally to make humanitarian representations on behalf of persons who have allegedly been victims of human rights violations within the fields of competence of UNESCO and whose cases call for urgent consideration.[95]

---

93 104 EX/Decision 3.3. See http://portal.unesco.org/en/ev.php-URL_ID=27969&URL_DO=DO_TOPIC&URL_SECTION=201.html (accessed 3 December 2012).

94 See in particular 19C/Resolution 12.1.

95 Paragraphs 8 and 9 of 104 EX/Decision 3.3 recognize the role played by the Director-General in this regard (see footnote 100).

Contacts and further information

To communicate with UNESCO, contact:

Struggle against Discrimination and Racism Section
Division of Human Rights, Human Security and Philosophy
Social and Human Sciences Sector
UNESCO
1 Rue Miollis
75732 Paris
France

Fax: 33 1 45 68 57 23

PART THREE
REGIONAL SYSTEMS

Where regional avenues for promoting and protecting the rights of members of minorities exist, they should often be the first port of call for minority rights activists. Regional bodies are likely to focus on issues of particular local interest, such as Roma in Europe or Afro-descendants in the Americas, and they are often accessible to minority advocates and NGOs.

Chapters XI-XV deal with the most important regional actors in Africa, Europe and the Americas, although they do not claim to be exhaustive.

In terms of international mechanisms in Asia and the Middle East and North Africa, the primary sources of support for minority rights remain the global institutions discussed in parts one and two of this *Guide*. Nevertheless, brief mention should be made of three regional institutions or mechanisms which might be useful in promoting and protecting the rights of persons belonging to minorities.

Asia has two subregional intergovernmental bodies which have human rights components: the Association of Southeast Asian Nations (ASEAN) and the South Asian Association for Regional Cooperation (SAARC).

Association of Southeast Asian Nations

In November 2007, ASEAN member States signed the ASEAN Charter, which sets out the purposes and principles of the Association.[96] While the Charter is not a human rights treaty, it states that one of the purposes of ASEAN is to "promote and protect human rights and fundamental freedoms" (art. 1 (7)) and that member States shall act in accordance with the principle of "respect for fundamental freedoms, the promotion and protection of human rights, and the promotion of social justice" (art. 2 (2)(i)). There is no specific reference to minorities in the Charter, but the ASEAN principles include "respect for the different cultures, languages and religions of the peoples of ASEAN, while emphasising their common values in the spirit of unity in diversity" (art. 2 (2)(l)).

Pursuant to article 14 of the Charter, the ASEAN Intergovernmental Commission on Human Rights (AICHR) was created in 2009.[97] Its functions are primarily promotional, and it is to pursue a "constructive and non-confrontational approach" (art. 2 (4)), bearing in mind the principle of "non-interference in the internal affairs of ASEAN Member States" (art. 2 (1)(b)). It is to "promote human rights within the regional context, bearing in mind national and regional particularities and mutual respect for different historical, cultural and religious backgrounds, and taking into account the balance between rights and responsibilities" (art. 1 (4)). It is to "uphold international human rights standards as prescribed by the Universal Declaration of Human Rights, the Vienna Declaration and Programme of Action, and international human rights instruments to which ASEAN Member States are parties" (art. 1 (6)).

The Commission's mandate also includes, inter alia:

- Developing an ASEAN Human Rights Declaration;
- Enhancing public awareness of human rights;

[96] Brunei Darussalam, Cambodia, Indonesia, the Lao People's Democratic Republic, Malaysia, Myanmar, the Philippines, Singapore, Thailand and Viet Nam.

[97] Available from www.asean.org/archive/publications/ASEAN-Charter.pdf (accessed 3 December 2012).

- Promoting capacity-building and providing advisory services and technical assistance;
- Preparing thematic studies;
- Obtaining information from ASEAN member States on the promotion and protection of human rights.

The Commission meets for at least 10 days annually and submits an annual report to the ASEAN Foreign Ministers Meeting. The Commission does not have the mandate to investigate cases of human rights abuses; however, NGOs prepared reports on human rights violations and made public statements at the time of its first session. Minority advocates should be able to contact its members (who are Government representatives, not independent experts) either through their national foreign ministries or the ASEAN Secretariat, as follows:

The ASEAN Secretariat
70A Jl. Sisingamangaraja
Jakarta 12110
Indonesia

Tel: 62 21 726 29 91; 62 21 724 33 72
Fax: 62 21 739 82 34; 62 21 724 35 04
Website: www.asean.org

South Asian Association for Regional Cooperation

The South Asian Association for Regional Cooperation (SAARC) aims to promote economic growth and development in the South Asian region. The SAARC Charter does not mention human rights. A number of SAARC treaties address human rights-related issues, however, and SAARC adopted a Social Charter in 2004.[98]

Among the principles, goals and objectives of the Social Charter are to "ensure tolerance, non-violence, pluralism and non-discrimination in respect of diversity within and among societies" (art. 2 (2)(vii)); "ensure that disadvantaged, marginalized and vulnerable persons and groups are included in social development" (art. 2 (2)(xi)); and "promote universal respect for and observance and protection of human rights and fundamental freedoms for all" (art. 2 (2)(xii)). The Social Charter does not create any body with the responsibility to monitor its provisions.

Arab Charter on Human Rights

The revised text of the Arab Charter on Human Rights, adopted in 2004 under the auspices of the League of Arab States, came into force in March 2008 following its ratification by Algeria, Bahrain, Jordan, Libya, the Palestinian Authority, the Syrian Arab Republic and the United Arab Emirates. Yemen, Qatar and Saudi Arabia have also since ratified it.

The Charter binds each State party to ensure to all individuals subject to its jurisdiction the right to enjoy the Charter rights "without distinction on grounds of race, colour, sex, language, religious belief, opinion, thought, national or social origin, wealth, birth or physical or mental disability" (art. 3 (1)). Article 25 (reflecting article 27 of the International Covenant on Civil and Political Rights) provides that "Persons belonging to minorities shall not be denied the right to enjoy their own culture, to use their own language and to [practise] their own religion. The exercise of these rights shall be governed by law". While the Charter does not define minorities, article 43 states, "Nothing in this Charter may be construed or interpreted as impairing the rights and freedoms ... set [forth] in the international and regional human rights instruments which the States parties

98 Available from www.saarc-sec.org/areaofcooperation/detail.php?activity_id=7 (accessed 3 December 2012).

have adopted or ratified, including the rights of women, the rights of the child and the rights of persons belonging to minorities".

The Charter establishes (art. 45 (1)) a monitoring body of independent experts, the Arab Human Rights Committee, to examine States parties' compliance with its principles. Article 48 requires States parties to submit periodic reports to the Committee on the measures they have taken to give effect to Charter rights. It further provides that the reports, comments and recommendations of the Committee are to be made public and disseminated widely.

CHAPTER XI

THE HUMAN RIGHTS SYSTEM OF THE AFRICAN UNION

Summary: The African Charter on Human and Peoples' Rights is a regional instrument designed to reflect the history, values, traditions and development of peoples in Africa. The Charter combines African values with international norms not only by promoting internationally recognized individual rights, but also by proclaiming collective rights and individual duties. This chapter outlines the rights contained in the Charter that are of particular interest to minorities and describes the work of the Charter's primary oversight body, the African Commission on Human and Peoples' Rights. While there is no minority-specific institution within the African human rights system, the Commission has adopted a very broad approach to minority issues. The work of the Commission is complemented by a transitional African Court on Human and Peoples' Rights, which is to be replaced by the African Court of Justice and Human Rights.

The African Union

In 2002, the Organization of African Unity, which was established in 1963 as a regional body dedicated primarily to the eradication of colonialism on the continent, became the African Union.[99] Almost all 54 States on the African continent are members of the African Union, the single exception being Morocco. The predecessor to the African Union, the Organization of African Unity, was principally concerned with relations between States and the fundamental objectives of preserving State sovereignty, territorial integrity and colonial boundaries. The Constitutive Act of the African Union is much more expansive. One of its objectives is "to promote and protect human and peoples' rights in accordance with the African Charter on Human and Peoples' Rights and other relevant human rights instruments" (art. 3 (h)). Another significant departure from the mandate of the Organization of African Unity is that the African Union has the right to "intervene in a Member State ... in respect of grave circumstances, namely war crimes, genocide and crimes against humanity" (art. 4 (h)).

The African Charter on Human and Peoples' Rights

The African Charter on Human and Peoples' Rights, also called the Banjul Charter, was adopted by the African States members of the Organization of African Unity in 1981 and entered into force five years later. It should be noted that the Charter is innovative in comparison with the other regional human rights instruments in placing special emphasis on the rights of "peoples". Although the Charter does not make specific reference to minorities, its protection of peoples' rights has been interpreted by the African Commission as according protection to minorities, as discussed below. Additionally, as with other international human rights instruments, there are a number of provisions in the Charter that are of particular significance to members of minority groups.

Both individual and peoples' rights are subject to the general provisions found in articles 1, 2 and 26.

Article 1 provides that "The Member States of the Organization of African Unity parties to the present Charter shall recognize the rights, duties and freedoms enshrined in this Chapter and shall undertake to adopt legislative or other measures to give effect to them".

[99] The Constitutive Act of the African Union was adopted by the Heads of State and Government of the Member States of the Organization of African Unity in July 2000 and entered into force on 26 May 2001.

Article 2 provides that "Every individual shall be entitled to the enjoyment of the rights and freedoms recognized and guaranteed in the present Charter without distinction of any kind such as race, ethnic group, color, sex, language, religion, political or any other opinion, national and social origin, fortune, birth or other status".

Article 26 provides that "States parties to the present Charter shall have the duty to guarantee the independence of the Courts and shall allow the establishment and improvement of appropriate national institutions entrusted with the promotion and protection of the rights and freedoms guaranteed by the present Charter".

Individual rights

Article 3 provides that every individual shall be equal before the law and shall be entitled to the equal protection of the law.

Article 7 guarantees the right to fair trial. In this context, a decision of the African Commission on Human and Peoples' Rights involved the protection of a linguistic minority in a bilingual state. The Commission ruled that, "since not all the citizens are fluent in both languages, it is the State's duty to make sure that, when a trial is conducted in a language that the accused does not speak, he/she is provided with the assistance of an interpreter. Failing to do that amounts to a violation of the right to a fair trial."[100]

Article 8 protects the right to practise the religion of one's choice. The Commission applied this provision to protect the Christian minority in the Sudan, noting that the State violated the authors' right to practise religion because non-Muslims did not have the right to preach or build their churches and were subjected to harassment, arbitrary arrest and expulsion.[101]

Article 12 guarantees the right to freedom of movement and residence within the borders of the State; the right to leave any country, including his or her own, and to return to it; and the right to seek asylum. It also prohibits the mass expulsion of non-nationals "aimed at national, racial, ethnic or religious groups".

Article 13 (3) protects the right of equal access to public property and services.

Article 17 (2) states that everyone "may freely take part in the cultural life of his community" and *article 17 (3)* provides that "[t]he promotion and protection of morals and traditional values recognized by the community shall be the duty of the State". In interpreting this provision, the Commission has noted that "Language is an integral part of the structure of culture; it in fact constitutes its pillar and means of expression par excellence. Its usage enriches the individual and enables him to take an active part in the community and in its activities. To deprive an individual of such participation amounts to depriving him of his identity."[102]

The guidelines adopted by the Commission to help States in preparing their periodic reports (discussed below) ask States to provide information on "measures and programmes aimed at promoting awareness and enjoyment of the cultural heritage of national ethnic groups and minorities and of indigenous sectors of the population".[103] With respect to the right to education

[100] Communication No. 266/2003, *Kevin Mgwanga Gunme et al.* v. *Cameroon* (2009).

[101] Communications Nos. 48/90, 50/91, 52/91 and 89/93 *Amnesty International and Others* v. *Sudan* (1999).

[102] Communications Nos. 54/91, 61/91, 98/93, 164/97-196/97 and 210/98, *Malawi African Association and Others* v. *Mauritania* (2000).

[103] Guidelines for National Periodic Reports, available from www.chr.up.ac.za/images/files/documents/ahrdd/theme02/african_commission_resolution_13.pdf (accessed 13 December 2012). The African Commission adopted a significantly simplified version of these initial guidelines at its 23rd Ordinary Session in April 1998. While the relationship between the two versions remains unclear, it is assumed that the simplified guidelines are in force.

set forth in article 17 (1) of the Charter, guideline 47 (e) draws States' attention to their obligation to report on "the promotion of understanding, tolerance and friendship among all nations and all racial, ethnic or religious groups" and on measures taken for special groups, including "children belonging to linguistic, racial, religious or other minorities, and children belonging to indigenous sectors of the population, where applicable".

The rights of peoples

The African Charter contains a series of group rights attributed to "peoples". A survey of the Commission's jurisprudence indicates that the Commission considers "peoples" to refer to identifiable ethnic communities, and it has not thus far distinguished between minorities and indigenous peoples in any of the cases that address peoples' rights.

Article 19 provides that "All peoples shall be equal; they shall enjoy the same respect and shall have the same rights. Nothing shall justify the domination of a people by another." The reporting guidelines for article 19 require more specifically that States give information on "the constitutional and statutory framework which seek to protect the different sections of national community", and refer to "precautions taken to proscribe any tendencies of some people dominating another as feared by the Article". Confronted by allegations of discriminatory practices against certain sections of the Mauritanian population, the Commission stated, "At the heart of the abuses alleged in the different communications is the question of the domination of one section of the population by another", thus affirming that the "peoples" referred to in the Charter include different groups within a State. On the merits of the case, the Commission concluded that it had insufficient information to conclude that there had been a violation of article 19.

Article 20 declares the right of all peoples to existence and proclaims their "unquestionable and inalienable right to self-determination. They shall freely determine their political status and shall pursue their economic and social development according to the policy they have freely chosen." Article 20 (2) states, "Colonized or oppressed peoples shall have the right to free themselves from the bonds of domination by resorting to any means recognized by the international community". The reporting guidelines for article 20 clarify that "[a]ll communities are allowed full participation in political activities and are allowed equal opportunities in the economic activities of the country both of which should be according to the choices they have made independently".

The African Commission has accepted cases brought by specific communities which assert their right to self-determination. In 1992, a claim was brought by the Katangese Peoples' Congress for recognition of the independence of Katanga, a province of (then) Zaire. Although the Commission found no violation of any Charter right, its decision recognized the population of Katanga as a people, defined as a group within the State of Zaire. The Commission stated, "In the absence of concrete evidence of violations of human rights to the point that the territorial integrity of Zaire should be called to question and in the absence of evidence that the people of Katanga are denied the right to participate in Government as guaranteed by Article 13 (1) of the African Charter, the Commission holds the view that Katanga is obliged to exercise a variant of self-determination that is compatible with the sovereignty and territorial integrity of Zaire."[104] The Commission further clarified its understanding of the concept of "people" in a 2009 decision concerning a claim by Southern Cameroonians that they were entitled to exercise their right to self-determination as "separate and distinct people". The Commission agreed that "the people of Southern Cameroon can legitimately claim to be a 'people'. Besides the individual rights due to Southern Cameroon, they have a distinct identity which attracts certain collective rights .... [T]he Commission finds that 'the people of Southern Cameroon' qualify to be referred to as a 'people' because they manifest numerous characteristics and affinities, which include a common history,

[104] Communication No. 75/92, *Katangese Peoples' Congress v. Zaire* (1995).

linguistic tradition, territorial connection, and political outlook. More importantly they identify themselves as a people with a separate and distinct identity. Identity is an innate characteristic within a people. It is up to other external people to recognize such existence, but not to deny it." Consistent with the Katanga decision, the Commission decided that, in the absence of proof of massive violations of human rights guaranteed in the Charter, the people of Southern Cameroon cannot engage in secession, but may only exercise a variant of self-determination – federalism, confederacy, local government, self-government – in conformity with State sovereignty and territorial integrity.[105]

Article 21 affirms the right of peoples to freely dispose of their wealth and natural resources. In another 2009 ruling, related to the forced displacement of the Endorois community from their ancestral lands, the Commission found violations of both articles 21 and 22 of the Charter. It stated that "a people inhabiting a specific region within a State can claim the protection of Article 21". The Commission held the view that "the Endorois have the right to freely dispose of their wealth and natural resources in consultation of the Respondent State", which "bears the burden for creating conditions favourable to a people's development".[106]

Article 22 sets forth the right of peoples to economic, social and cultural development "with due regard to their freedom and identity and in the equal enjoyment of the common heritage of mankind".

Article 23 enshrines peoples' right to peace and security.

Article 24 provides that "All peoples shall have the right to a general satisfactory environment favourable to their development". In a case involving the Ogoni community in Nigeria, the Commission ruled that "the right to a general satisfactory environment ... requires the State to take reasonable and other measures to prevent pollution and ecological degradation, to promote conservation, and to secure an ecologically sustainable development and use of natural resources" and must also include "environmental and social impact studies prior to any major industrial development, undertaking appropriate monitoring and providing information to those communities exposed to hazardous materials and activities and providing meaningful opportunities for individuals to be heard and to participate in the development decisions affecting their communities".[107]

The African Commission on Human and Peoples' Rights

The African Commission on Human and Peoples' Rights is the monitoring body for the African Charter. It is composed of 11 members "chosen from amongst African personalities of the highest reputation, known for their high morality, integrity, impartiality, and competence in matters of human and peoples' rights". Members of the Commission serve in their individual capacities and are therefore expected to act independently while serving as commissioners. They are elected by the Summit of Heads of State and Government of the African Union for a renewable mandate of six years.

The African Commission meets twice a year in ordinary sessions of 15 days each, either in its headquarters in Banjul, the Gambia, or in the territory of a State party at the latter's invitation. It may also organize extraordinary sessions at the request of its members or of the Chair of the Commission of the African Union.

---

105 Communication No. 266/2003, *Kevin Mgwanga Gunme et al.* v. *Cameroon* (2009).

106 Communication No. 276/2003, *Centre for Minority Rights Development (Kenya) and Minority Rights Group International on behalf of Endorois Welfare Council* v. *Kenya* (2009).

107 Communication No. 155/96, *The Social and Economic Rights Action Center and the Center for Economic and Social Rights* v. *Nigeria* (2001).

The broad mandate of the African Commission is set out in article 45 of the Charter. It includes the promotion of human rights, through studies, research, the organization of seminars and dissemination of information; making its views and recommendations known to Governments; formulating and laying down principles and rules to guide African Governments in their domestic legislation; interpreting the provisions of the Charter; and ensuring the protection of human and peoples' rights, as laid down in the Charter.

Minority advocates should be able to raise relevant issues at Commission sessions and through the submission of formal communications under the Charter. The Commission's promotional role also offers numerous opportunities for education and dissemination of information on minority rights and those general human rights which are of particular importance to members of minority groups.

Promotional activities

Promotional activities are at the heart of the African Commission's mandate, and individual members report at each session on the initiatives they have taken to promote human rights in various African countries assigned to them. The Commission has carried out this mandate by conducting missions whereby commissioners visit States to disseminate information about the role of the African Commission and participate in workshops to raise awareness about the Charter and other key human rights instruments in Africa.[108] The Commission has also employed other mechanisms, such as special rapporteurs and working groups, to carry out its promotional mandate and undertake specific activities on various thematic issues of concern. Currently there are special rapporteurs on prisons and conditions of detention; refugees, asylum seekers, migrants and internally displaced persons; human rights defenders; the rights of women; freedom of expression and access to information. The Commission has also established a committee for the prevention of torture, and working groups on the death penalty, and on extractive industries, environment and human rights violations. Two working groups that may be of particular concern to minorities are discussed below.

The Working Group of Experts on Indigenous Populations/Communities in Africa was established in 2000 with a mandate "to examine the concept of indigenous peoples and communities in Africa"; "study the implications of the African Charter on Human Rights [and the] well being of indigenous communities especially with regard to the right to equality (Art. 2 and 3), the right to dignity (Art. 5), the protection against domination (Art. 19), self-determination (Art. 20) and the promotion of cultural development and identity (Art. 22)"; and "consider appropriate recommendations for the monitoring and protection of the rights of indigenous communities".[109] Its renewed mandate includes gathering information on violations of indigenous peoples' human rights, undertaking country visits (with the permission of the country concerned), and formulating recommendations on appropriate measures to prevent and remedy violations of indigenous peoples' human rights.[110]

A comprehensive report submitted by the Working Group to the Commission in 2003 examines the human rights situation of indigenous peoples in Africa, analyses the African Charter and its

[108] The major human rights instruments in Africa include the African Charter on Human and Peoples' Rights, the African Charter on the Rights and Welfare of the Child, the Protocol to the African Charter on Human and Peoples' Rights on the establishment of an African Court on Human and Peoples' Rights, and the Protocol to the African Charter on Human and Peoples' Rights on the Rights of Women in Africa (Maputo Protocol).

[109] Resolution on the Rights of Indigenous Populations/Communities in Africa adopted at the 28th Ordinary Session of the African Commission on Human and Peoples' Rights, Cotonou, Benin, 6 November 2000.

[110] Resolution on the adoption of the Report of the African Commission's Working Group on Indigenous Populations/Communities adopted at the 34th Ordinary Session of the African Commission on Human and Peoples' Rights, Banjul, the Gambia, 20 November 2003.

jurisprudence regarding the concept of "peoples" and identifies criteria to distinguish minorities from indigenous peoples. The report states that "the major and crucial difference between minority rights and indigenous rights is that minority rights are formulated as individual rights whereas indigenous rights are collective rights. The specific rights of persons belonging to national or ethnic, religious or linguistic minorities include the right to enjoy their own culture, to practise their own religion, to use their own language, to establish their own associations, to participate in national affairs etc. These rights may be exercised by persons belonging to minorities individually as well as in community with other members of their group."[111] The Commission also has underscored the importance of the United Nations Declaration on the Rights of Indigenous Peoples, noting in a 2007 communiqué that "the Declaration will become a very valuable tool and a point of reference for the African Commission's efforts to ensure the promotion and protection of indigenous peoples' rights on the African continent".[112]

Despite this flexible approach to the concept of "indigenous", the Working Group remains concerned not with the issue of minority rights per se but rather with indigenous peoples' issues. In the light of the different rights which may be important to minorities, some minority groups have called for the creation of a separate forum to consider issues specific to them.

The Working Group on Economic, Social and Cultural Rights was established in late 2004 with a mandate to develop draft principles and guidelines on economic, social and cultural rights; elaborate State reporting guidelines pertaining to economic, social and cultural rights; and undertake studies and research.[113] The two main documents – Draft Principles and Guidelines on Economic, Social and Cultural Rights and State Party Reporting Guidelines on Economic, Social and Cultural Rights – were officially launched during the Commission's 50th Ordinary Session in Banjul, the Gambia, on 24 October 2011.[114]

Protective activities

The Commission also has a protective mandate under the Charter, which is exercised through examination of periodic country reports, consideration of complaints (communications) submitted to it by individuals and NGOs, and fact-finding missions.

Periodic reports

Article 62 requires every State party to the Charter to submit a report every two years on the measures it has taken to give effect to the rights recognized in the Charter. However, compliance with this requirement has been problematic: 12 States[115] have never submitted a report, and most have submitted only one or two.[116] The existing guidelines contain a number of references related to the protection of ethnic and other groups, as discussed above. Minorities can contribute to the Commission's consideration of these reports by submitting their own shadow reports, which

[111] Report of the Working Group of Experts on Indigenous Populations/Communities adopted by the African Commission at its 28th Ordinary Session, Cotonou, Benin, 2003. Available from http://pro169.org/res/materials/en/identification/ACHPR%20Report%20on%20indigenous%20populations-communities.pdf (accessed 4 December 2012).

[112] ACHPR/Res.121 (XXXXII) 07.

[113] Resolution on Economic, Social and Cultural Rights in Africa adopted at the 36th Ordinary Session of the African Commission on Human and Peoples' Rights, Dakar, Senegal, 7 December 2004.

[114] Available from www.achpr.org.

[115] The Comoros, Côte d'Ivoire, Djibouti, Equatorial Guinea, Eritrea, Gabon, Guinea-Bissau, Liberia, Malawi, Sao Tome and Principe, Sierra Leone and Somalia.

[116] The status of submission of all reports is available from www.achpr.org/english/_info/statereport_considered_en.html.

can provide an alternative source of information and may assist the commissioners in asking questions of the State about the situation of minorities and drafting their concluding observations.

Complaints from individuals and NGOs

The African Charter does not explicitly speak of "individual and NGO complaints" but uses the term "other communications" to distinguish these communications from those submitted by States.[117] In practice, however, any individual or organization may submit a communication; one needs not be African, a resident of the State complained against, or even a victim, and communications have been filed by international organizations and individuals based outside Africa. Individual members of a minority may complain on their own behalf or on behalf of the group to which they belong.

Complainants need not have the permission of the alleged victim(s) in order to submit a communication. This permits NGOs or others to file complaints even when all of the victims may not be known. However, NGOs should be responsible and put the safety of the alleged victims first, which includes seeking the permission of alleged victims to submit a communication; this can be vital, especially if the cooperation of the victim will later be necessary. The Commission has stated that "in a situation of grave and massive violations, it may be impossible to give a complete list of names of all the victims. It will be noted that article 56(1) demands simply that communications should indicate the names of those submitting and not those of all the victims of the alleged violations."[118]

Every communication should be as detailed as possible, comprehensive and verified as far as possible. Where possible, NGOs should submit statements or affidavits from the author(s) of the complaint, witnesses, family members and others who have relevant information about the specific issues raised. If the authorities are involved, information such as the number and kind of police or security services, or details of any arrest or search should be included. In addition, texts of relevant laws and directives, legal judgements and copies of any publications or documents which may have been seized should be annexed to the communication. If the situation does not obviously constitute a human rights violation, the applicant should try to refer to relevant international opinions to support the claim that the act violates the norms of the African Charter.

Admissibility criteria

Seven criteria set forth in article 56 of the Charter must be satisfied for a complaint to be considered on its merits by the Commission:

- The communication must not be anonymous, although it may be requested that the identity of the author not be disclosed. For practical reasons, the Commission must be able to contact the author.
- The communication must allege violations of rights that are protected by the Charter and must be compatible with the Constitutive Act. This provision prohibits any claim for secession, which would be counter to the Constitutive Act's reaffirmation of the territorial integrity of States.
- The communication must not have manifestly political motivations or be written in "disparaging or insulting language".
- The communication should not be based exclusively on media reports, but reliance to some degree on the media is permissible. The complainant should attempt to verify the

[117] Detailed provisions for the latter are set out in articles 47-54.

[118] Communications Nos. 54/91, 61/91, 96/93, 98/93, 164/97-196/97 and 210/98, *Malawi Africa Association and Others* v. *Mauritania* (2000), para. 79. The Commission reiterated this finding in its Communication No. 266/03, *Kevin Mgwanga Gunme et al.* v. *Cameroon* (2009), para. 67.

truth of media reports independently, where possible. Local remedies must have been exhausted prior to submission of the communication, unless the national procedures are inadequate or unduly prolonged. The Commission has stressed that theoretically available remedies must, in fact, be available, effective and sufficient. "A remedy is considered available if the petitioner can pursue it without impediment, it is deemed effective if it offers a prospect of success, and it is found sufficient if it is capable of redressing the complaint."[119]

- The Commission distinguishes between cases in which the complaint deals with violations against identified individual victims and those alleging widespread violations in which it may be impossible for the complainants to identify all the victims. In the latter case, there is no need to exhaust domestic remedies. "The Commission does not believe that the condition that internal remedies must have been exhausted can be applied literally to those cases in which it is 'neither practicable nor desirable' for the complainants or the victims to pursue such internal channels of remedy in every case of violation of human rights. Such is the case where there are many victims."[120]
- The communication must be submitted "within a reasonable period from the time local remedies are exhausted or from the date the Commission is seized of the matter." The Commission has not yet rejected a communication for being submitted too late, and it once declared a communication admissible that was initiated after more than 16 years of fruitless domestic proceedings.
- The Commission will not admit cases that have been settled by the State(s) involved in some other manner. However, this provision applies only if the settlement concerns the same parties and the same facts as those before the Commission.

Investigation and decisions on the merits

All communications received by the Secretariat are transmitted to the Commission, which determines whether or not to consider a communication, based on the above criteria. While article 55 empowers a simple majority of the Commission to make that determination, in practice the Commission usually acts by consensus. The Commission will inform the applicant if it does not take up a case. Individual communications are confidential and are examined in closed sessions.

The Commission does not always distinguish clearly between admissibility and action on the merits, but the State concerned is given the opportunity to respond to the allegations prior to the Commission's deliberations; the complainant may then reply in writing to the State's response. If the State does not respond or does not contest the allegations, the Commission decides whether or not to accept the allegations as true based on the evidence before it and on any other information that the Commission may acquire during its investigation. If the applicant ceases to communicate with the Commission, the Commission may treat that silence as a wish to withdraw the communication. However, the Commission will try to establish whether the silence is indicative of a lack of interest or whether it reflects circumstances beyond the person's control that prevent him or her from pursuing the application.

Article 46 of the Charter gives the Commission broad authority to "resort to any appropriate method of investigation" in the course of its work. The Commission normally invites all the parties to attend or be represented at a hearing on the merits of those cases that have been declared

[119] Communications Nos. 147/95 and 149/96, *Dawda Jawara* v. *The Gambia* (2000).

[120] Communications Nos. 54/91, 61/91, 98/93, 164/97-196/97 and 210/98, *Malawi African Association and Others* v. *Mauritania* (2000).

admissible. An author, his or her legal representative and the State are entitled to be represented at the hearing.

Since 1994, the Commission has undertaken a number of on-site investigations of communications, although these may occur only with the consent of the State concerned. Reports from such missions are adopted as part of the proceedings and may also be published by the Commission separately, prior to a final decision on the communication. The Commission also may take into account information provided by United Nations special procedures (see chap. IV) in determining whether allegations contained in individual complaints are well founded.

After hearing the parties and completing any investigation, the Commission deliberates, reaches its decision and adopts its report in the case.[121] All of these actions are taken in camera. However, NGOs recognized as observers "may be invited specially to be present at closed sessions dealing with issues of particular interest to them".[122] The Commission's conclusions are not legally binding on States, but the Commission does reach direct conclusions that a State has (or has not) violated specific articles of the Charter. If the Commission concludes that Charter rights have been violated, it adopts recommendations and indicates appropriate remedial measures for the harm suffered by the victim(s). The recommendations of the Commission are sent to the parties and annexed to the Commission's annual report, publication of which is approved every year by the Assembly of the African Union.

At any time, a case may be closed if the parties reach a settlement. Although the Commission is not specifically directed under the Charter to seek such a "friendly settlement", the Commission has made it clear that this is its preferred course. "The main goal of the communications procedure before the Commission is to initiate a positive dialogue, resulting in an amicable resolution between the complainant and the State concerned, which remedies the prejudice complained of. A pre-requisite for amicably remedying violations of the Charter is the good faith of the parties concerned, including their willingness to participate in a dialogue."[123]

Fact-finding missions

The African Commission also undertakes fact-finding missions to investigate allegation of serious and massive human rights violations within a member State, as provided for in article 58 of the Charter (which refers to these as "special cases"). Reports on two such missions, to the Sudan (2004) and Zimbabwe (2002), have been published.[124] The report on a third mission, to Mali and Mauritania, was not made public.

The role of NGOs

The African Charter makes no express reference to NGOs, but the rules of procedure of the Commission authorize it to grant observer status to NGOs. Currently, 414 NGOs have formal

[121] Since 1994, the Commission has published its decisions (on both admissibility and merits) on individual complaints as an annex to the annual activity reports it submits to the Assembly of Heads of State of the African Union (available from www.achpr.org). The Institute for Human Rights and Development in Africa (IHRDA) has also published the African Commission's decisions on communications, in two volumes covering the periods 1994-2001 and 2002-2007 respectively (available from ww.ihrda.org/documents).

[122] Resolution on the Criteria for Granting and Enjoying Observer Status to Non-governmental Organizations Working in the Field of Human Rights with the African Commission on Human and Peoples' Rights adopted at the 25th Ordinary Session of the African Commission on Human and Peoples' Rights, Bujumbura, Burundi, 5 May 1999.

[123] Communications Nos. 25/89, 47/90, 56/91 and 100/93, *Free Legal Assistance Group and Others* v. *Zaire* (1995).

[124] Available from www.achpr.org/english/_info/reports_en.html (accessed 4 December 2012).

observer status with the Commission. The Commission had also granted "affiliate status" to 22 national human rights institutions.

In May 1999, the Commission adopted a resolution on the criteria for granting NGOs observer status (see above). NGOs applying for observer status should have objectives and activities which are consistent with the fundamental principles and objectives of the Charter of the Organization of African Unity and the African Charter, and, naturally, work in the area of human rights. An NGO must send a written application to the Secretariat of the Commission at least three months prior to an ordinary session of the Commission, providing "its statutes, proof of its legal existence, a list of its members, its constituent organs, its sources of funding, its last financial statement, as well as a statement on its activities". The statement of activities should cover "the past and present activities of the organization, its plan of action and any other information that may help to determine the identity of the organization, its purpose and objectives, as well as its field of activities".

The Commission has been generous in granting observer status to NGOs and such status can be sought by any minority rights organization in Africa. Having observer status entitles an NGO to receive public documents and to participate in the public sessions of the Commission and its subsidiary bodies. The Commission may consult with NGOs either directly or through committees set up for this purpose. NGOs may distribute their documents, make oral interventions under agenda items considered in public session and participate in working groups established by the Commission.

The annex of the resolution on observer status also permits observers to request to have issues of particular interest to them included in the provisional agenda of the Commission. This might be a particularly useful tool for NGOs which would like to see more attention paid to issues of minority rights and non-discrimination.

The rules of procedure do not require that documentation, other than the provisional agenda, be distributed to NGOs in advance of the Commission's sessions. However, all general distribution documents are available to everyone at a session and NGOs should request relevant documentation so that they can prepare their contribution to the debate.

NGOs cannot take the floor when States report to the Commission on the implementation of the Charter. However, as noted above, they can provide alternative reports on States under consideration by the Commission. Similarly, NGOs can take the floor during the general debate on the reports of special rapporteurs.

Sessions of the Commission are preceded by a three-day Forum of Non-governmental Organizations, organized by the African Centre for Democracy and Human Rights Studies, which is based in Banjul, the Gambia.[125] These have been important meetings for both NGOs and members of the Commission, and they are among the most significant and practical ways in which NGOs can help strengthen the African human rights system. The Forum adopts resolutions on thematic issues and the thematic group on indigenous peoples has proposed a number of resolutions over the years. Unfortunately, the thematic group on minorities does not meet regularly and is therefore not systematic in issuing resolutions to be taken up by the NGO Forum and forwarded to the Commission. Minority representatives and organizations should be aware that the Forum is an effective means of raising issues of concern with the Commission.

The African Court on Human and Peoples' Rights

The African Charter does not provide for a human rights court, but a protocol to create such a court was adopted by the Organization of African Unity in 1998 and entered into force in 2004.

[125] See www.acdhrs.org.

It was not until 2006, however, that the African Court on Human and Peoples' Rights began functioning. The Protocol has been ratified by 26 of the 54 States of the African Union.[126] Pursuant to article 5 of the Protocol, only States, the African Commission and African intergovernmental organizations have an automatic right to submit cases to the Court. However, five of the ratifying States – Burkina Faso, Ghana, Malawi, Mali and the United Republic of Tanzania – have made the declaration required under article 34 (6) of the Protocol to grant the Court the competence to receive cases from individuals and NGOs. The Court delivered its first decision in December 2009. The Court is empowered to issue advisory opinions on legal matters relating to the Charter or any other relevant human rights instruments, if requested to do so by a member State of the African Union, an organ of the African Union or any African organization recognized by the African Union (which includes eight regional economic commissions). Although not expressly stated in the Constitutive Act to be organs of the African Union, the African Commission and the African Committee of Experts on the Rights and Welfare of the Child are, through a decision of the Assembly, recognized as institutions within the framework of the African Union.

Article 2 of the Protocol establishing the Court states that the Court shall "complement the protective mandate of the African Commission". The Commission is entitled to submit cases to the Court (art. 5 (1)) and the Court may request the opinion of the Commission or transfer cases to it (arts. 6 (1) and 6 (3)). The two organs harmonized their interim rules of procedure in October 2009, including provisions on consultation between the Court and the Commission, seizure of the Court by the Commission, admissibility, representation of the Commission before the Court and the content of applications made to the Court.

The African Court of Justice and Human Rights

In July 2008, the African Union adopted another protocol, to create a single African Court of Justice and Human Rights, based in Arusha in the United Republic of Tanzania, to replace the present African Court on Human and Peoples' Rights and the Court of Justice of the African Union.[127] The Protocol entered into force on 11 February 2009 after it had been ratified by 15 States.

Contacts and further information

Secretariat of the African Commission on Human and Peoples' Rights
No. 31 Bijilo Annex Layout
Kombo North District
Western Region
P.O. Box 673
Banjul
The Gambia

Tel: 220 441 05 05; 220 441 05 06
Fax: 220 441 05 04
E-mail: achpr@achpr.org

The websites of the African Union (www.au.int) and the African Court on Human and Peoples' Rights (www.african-court.org) contain all relevant documents on the African courts. The texts

126 Algeria, Burkina Faso, Burundi, the Comoros, the Congo, Côte d'Ivoire, Gabon, the Gambia, Ghana, Kenya, Libya, Lesotho, Malawi, Mali, Mauritania, Mauritius, Mozambique, the Niger, Nigeria, Rwanda, Senegal, South Africa, the United Republic of Tanzania, Togo, Tunisia and Uganda.

127 Available from www.au.int/en/sites/default/files/PROTOCOL_STATUTE_AFRICAN_COURT_JUSTICE_AND_HUMAN_RIGHTS.pdf (accessed 4 December 2012).

of treaties, conventions, protocols and charters of the Organization of African Unity and the African Union are available from www.au.int/en/treaties/status.

Useful publications on the human rights system of the African Union include: I. Kane, *Protecting the Rights of Minorities in Africa: A Guide for Human Rights Activists and Civil Society Organizations* (Minority Rights Group International, 2008); M. Evans and R. Murray (eds.), *The African Charter on Human and Peoples' Rights: The System in Practice 1986-2006*, 2nd ed. (Cambridge, 2008); H. B. Jallow, *The Law of the African (Banjul) Charter on Human and Peoples' Rights* (Trafford, 2007); and K. O. Kufuor, *The African Human Rights System: Origin and Evolution* (Palgrave Macmillan, 2010).

CHAPTER XII

THE COUNCIL OF EUROPE

Summary: Three Council of Europe treaties, the Convention for the Protection of Human Rights and Fundamental Freedoms (also known as the European Convention on Human Rights), the Framework Convention for the Protection of National Minorities, and the European Charter for Regional or Minority Languages, provide multiple opportunities for persons belonging to minorities to raise individual cases of discrimination (under the European Convention on Human Rights) and broader minority issues (under the other two treaties). The Council of Europe's non-treaty mechanisms provide additional avenues for bringing minority issues to the attention of Governments and the public. The Council has also established specific bodies dealing with racism and intolerance, and with Roma and Travellers.

Based in Strasbourg, France, the Council of Europe is an intergovernmental organization composed of 47 States.[128] Its objectives are to:

- Protect human rights, pluralist democracy and the rule of law;
- Promote awareness and encourage the development of Europe's cultural identity and diversity;
- Seek solutions to problems facing European society, including discrimination against minorities, xenophobia, intolerance, environmental protection, human cloning, HIV/AIDS, drugs, organized crime and other problems;
- Help consolidate democratic stability in Europe by backing political, legislative and constitutional reform.

The Council is governed by an intergovernmental Committee of Ministers and an indirectly elected Parliamentary Assembly. The Council of Europe should not be confused with the European Council, an official institution of the European Union, although all the 27 European Union States are also members of the Council of Europe.

The Convention for the Protection of Human Rights and Fundamental Freedoms

The Convention for the Protection of Human Rights and Fundamental Freedoms (also known as the European Convention on Human Rights) entered into force in 1953, inaugurating the first regional human rights system. It has been revised several times through a series of protocols and, in 1998, the European Court of Human Rights became the first full-time human rights court in the world. All the member States of the Council of Europe are parties to the Convention. The right of individual petition is inherent in the Convention system, and the Court's judgements are legally binding on the States parties.

The 47 judges of the Court are elected by the Parliamentary Assembly. Cases are heard by chambers of seven judges, and important cases may be referred to a Grand Chamber of 17 judges. The execution of the Court's judgements is overseen by the Committee of Ministers.

[128] Albania, Andorra, Armenia, Austria, Azerbaijan, Belgium, Bosnia and Herzegovina, Bulgaria, Croatia, Cyprus, the Czech Republic, Denmark, Estonia, Finland, France, Georgia, Germany, Greece, Hungary, Iceland, Ireland, Italy, Latvia, Liechtenstein, Lithuania, Luxembourg, Malta, Monaco, Montenegro, the Netherlands, Norway, Poland, Portugal, the Republic of Moldova, Romania, the Russian Federation, San Marino, Serbia, Slovakia, Slovenia, Spain, Sweden, Switzerland, the former Yugoslav Republic of Macedonia, Turkey, Ukraine, and the United Kingdom of Great Britain and Northern Ireland.

In appropriate circumstances, an applicant may be awarded legal aid by the Court and, in the event of a finding of violation, may also recover necessary expenses incurred in the preparation of the case. However, this assistance only becomes potentially available after the respondent Government has been asked for its observations on the admissibility of the application. Unlike in some domestic legal systems, applicants cannot be required to pay legal costs incurred by the State against which a claim is brought.

The Court considers a large number of individual cases as well as inter-State cases (rarely), and its jurisprudence is enormous.[129] In recent years, 40,000 to 50,000 applications have been lodged annually. The summary below can only outline certain issues that have arisen in connection with minorities in cases before the Court.

The Convention contains no minority rights provision akin to article 27 of the International Covenant on Civil and Political Rights. Therefore, there is no way in which members of minority groups can directly claim "minority rights" before the European Court of Human Rights. Nevertheless, a number of rights guaranteed by the Convention may be invoked in relation to the protection of minorities.

The Convention and minority rights

Many of the rights contained in the Convention for the Protection of Human Rights and Fundamental Freedoms are relevant to minorities, but the phrase "national minority" appears in only two of its articles.

Article 14 states that "The enjoyment of the rights and freedoms set forth in this Convention shall be secured without discrimination on any ground such as sex, race, colour, language, religion, political or other opinion, national or social origin, association with a national minority, property, birth or other status".

Article 14 is not a free-standing right to non-discrimination, and it may be raised only in connection with another Convention right. Despite its limitations, article 14 has in recent years been invoked successfully to address concerns of minorities, in particular Roma. In *Gaygusuz* v. *Austria* (1996) the Court found a violation of article 14 read in conjunction with article 1 of Protocol No. 1 with respect to the difference in treatment between Austrians and non-Austrians as regards their entitlement to emergency assistance. In *Nachova* v. *Bulgaria* (2005) the Court found for the first time a violation of the principle against racial discrimination contained in article 14 (read in conjunction with art. 2, on the right to life) in that the authorities had failed to investigate possible racist motives behind the shooting of Roma by military police. In *D. H. and Others* v. *the Czech Republic* (2007) the Court further developed its jurisprudence under article 14, finding that the disproportionately high placement of Romani students in so-called "special schools" for children with mental disabilities violated the right to be free from racial discrimination (read in conjunction with art. 2 of Protocol No. 1, on the right to education). This was further upheld in *Oršuš and Others* v. *Croatia* (2010) when the Court ruled that "the placement, at times, of the applicants in Roma-only classes during their primary education had not been justified, in violation of Article 14 taken together with Article 2 of Protocol No. 1". In *Religionsgemeinschaft der Zeugen Jehovas and Others* v. *Austria* (2008) the Court found a violation of article 14 read in conjunction with article 9 as regards the way in which religious communities were granted the status of a religious society.

Protocol No. 12, which entered into force in 2005, creates a general prohibition against discrimination in the application of any right guaranteed by law or by any public authority. Thus,

[129] See www.echr.coe.int.

it is no longer necessary to link an allegation of discrimination to a specific substantive right set out in the Convention.

Discrimination is not limited to those cases where a person or group is treated worse than another group. It may also constitute discrimination to treat different groups as if they were alike, that is, to treat a minority and a majority alike may discriminate against the minority. The Court has endorsed positive measures taken to improve the situation of minorities as being compatible with the principle of non-discrimination. The Court has stressed that "democracy does not simply mean that the views of the majority must always prevail: a balance must be achieved which ensures the fair and proper treatment of minorities and avoids any abuse of a dominant position" (*Chassagnou and Others* v. *France* (1999) and *Gorzelik and Others* v. *Poland* (2004)).

In 2009, the Court ruled that provisions in the constitution of Bosnia and Herzegovina that restricted certain political offices to members of the three "constituent peoples" of the State (Bosniacs, Croats and Serbs) violated article 14 of the Convention, taken in conjunction with article 3 of Protocol No. 1 which guarantees elections "which will ensure the free expression of the opinion of the people", as well as the general prohibition of discrimination under article 1 of Protocol 12. The applicants were of Roma and Jewish origin, respectively, and thus were ineligible under the law of Bosnia and Herzegovina to stand for election to one house of the parliament or to the presidency of Bosnia and Herzegovina (*Sejdic and Finci* v. *Bosnia and Herzegovina* (2009)).

A number of cases brought under the Convention have dealt with linguistic rights. The Strasbourg institutions have consistently held that there is no right to use a particular language in making contact with Government authorities, but, in the context of judicial proceedings, everyone has the right to be informed promptly, in a language he or she understands, of the reasons for arrest (art. 5 (2)) and the nature of any criminal charge (art. 6 (3)(a)); there also is a right to a free interpreter if a defendant cannot speak or understand the language used in court (art. 6 (3)(e)).

Article 8 of the Convention provides for the right to respect for an individual's private and family life, home and correspondence. In *Yordanova and Others* v. *Bulgaria*, concerning a planned eviction of Roma from a settlement in Sofia, the Court held that in the context of article 8, the applicants' specificity as a socially disadvantaged group, as well as their particular needs, had to be considered in the proportionality assessment and that the enforcement of the removal order against the applicants would constitute a violation of article 8.

Article 10 guarantees the right to freedom of expression and thus protects the right to use a minority language in private or among members of a minority group. Minorities have a right to publish their own newspapers or use other media without interference by the State or others.

Protocol 2, article 2, states that no person shall be denied the right to education. The education of children belonging to the group is another means of protecting a minority's identity. While under the Convention there is no right per se to education in one's mother tongue, the discontinuance of mother-tongue education may in certain circumstances violate the right to education (*Cyprus* v. *Turkey* (2001)).

Article 9 enshrines the right to freedom of thought, conscience and religion. The individual right to freedom of religion includes the right to manifest that religion, which implies that a minority is to have the necessary degree of control over community religious matters. The Court has held that the State must not interfere in the internal affairs of a church and that "freedom of thought, conscience and religion is one of the foundations of a 'democratic society' within the meaning of the Convention. The pluralism indissociable from a democratic society, which has been dearly won over the centuries, depends on it" (*Serif* v. *Greece* (1999)).

The State may limit manifestation of a minority's religion only for reasonable and objective reasons.

> [W]here the organisation of the religious community is at issue, Article 9 must be interpreted in the light of Article 11 of the Convention which safeguards associative life against unjustified State interference. Seen in this perspective, the believer's right to freedom of religion encompasses the expectation that the community will be allowed to function peacefully, free from arbitrary State intervention. Indeed, the autonomous existence of religious communities is indispensable for pluralism in a democratic society and is thus an issue at the very heart of the protection which Article 9 affords. It directly concerns not only the organisation of the community as such but also the effective enjoyment of the right to freedom of religion by all its active members. Were the organisational life of the community not protected by Article 9 of the Convention, all other aspects of the individual's freedom of religion would become vulnerable (*Hasan and Chaush* v. *Bulgaria* (2000)).

Furthermore, according to the Court, "a minority group is, in principle, entitled to claim the right to respect for the particular life style it may lead as being 'private life', 'family life' or 'home'" under article 8 of the Convention (*G. and E.* v. *Norway* (1983)).

The Court has recently recalled, referring to the Framework Convention for the Protection of National Minorities, that "there is an emerging international consensus amongst the Contracting States of the Council of Europe recognising the special needs of minorities and an obligation to protect their security, identity and lifestyle ... , not only for the purpose of safeguarding the interests of the minorities themselves but to preserve a cultural diversity that is of value to the whole community .... [T]he force of the collective beliefs of a community that is well defined culturally cannot be ignored" (*Munoz Diaz* v. *Spain* (2009)). In this case, the Court found it to be disproportionate for Spain – which had issued the applicant and her Roma family with a family record book, granted them large-family status, afforded health-care assistance to her and her six children and collected social security contributions from her Roma husband for over 19 years – to refuse to recognize the effects of their Roma marriage when it came to a survivor's pension.

Procedure for individual applications

Filing an application

In order to successfully lodge a case with the Court, an applicant must fulfil certain admissibility criteria.[130] Most complaints are dismissed at the admissibility stage, and, since a complaint cannot be lodged twice on substantially the same facts, it is imperative that the complaint meet the criteria on the first application.

The Court has its own application form (available from the Registrar of the Court in all the official languages of the Contracting States), which must be completed and returned to the Court. Besides the personal details of the applicant and his or her legal representative, the applicant must provide information including:

- A detailed account of the facts;
- Detailed submissions on the Convention rights which have allegedly been violated;
- Evidence of the remedies already sought at the national level including dates and details of judgements;
- The remedy sought from the Court.

Copies of all supporting documents must be included with the application.

[130] Guidance for those wishing to apply to the European Court of Human Rights is available from www.echr.coe.int/ECHR/EN/Header/Applicants/Apply+to+the+Court/Application+pack (accessed 4 December 2012).

The Court cannot accept anonymous complaints, and the name of the applicant will be given to the State. The proceedings of the Court are public, although confidentiality may be maintained in appropriate cases by referring to an applicant only by initials. States have an obligation not to obstruct the application and to cooperate with the Court in its investigation.

In order to initiate proceedings under the Convention, an applicant should allege a violation of one or more rights guaranteed under the Convention or one of its Protocols. A complaint may involve action taken by the State itself or by a State organ, such as the armed forces, police forces, courts or other public bodies. Only rarely has the Court allowed a complaint alleging that a private party has caused the harm; in those instances either the State had delegated a public function to the private body or it was the duty of the State to deter such actions by third parties.

The Convention protects everyone within the jurisdiction of the State. The nationality of the applicant is not important; indeed, a claim may even be made by a stateless person. An application may be brought if action by one State may result in a violation of rights in another State, even if the latter is not a party to the Convention. The most common example of this situation is when a person seeks to prevent deportation or extradition to a State in which there is a danger of torture or death.

The "victim" requirement

In order to file a case under the Convention, the complainant must have suffered personally from the alleged violation. This might be as a direct result of State action, for example, if the applicant personally suffered torture, had a publication seized by the Government or was prohibited from exercising his or her religion. A violation may cause personal harm also to the relatives of those whose rights were directly violated; for example, parents could claim harm if their child were detained or otherwise mistreated.

Potential victims also may file a case in some circumstances. The Court has accepted the argument that an applicant is a victim if there is a risk of their being directly affected by a State action, such as enforcement of statutes outlawing homosexuality or requiring sex education in schools, contrary to the wishes of the parents. However, the applicant must show that there is real personal risk, not just a theoretical possibility, of being a victim in the future. A general complaint about a law or a measure is inadmissible, as is a complaint on behalf of other people (unless they are clearly identified and the applicant is their official representative).

Individuals, groups of individuals and NGOs may file applications. If a group or NGO lodges a complaint, it must still fulfil the "victim" requirement. Clearly, where the organization is itself the victim of the breach (if a school is closed or an organization is subjected to improper police surveillance, for example), this will be sufficient. Trade unions, companies, religious bodies, political parties and the inhabitants of a town have been found by the Court to fulfil the "victim" requirement. Where members of a group or association are the victims, it may be advisable to lodge both an individual and a group complaint. Should the group complaint fail the admissibility test, the case may succeed on the individual complaint.

A group need not be formally registered or recognized by the State in order to bring a claim. Moreover, where lack of recognition denies access to domestic courts and prevents a minority group acting to defend its rights, it may amount to a denial of fair trial or an effective remedy (arts. 6 and 13 respectively) that could itself be challenged under the Convention.

Other admissibility requirements

As is generally true for international human rights procedures, applicants must show that they have tried to seek a remedy for the alleged breach from the State concerned. In rare cases, there may be no suitable and effective remedy for violation of a particular Convention right.

However, if a remedy that should have been sought by the applicant has not been sought, the Court will declare the case inadmissible. Only "effective" remedies capable of remedying the violation completely must be exhausted, and this normally includes both judicial and administrative procedures. Discretionary remedies (such as seeking clemency after a conviction) do not generally have to be pursued.

Once a final judgement in the relevant domestic proceedings is received, the applicant must lodge a complaint with the European Court of Human Rights within six months. Where a law in force constitutes a continuing violation, the application may be made at any time. If the applicant is initially unaware of the violation, the six-month limit begins from the date he or she acquires actual knowledge. It is important to note that the application cannot have been previously submitted to another body of international investigation, such as the United Nations Human Rights Committee.

Finally, the application must claim violation of a right that is actually protected under the Convention. For example, a claim of ethnic or religious discrimination in the administration of a State's social security scheme would not be admissible, because there is no right under the Convention to social security. However, this limited interpretation of discrimination was expanded by the entry into force of Protocol No. 12 to the Convention.

Investigation and decision

There may be an exchange of written pleadings on both admissibility issues and the substantive merits of an application. Each party may comment on the submissions made by the other party. The process is usually by way of written pleadings only, although the Court may decide to hold an oral hearing on admissibility or the merits or both. Again, each side is represented at any hearing, and the entire procedure is based on equality between the applicant and the State as party.

NGOs may be asked to provide expert evidence or to appear as witnesses, and minority rights advocates should be aware of the possibility of submitting an amicus curiae brief to the Court if a case is of particular concern. This procedure is called a third-party intervention and may be sought once a case has been communicated to the respondent State for its observations. It offers the possibility of providing useful information to the Court on an issue that may have a direct impact on minority rights beyond the scope of the particular case at hand. An NGO interested in intervening should write to the President of the Court for permission within 12 weeks of communication of the case to the State concerned, information about which can be obtained from the Court's website.

The Court examines the merits of the case through the written pleadings, and it may hear witnesses or even travel to the country concerned if it is deemed necessary. The Court will seek to reach a friendly settlement, if that is possible, but this happens only if both sides agree.

The Court's deliberations are in private, but its judgement is public and is communicated immediately to both parties. The Court has limited its judgements to determining whether or not there has been a violation of the Convention and awarding monetary damages and costs when a violation is found. The Court does not, in principle, issue orders to Governments, for example, to release a prisoner or change its laws. However, in recent years it has shifted somewhat in this respect, for example, by indicating that an unlawfully detained person should be released (*Ilaşcu and Others* v. *Moldova and Russia* [GC] (2004)). As noted above, the Court's judgement is legally binding on States parties to the Convention. Ensuring compliance with a decision of the Court is a matter for the Committee of Ministers under article 46.2 of the Convention, although the great majority of States do comply with judgements readily.

A seven-judge chamber may relinquish jurisdiction over a case in favour of a grand chamber of 17 judges where the case involves a serious issue of general importance or a serious question affecting the interpretation or application of the Convention. A chamber judgement does not become final for a period of three months. During this period either party may request referral to the Grand Chamber and such a request is examined by a panel of five judges.

Urgent cases

The Court may grant priority to urgent cases. The Court may also grant interim measures where there is an imminent, real and serious risk to the life of the applicant or of serious ill-treatment. The Court may indicate that the State should either refrain from or undertake certain actions to protect the applicant. The measures sought and the reasons for seeking them must be indicated on the application form.

Impact of the Strasbourg system on minority rights

The preceding summary suggests ways in which the Convention for the Protection of Human Rights and Fundamental Freedoms can protect minority rights; however, this is not the primary purpose of the Convention. There is a risk that, if a minority group tries to assert "minority rights" per se, the claim might be dismissed as beyond the scope of the Convention and therefore "manifestly ill founded". Furthermore, even where a violation is found, it is still up to the State to provide remedies beyond damages, such as amending an offending piece of legislation. The Court does not act as an appellate court from domestic decisions, and it will only consider whether or not a State has fulfilled its obligations under the Convention, not whether it might have adopted different or even better policies.

Contacts and further information

The Registrar
European Court of Human Rights
Council of Europe
F-67075 Strasbourg Cedex
France

Tel: 33 388 41 20 18
Fax: 33 388 41 27 30
Website: www.echr.coe.int

The essential publication containing the European Convention, rules of procedure of the European Court of Human Rights and other information is *European Convention on Human Rights: Collected Texts* (Council of Europe, 1998). Individual decisions and judgements of the Court are issued in soft cover format and are collected in *Reports of Judgments and Decisions*. The Council of Europe also publishes an annual *Yearbook of the European Convention on Human Rights*, which contains a selection of the most important cases and information on the Convention's application in domestic law.

A number of books have been written on the Strasbourg system, concerning both specific rights and the system as a whole. Two authoritative analyses are: D. J. Harris, M. O'Boyle, E. P. Bates and C. M. Buckley, *Law of the European Convention on Human Rights*, 2d ed. (2009); and P. Van Dijk, F. Van Hoof, A. Van Rijn and L. Zwaak, *Theory and Practice of the European Convention on Human Rights* (2006).

Framework Convention for the Protection of National Minorities

The Framework Convention for the Protection of National Minorities is the first legally binding multilateral instrument devoted to the protection of minorities and is regarded as setting forth the most comprehensive international standards in the field of minority rights thus far. It entered into force in 1998 and has been ratified by 39 States.[131] As the title indicates, the Framework Convention seeks to ensure that the signatory States respect the rights of national minorities; undertake to combat discrimination; promote equality; preserve and develop the culture and identity of national minorities; guarantee certain freedoms in relation to access to the media, minority languages and education; and encourage the participation of national minorities in public life.

The Framework Convention may be ratified by member States of the Council of Europe, and non-member States may join at the invitation of the Committee of Ministers. Commitment to accession to the Convention is regularly required of States applying for membership in the Council of Europe.

The substantive provisions of the Convention

Article 4.1 of the Framework Convention proclaims the fundamental principles of non-discrimination and equality.

Article 4.2 makes it clear that State obligations may also require positive measures on the part of the State and not merely abstention from discrimination. States are to adopt, "where necessary", measures to promote "full and effective equality between persons belonging to a national minority and those belonging to the majority", taking "due account of the specific conditions" of national minorities. Article 4.2 is a key provision, since it provides the basis for the succeeding provisions which spell out in greater detail the measures that States should take in specific areas.

Article 4.3 clarifies that any measures taken to promote effective equality are not to be considered themselves as discrimination.

Article 15 provides that "The Parties shall create the conditions necessary for the effective participation of persons belonging to national minorities in cultural, social and economic life and in public affairs, in particular those affecting them".

The remaining substantive provisions of the Framework Convention cover a wide range of issues. States agree to:

- Promote the conditions necessary for minorities to maintain and develop their culture and identity (art. 5);
- Encourage tolerance, mutual respect and understanding among all persons living on their territory (art. 6);
- Protect the rights to freedom of assembly, association, expression, thought, conscience and religion (arts. 7, 8 and 9);
- Facilitate access to mainstream media and promote the creation and use of minority media (art. 9);
- Recognize the right to use a minority language in private and in public and to display

[131] Albania, Armenia, Austria, Azerbaijan, Bosnia and Herzegovina, Bulgaria, Croatia, Cyprus, the Czech Republic, Denmark, Estonia, Finland, Georgia, Germany, Hungary, Ireland, Italy, Latvia, Liechtenstein, Lithuania, Malta, Montenegro, the Netherlands, Norway, Poland, Portugal, the Republic of Moldova, Romania, the Russian Federation, San Marino, Serbia, Slovakia, Slovenia, Spain, Sweden, Switzerland, the former Yugoslav Republic of Macedonia, Ukraine, and the United Kingdom of Great Britain and Northern Ireland.

information in the minority language (arts. 10 and 11);

- Officially recognize surnames and first names in the minority language (art. 11);
- "Endeavour to ensure" the right to use the minority language before administrative authorities and to display bilingual topographical indications in the minority language, in areas inhabited by national minorities "traditionally" or "in substantial numbers" (arts. 10 and 11);
- Foster knowledge of the culture, history, language and religion of both majority and minorities (art. 12);
- Recognize the rights of minorities to set up and manage their own educational establishments and learn their own language (arts. 13 and 14);
- "Endeavour to ensure" that there are adequate opportunities to be taught in the minority language, in areas traditionally inhabited by national minorities or where they live in "substantial numbers" (art. 14);
- Refrain from measures which alter the proportions of the population in areas inhabited by minorities (art. 16);
- Refrain from interfering with the rights of members of minorities to maintain contacts across frontiers and participate in the activities of national and international NGOs (art. 17).

Definition

The Framework Convention does not define "national minority", although several States have set out their own definition when they ratified it. Many of these definitions (attached as declarations at the time of ratification) exclude non-citizens and migrants from protection under the Framework Convention, and some identify the specific groups to whom the Convention will apply. Liechtenstein, Luxembourg and Malta are parties to the Framework Convention, but each declared that there are no national minorities within their respective territory.

Although States have a margin of appreciation in deciding to whom the Framework Convention applies, this issue will be assessed as part of the international monitoring process created for the Framework Convention, discussed below. But a first step by any NGO which wishes to participate in the monitoring process should be to determine whether the State concerned has made a declaration concerning the groups to which it will apply the Framework Convention.[132]

Implementation and monitoring

The Framework Convention creates an Advisory Committee, a body of 18 independent experts elected by the Committee of Ministers from candidates proposed by States parties, which is responsible, together with the Committee of Ministers, for monitoring implementation of the Convention and adopting country-specific recommendations. Advisory Committee members are to be recognized experts in the field of minority protection; they serve in their individual capacity and must be independent and impartial. The fact that they do not represent their Governments is important, since the Committee of Ministers is a political body of Government representatives. The involvement of an impartial expert body in assessing minority issues facilitates the task of the Committee of Ministers, and the Committee of Ministers (which, as the highest decision-making body in the Council of Europe, has many other duties) relies heavily on the work of the Advisory Committee.

The Advisory Committee's activities begin with the analysis of State reports, which are submitted within one year of the entry into force of the Framework Convention for that State and every five

[132] An up-to-date list of such declarations is available from www.coe.int/minorities.

years thereafter. The Advisory Committee may also invite the Committee of Ministers to request ad hoc reports in order to address situations that arise between periodic reports of a State party. The initial reports should contain full information on the legislative and other measures adopted by the State to realize the principles of the Convention. Detailed guidelines have been adopted by the Committee of Ministers for the initial reports, as well as for subsequent reports. Drafting the reports usually involves a process of consultation with minority organizations and NGOs, which are also encouraged to submit alternative reports or information to the Committee. While the Secretariat of the Framework Convention actively reaches out towards minority organizations and NGOs, interested organizations are also encouraged to initiate contact. Once it is received by the Council of Europe, the State report is automatically made public and posted on the Council's website.

In its examination of State reports, the Advisory Committee makes use of a wide variety of written sources of information from State and non-State actors. It has also developed the practice of carrying out country visits, during which it meets with Government officials, parliamentarians, representatives of minorities, NGOs and other relevant interlocutors.

Following its examination of a State's report and, in most cases, a country visit, the Advisory Committee adopts an "opinion", which is transmitted to the State concerned and to all Council of Europe member States. The State concerned has an opportunity to comment on the Committee's opinion, and it may decide to make it public at this stage. In preparing its response, the State concerned may also choose to engage in further consultations with minority organizations and NGOs.

The Committee of Ministers of the Council of Europe has the final responsibility in monitoring the Framework Convention (art. 26). Following the adoption of an opinion by the Advisory Committee, the Committee of Ministers adopts a resolution containing conclusions and recommendations (which are normally closely based on the Committee's opinion) to the State concerned on implementation of the Framework Convention. The preparation of this resolution provides an opportunity for other States, including non-parties, to express themselves on the situation. This resolution is made public, together with any comments by the State party and the Advisory Committee opinion, if the latter had not been made public earlier.

In order to encourage discussions on measures to improve minority protection, the Secretariat of the Framework Convention organizes meetings in States for which monitoring has been completed. These follow-up meetings have proved an excellent opportunity to bring together all the actors concerned by the implementation of the Framework Convention, both governmental and non-governmental, and to examine ways to put into practice the results of the monitoring.

NGO participation at the domestic level

NGOs can encourage changes in domestic legislation and practice in accordance with the principles set forth in the Framework Convention. They can present their own ideas concerning the interpretation of the Convention and raise public awareness about the country's obligations under it. This can create a new climate in which the State is expected to take steps to comply with its obligations, irrespective of the presence of international monitoring bodies. Public awareness can be increased, for example, by translating and disseminating the text of the Framework Convention and related documents. The latter should include the official State report, any comments by NGOs and, once they are available, the opinions of the Advisory Committee and the conclusions and recommendations of the Committee of Ministers.

It may also be possible for NGOs and minority communities to be directly involved in the preparation of a State's report. NGOs should be aware of which Government body is responsible for preparing the report and contact it to see if information or comments can be submitted while the report is still in draft form. States may involve NGOs in the drafting of the report itself.

NGOs will need to consider the degree to which they want to cooperate in the official reporting process, as opposed to the possibility of submitting comments or alternative reports to the Advisory Committee. Participating in a report's preparation and commenting on it later are not mutually exclusive, and NGOs can choose to do both. The positive side of NGO participation in the preparation of a State report is that it creates an opportunity to engage in direct dialogue with the Government and to contribute to the interpretation of the Framework Convention's provisions in the context of the country concerned. On the other hand, NGO involvement might be perceived as endorsing a State's report, which may not be the case.

In the States that are not yet a party to the Framework Convention, NGO advocacy and lobbying can focus on the need for its ratification.

The role of NGOs in monitoring

NGOs and minority associations have a key role in monitoring the Framework Convention, which is made explicit by Council of Ministers resolution 97 (10), which allows the Advisory Committee to receive and invite information from sources other than States.

In practice, NGOs and minority associations, in many cases with support from international NGOs, have very often used this opportunity to provide the Advisory Committee with well-researched reports which provide information about the practical implementation of the Framework Convention. Such information, as well as direct contacts with NGOs, has been welcomed by the Advisory Committee and constitutes an essential part of the Committee's monitoring tasks.

NGOs and minorities may contribute to the monitoring of the Framework Convention at various stages of the procedure. For example, NGOs may:

- Provide information to the Advisory Committee through written submissions at the time a State's report is due, including shadow reports that may cover the situation of one or several minorities, focus on selected articles or topics or provide information on all articles of the Framework Convention;[133]
- Send information to the Advisory Committee at any time regarding specific issues of concern to minorities and relevant to implementation of the Framework Convention;
- Meet with the Advisory Committee during its country visit;
- Use the Framework Convention as a tool for dialogue, in order to communicate with State authorities during preparation of the State report, obtain information on the implementation of the Framework Convention and participate in follow-up meetings once the monitoring results are made public;
- Encourage the State to publish the opinion of the Advisory Committee as soon as possible, as well as to translate it into local languages;
- Increase awareness of minority rights by organizing training sessions for NGOs and minorities on the Framework Convention;
- Contribute to the consultations undertaken by the Advisory Committee when it prepares commentaries on specific themes.

[133] If an NGO would like to submit a full alternative or "shadow" report, it should consider cooperating with other national or international NGOs. This will minimize duplication of work and may provide more representative and comprehensive information, which will give the report greater credibility. At a minimum, it is important to be aware of what other NGOs are doing in order to prevent presenting conflicting information.

NGOs can send information at any time to the Secretariat of the Framework Convention at the Council of Europe, which will forward the information to members of the Advisory Committee. However, it is best to submit information when the Advisory Committee is actively considering a State's report. Therefore, NGOs should study the report (which is made public as soon as the Committee receives it, if it is not made public earlier by the State itself), decide what information provided by the Government should be supplemented or challenged, and submit comments in time for them to be considered when the Committee examines the State's report. Information on the schedule for State reports and when they have actually been received may be obtained from the Council of Europe's website, and the Secretariat can provide information as to when NGO comments must be received in order for the Committee to take them into account. If possible, NGO submissions should be in either French or English, the working languages of the Committee.

When submitting information, whether comments or a full alternative report, NGOs should refer whenever possible to specific information that might be missing or incorrect in a State's report. The information provided by the NGO should be factual, complete and detailed, and it should refer whenever possible to specific articles of the Framework Convention. Demographic and statistical information is very valuable, if it is not included in the State's report, and it may help the Committee to compare the situation of minorities at different times. Finally, NGOs may also present their own recommendations for actions the Government should take to implement the Framework Convention.

Contacts and further information

Secretariat of the Framework Convention for the Protection of National Minorities
F–67075 Strasbourg Cedex
France

Tel: 33 3 88 41 20 00
Fax: 33 3 90 21 49 18
E-mail: minorities.fcnm@coe.int
Website: www.coe.int/minorities

European Charter for Regional or Minority Languages

The European Charter for Regional or Minority Languages was adopted in 1992 and entered into force in 1998. The Charter, ratified by 25 States,[134] seeks to protect and promote regional and minority languages and to enable speakers of a regional or minority language to use it in private and public life. Its overriding purpose is cultural, and it concerns itself with regional and minority languages, non-territorial languages and less widely used official languages, rather than minority rights per se.

The Charter's preamble begins by setting out the main objectives and principles that States undertake to apply to all regional or minority languages existing within their national territory, "[s]tressing the value of interculturalism and multilingualism". It then identifies a series of concrete measures designed to facilitate and encourage the use of specific regional or minority languages in public life (part III). These are intended to ensure, as far as is reasonably possible, that regional or minority languages are used in education, media, legal and administrative contexts, economic and social life, cultural activities and transfrontier exchanges. At the time of ratifying

[134] Armenia, Austria, Bosnia and Herzegovina, Croatia, Cyprus, the Czech Republic, Denmark, Finland, Germany, Hungary, Liechtenstein, Luxembourg, Montenegro, the Netherlands, Norway, Poland, Romania, Serbia, Slovakia, Slovenia, Spain, Sweden, Switzerland, Ukraine, and the United Kingdom of Great Britain and Northern Ireland.

the Charter, States must indicate specifically to which languages part III of the Charter will apply; all languages which fall under the definition of a regional or minority language are covered by part II (see below).

As defined by the Charter, "regional or minority languages" are languages traditionally used within a given territory of a State by nationals of that State who form a group numerically smaller than the rest of the State's population; they are different from the official language(s) of that State, and they include neither dialects of the official language(s) of the State nor the languages of migrants. The expression "territory in which the regional or minority language is used" means the geographical area in which the said language is the mode of expression of a number of people sufficient to justify the adoption of protective and promotional measures, as provided for in the Charter.

The expression "non-territorial languages" means languages used by nationals of the State which differ from the language(s) used by the rest of the State's population but which, although traditionally used within the State's territory, cannot be identified with a particular area thereof; examples are Romani and Yiddish.

The demographic situation of the languages covered by the Charter differs greatly, and they exist in a very wide range of social, political and economic contexts. Accordingly, the Charter facilitates adapting the scope of the protection afforded to suit the particular situation of each language, including taking into account the costs of protection.

Part II of the Charter sets out eight fundamental principles and objectives upon which States must base their policies, legislation and practice, and which are regarded as providing the necessary framework for the preservation of the languages concerned:

- Recognition of regional or minority languages as an expression of cultural wealth;
- Respect for the geographical area of each regional or minority language;
- The need for resolute action to promote such languages;
- Facilitation and/or encouragement of the use of such languages, in speech and writing, in public and private life;
- Provision of appropriate forms and means for the teaching and study of such languages at all appropriate stages;
- Promotion of relevant transnational exchanges;
- Prohibition of all forms of unjustified distinction, exclusion, restriction or preference relating to the use of a regional or minority language and intended to discourage or endanger its maintenance or development;
- Promotion by States of mutual understanding between all the country's linguistic groups.

Part III (arts. 8-14) lays down detailed measures in a number of fields, offering States a choice of 68 concrete undertakings in seven areas of public life. States undertake to apply only those provisions of part III to which they have subscribed, so the precise obligations accepted are likely to vary from State to State; they may also vary from language to language within a particular State. In the United Kingdom of Great Britain and Northern Ireland, for example, different provisions in part III apply to Welsh, Scottish-Gaelic and Irish respectively, while only part II applies to Scots, Ulster Scots, Cornish and Manx Gaelic.

States must select at least 35 undertakings in respect of each language that they have designated as falling within the scope of part III of the Charter. Many of the Charter's provisions consist of several options, of varying degrees of rigour, one of which has to be chosen "according to the situation of each language". States are encouraged to add to or upgrade their commitments under the Charter at a later date, as their legal situation develops or as their financial circumstances allow (art. 3 (2)).

The areas of public life, each corresponding to an article of part III, from which these specific undertakings must be chosen, are:

- Education;
- Judicial authorities;
- Administrative authorities and public services;
- Media;
- Cultural activities and facilities;
- Economic and social life;
- Transfrontier exchanges.

Implementation and monitoring

Members of a committee of independent experts, composed of one member for each State party, are appointed by the Committee of Ministers of the Council of Europe from "a list of individuals of the highest integrity and recognised competence in the matters dealt with in the Charter, who shall be nominated by the Party concerned". As pointed out in the explanatory report of the Charter (para. 131), "by placing emphasis on the intrinsically personal trait of the 'highest integrity', the Charter makes clear that the experts appointed to the committee, in carrying out their task, should be free to act independently and not be subject to instructions from the governments concerned."

State reports on implementation of the Charter are to be submitted on a regular basis. The first report must be submitted within one year of the entry into force of the Charter for the State, and subsequent reports are to be submitted every three years thereafter.

Once a State has submitted its report, the monitoring procedure begins. The committee of experts has developed innovative working methods and makes full use of the broad powers available to it to obtain and solicit information from non-official sources, particularly NGOs, under article 16.2 of the Charter. The committee carries out on-site visits, during which members visit the State being monitored to meet with both Government officials and representatives of the linguistic communities.

Based on the information gathered, the committee adopts a report and submits it to the Committee of Ministers, which formulates recommendations to the State based upon the report and comments by the State. These reports are made public and are usually translated into the official language of the State.[135]

The role of NGOs in monitoring

The committee of experts places great importance on the active role of NGOs in the monitoring procedure and sees NGOs as equal and essential partners in the dialogue between the States and the Council of Europe. NGOs have the opportunity to provide the committee with their views on the situation of regional or minority languages in the country concerned, in much the same way as they participate in the work of the Advisory Committee to the Framework Convention. NGOs and others should feel free to contact the committee of experts at any time to provide relevant information.

[135] Available from www.coe.int/t/dg4/education/minlang/Report/default_en.asp (accessed 4 December 2012).

To facilitate the involvement of NGOs in the monitoring process, in 2004, the Council of Europe published *The European Charter for Regional or Minority Languages: Working Together: NGOs and Regional or Minority Languages.*

Contacts and further information

Council of Europe
European Charter for Regional or Minority Languages
Directorate General IV – Education, Culture and Heritage, Youth and Sport
F–67075 Strasbourg Cedex
France

Tel: 33 3 88 41 31 86
Fax: 33 3 88 41 27 88
E-mail: minlang.secretariat@coe.int
Website: www.coe.int/minlang

European Commission against Racism and Intolerance

The European Commission against Racism and Intolerance (ECRI) is a monitoring body created by the Council of Europe to combat racism, xenophobia, antisemitism and intolerance. Its mandate covers all forms of discrimination and prejudice against persons or groups of persons on grounds of race, colour, language, religion, nationality, or national or ethnic origin.

The Commission was established at the first Summit of Heads of State and Government of the Council of Europe and endowed with a Statute by the Committee of Ministers in 2002, which consolidated its role as an independent human rights organ. It conducts country-by-country monitoring, makes general policy recommendations and promotes awareness-raising. Its members are appointed on the basis of their expertise in the fields covered by its mandate, and they serve in their individual capacity in an independent and impartial manner.

In the course of its country-specific work, the Commission examines the situation of racism and intolerance in each of the Council of Europe member States. Its findings, along with recommendations on ways of dealing with the problems identified, are published in country reports. These are drawn up following analyses of information provided in writing by the State and NGOs and a country visit, during which Commission delegates meet relevant Government and civil society stakeholders. Before finalizing a report on a country, the Commission engages in a confidential dialogue with its authorities. All States are considered in the same manner, in five-year monitoring cycles (covering nine to 10 countries per year). The fourth monitoring cycle, which started in 2008, focuses on the implementation of previous cycles' recommendations. Three specific recommendations are designated as priorities for each State, on which they are to report progress two years after the publication of their fourth-cycle report.

The Commission also addresses general policy recommendations to all member States, which provide guidelines for Government policymakers in their fight against racism and related forms of discrimination. The Commission has adopted 12 such recommendations on, for example, effective legislative responses, specialized bodies, Roma, Islamophobia, the Internet, combating racism while fighting terrorism, antisemitism, education, policing and sports.

For the fight against racism to be effective, the message must filter down to the general population. Awareness-raising is, therefore, crucial. In 2002, the Commission adopted a programme of action that includes developing contacts with all interested NGOs, initiating round-table sessions in States to discuss the impact of the Commission's country reports, and organizing annual seminars for specialized bodies on topics of common interest (such as mediation, positive measures and integration).

Contacts and further information

The Secretariat
European Commission against Racism and Intolerance
Council of Europe
Directorate General of Human Rights and Legal Affairs-DGHL
F–67075 Strasbourg Cedex
France

Tel: 33 3 88 41 29 64
Fax: 33 3 88 41 39 87
E-mail: ecri@coe.int
Website: www.coe.int/t/dghl/monitoring/ecri/default_en.asp

Commissioner for Human Rights

The Commissioner for Human Rights is an independent institution within the Council of Europe, created in 1999 and mandated to promote awareness of and respect for human rights in all Council of Europe States.

Mandate

The objectives of the Commissioner for Human Rights are laid out in Committee of Ministers resolution (99) 50, in which the Commissioner is mandated to:

- Foster the effective observance of human rights and assist member States in the implementation of Council of Europe human rights standards;
- Promote education in and awareness of human rights in Council of Europe member States;
- Identify possible shortcomings in laws and practices concerning human rights;
- Facilitate the activities of national ombuds institutions and other human rights bodies;
- Provide advice and information regarding the protection of human rights throughout the region.

The Commissioner's work focuses on encouraging reforms that will achieve tangible improvement in human rights promotion and protection. The Commissioner cannot act upon individual complaints. However, he or she may receive information from any source, including individuals and NGOs, and can take wide-ranging initiatives on the basis of such information if it reveals a systematic human rights problem within a particular country. Among the specific themes to which the Commissioner devotes attention are the eradication of discrimination and the rights of children and migrants.

The Commissioner cooperates with a broad range of international and national institutions, as well as human rights monitoring mechanisms. The most important intergovernmental partners of the Commissioner include the United Nations and its specialized agencies, the European Union and OSCE (see chap. XIII). The Commissioner also cooperates closely with leading human rights NGOs, universities and think tanks.

Activities of the Commissioner for Human Rights

The Commissioner seeks to engage in ongoing dialogue with Council of Europe member States and conducts official country visits to examine and evaluate the human rights situation when he or she deems it necessary. These visits commonly include meetings with the highest representatives of Government, parliament and the judiciary, as well as leading members of human rights institutions and civil society. During country visits, the Commissioner engages in dialogue with minority representatives and organizations representing them. The Commissioner's reports contain both an analysis of human rights practices and detailed recommendations for improvement. The reports are published and widely circulated in the policymaking and NGO communities and the media. By 2008, all member States of the Council of Europe had been visited by the Commissioner and an evaluation report had been published on every country.

A few years after an initial visit to a country, the Commissioner or a staff member carries out a follow-up visit to assess the progress made in implementing the recommendations or a more focused visit to review priority concerns. The Commissioner issues a follow-up report, which is also widely publicized. Shorter visits may be made to countries or regions in order to strengthen relations with the authorities and examine specific human rights issues, although these visits do not necessarily result in a public report.

When it is appropriate, the Commissioner makes recommendations regarding a specific human rights issue in a single member State or in several States. On the request of national bodies or on his or her own initiative, the Commissioner may also give an opinion on draft laws and specific practices. In 2004, for example, the Commissioner issued an opinion on the creation of a national body for counteracting discrimination in Poland.[136]

To promote awareness of human rights in member States, the Commissioner is involved in organizing seminars and events on human rights themes, and seeks to maintain a permanent dialogue with Governments, civil society organizations and educational institutions. The seminars and events usually lead to the publication of recommendations, opinions or reports by the Commissioner on issues discussed.[137]

The Commissioner cooperates closely with national ombudsmen or women, national human rights institutions and other Government institutions concerned with the protection of human rights, and maintains close working relations with the Ombudsman of the European Union. The Commissioner encourages the establishment of such bodies in Council of Europe member States where they do not yet exist.

The situation of minorities has been assessed in most of the country reports issued by the Commissioner. Particular attention has been paid to Roma and Travellers, due to the persistent, systemic discrimination they encounter. A general report on the human rights situation of Roma, Sinti and Travellers was published in 2006, and a subsequent study, *Recent Migration of Roma in Europe* (carried out in cooperation with the OSCE High Commissioner on National Minorities) in 2009.[138] The Commissioner's Office has also organized seminars with outside partners on Roma-related questions.

The Commissioner's country monitoring on minorities has often built on the work of the Advisory Committee of the Framework Convention for the Protection of National Minorities and the committee of experts of the European Charter for Regional or Minority Languages, which are described above. However, the Commissioner also assesses the situation of minorities in countries which have not yet adhered to these instruments. The Commissioner has evaluated member States' approaches to including or excluding minorities falling under the protection of international instruments.

---

136 Available from https://wcd.coe.int/ViewDoc.jsp?id=980009&Site=CommDH&BackColorInternet=FEC65B&BackColorIntranet=FEC65B&BackColorLogged=FFC679 (accessed 4 December 2012).

137 Available from www.coe.int/t/commissioner/Activities/themes/default_en.asp (accessed 4 December 2012).

138 Available from https://wcd.coe.int/wcd/ViewDoc.jsp?id=1536357. The 2006 report is available from https://wcd.coe.int/com.instranet.InstraServlet?command=com.instranet.CmdBlobGet&InstranetImage=320815&SecMode=1&DocId=941416&Usage=2 (both accessed 4 December 2012).

Many national and international NGOs representing minorities or working for the realization of their rights provide information to the Commissioner's Office on a regular basis. They also make use of the Commissioner's findings and recommendations in their own work.

Contacts and further information

Office of the Commissioner for Human Rights
Council of Europe
F–67075 Strasbourg Cedex
France

Tel: 33 3 88 41 34 21
Fax: 33 3 90 21 50 53
E-mail: commissioner@coe.int
Website: www.coe.int/t/commissioner/Default_en.asp

Council of Europe engagement on Roma issues

The Council of Europe estimates the number of Roma presently resident in Europe at between 10 million and 12 million. Roma are among the most deprived of all communities, with many living in extreme poverty, facing racism and discrimination on a daily basis, and being excluded from the normal life – and protection of fundamental rights – that other people take for granted.

In October 2010, the Secretary-General of the Council of Europe launched an initiative to bring the member States to agree on priorities for better social inclusion of Roma and respect for their human rights. From 2011, a dedicated team has worked on the issue, led by the Special Representative of the Secretary-General for Roma issues. It acts as the hub for a range projects, discussed below.

Capacity-building and awareness-raising

Training programme for mediators

Mediators build a bridge between Roma communities and local public institutions. They work to enrol Roma children in local schools, ensure that families obtain proper health care, obtain identity cards, secure decent housing and find jobs. The ROMED training programme for mediators for the Roma community began in October 2010 and the European Commission joined the programme in July 2011. Specialized training took place in 21 countries during 2011 and 2012.

A new training curriculum for mediators (available in 16 languages) has been drawn up, together with the European Code of Ethics for Mediators to protect mediators against abuse and to enhance the quality of services provided. A European pool of 38 ROMED trainers has been created, 21 of whom are of Roma origin.

The European Database on Mediators is a valuable resource with up-to-date information on various aspects of Roma mediation in a number of countries.[139]

Training for lawyers defending Roma

Since 1996, the Council of Europe and the European Roma Rights Centre (ERRC) have organized training sessions to encourage and assist advocates in bringing cases involving Roma before the European Court of Human Rights (see above) and the European Committee for Social Rights (under the European Social Charter mechanism for collective complaints). The Programme for

[139] Available from www.coe-romed.org.

Lawyers Defending Roma has been implemented in France, Greece, Italy and Turkey and training continues in Romania and Bulgaria.

Combating anti-gypsyism

Dosta! – "Enough!" in the Romani language – is the slogan of the Council of Europe campaign to change attitudes and have people discover the true potential of the Roma people. Launched in 2008, the campaign has been implemented in 14 countries to date. The multilingual website of the Dosta! campaign is regularly updated with new information and documentation, including leaflets, posters, television and radio spots and a toolkit for campaigning against stereotypes.[140]

Recognition of the Roma genocide

The Council of Europe, in cooperation with the Contact Point for Roma and Sinti Issues within the Office for Democratic Institutions and Human Rights (ODIHR) of OSCE (see chap. XIII), has a project to enhance recognition and increase awareness of the genocide of Roma and Sinti during the Second World War. The project includes the production of teaching materials on Roma history and culture and the organization of events and meetings. A website devoted to Roma remembrance comprises a database on this period of Roma history, with a virtual library of the best-known and most useful publications, and an interactive map indicating special or distinctive features by country; and information on curricula, available teaching materials, school textbooks, places of remembrance, and innovative practices introduced by ministries, civil society, international organizations, museums and schools.[141]

Analysis and exchange of policies and good practices

Database on policies and good practices

A database established in 2011 includes examples of policies, strategies and "promising", "demonstrated" and "replicated" (or best) practices relating to Roma at national, regional or local levels. It integrates information in cooperation with member States, the Congress of Local and Regional Authorities, the Office of the Commissioner for Human Rights, and international partners such as the Decade for Roma Inclusion, European Commission, European Union Agency for Fundamental Rights and ODIHR.

The Council of Europe Roma portal (www.coe.int/roma) reflects the transversal approach taken and includes a link to all Roma-related texts adopted by various Council of Europe bodies and updated information on Roma-related projects.

Ad hoc Committee of Experts on Roma Issues

An intergovernmental body dealing with Roma issues was first set up in 1995. Following the adoption of the Strasbourg Declaration on Roma in October 2010, intergovernmental work on Roma issues has been strengthened and new terms of reference adopted for an Ad hoc Committee of Experts on Roma Issues (CAHROM), which is answerable directly to the Committee of Ministers of the Council of Europe.

The terms of reference place emphasis on the analysis and evaluation of the implementation of national policies and thematic exchanges of experience and good practices. The Committee has established three thematic groups of countries, based on the role of local and regional authorities in implementing national strategies and action plans for Roma, on absenteeism and school dropout of Roma children and on social housing for Roma.

140 See www.dosta.org.

141 See www.opusidea.eu/trr/.

In 2011, CAHROM adopted an opinion on Parliamentary Assembly recommendation 1941 (2010) on Roma asylum seekers in Europe. It also approved an implementation report on the Committee of Ministers recommendation on Roma employment[142] which includes member States' good practices in this field, as well as a draft declaration on the rise of anti-Gypsyism and racist violence against Roma in Europe which was adopted by the Committee of Ministers on 1 February 2012. CAHROM is currently also drafting a recommendation on mediators, to encourage the use of mediators and establish basic principles for effective mediation which has maximum impact.[143]

European Alliance of Cities and Regions for Roma Inclusion

A European Alliance of Cities and Regions for Roma Inclusion was agreed to at the Summit of Mayors in September 2011. Its aim is to help cities and regions increase their capacities for Roma inclusion, provide advice and support the exchange of experiences and practices. A core group of 11 cities and regions has been entrusted with setting up the Alliance.

The role of local and regional authorities in the social inclusion of Roma is of paramount importance as most problems related to Roma health, education, employment and housing are, in general, the responsibility of these authorities.

Education of Roma Children in Europe

The future of Roma communities depends on the schooling of their children, as education is a key factor in comprehending the situation and achieving social integration. In 2002, the Council of Europe began the Education of Roma Children in Europe project, which supports the integration of Roma communities into the mainstream education system. Roma themselves were actively involved in initiating the project, including its design and execution. The project has developed a teaching kit to prepare Roma children who have not attended nursery school to better cope with their first primary school class; training seminars devoted to Roma issues, within the framework of the Council of Europe's Pestalozzi programme for education professionals; a guide for Roma mediators or school assistants; teaching materials for use in classes of Roma and non-Roma children, designed to foster mutual understanding; and development of material on the Roma genocide during the Second World War.[144]

Teaching and learning of the Romani language

The Council of Europe Language Policy Division fosters the teaching and learning of the Romani language in Europe through its Curriculum Framework for Romani.[145] It draws on the Council's Common European Framework of Reference for Languages, which focuses on ages 4-16, can be adapted to local contexts and needs, and is designed for practitioners, manual designers and policy decision makers. Supplementing the Curriculum Framework are two European Language Portfolio models (for ages 6-11 and 11-16), each comprising a personal document for the learner and a handbook for teachers. Translation of these materials into additional Romani dialects and national or official languages is encouraged.

---

142 Recommendation Rec(2001)17 on improving the economic and employment situation of Roma/Gypsies and Travellers in Europe.

143 Further information on CAHROM is available from www.coe.int/roma.

144 See www.romagenocide.org. Further information on the project, which was concluded in 2009, is available from www.coe.int/t/dg4/education/roma/default_en.asp (accessed 4 December 2012).

145 See www.coe.int/t/dg4/linguistic/Source/Rom_CuFrRomani2008_EN.pdf (accessed 4 December 2012).

International Task Force for the Education of Roma

The International Task Force for the Education of Roma (ITFER) is composed of representatives of the Council of Europe, UNICEF, the European Commission, UNESCO, ODIHR, the Fundamental Rights Agency, Open Society and the International Step by Step Association. It aims at developing and ensuring the close coordination of European and international initiatives on all levels of education for Roma, Sinti and Travellers and reinforcing cooperation among its representatives' member States.

Route of Roma Culture and Heritage

The objective of the Route of Roma Culture and Heritage is to increase the knowledge of Europeans about Roma history, culture, values and lifestyle; encourage the contribution of Roma to Europe's cultural life and diversity; and contribute to reversing negative stereotypes of Roma. The first phase of the project is the development of a network of organizations (including associations, museums, documentation and cultural centres, art and education institutions, festivals) which work to develop activities in common. The second phase will develop a series of tourist itineraries across Europe which will promote better understanding of Roma culture.[146]

Cooperation with international partners

The Council of Europe cooperates with both intergovernmental and non-governmental organizations and with Romani NGOs. It has a partnership agreement with the European Roma and Travellers Forum.

The Informal Contact Group of International Organisations and Institutions dealing with Roma issues is an informal mechanism of consultation and cooperation among representatives of the European Union, the Council of Europe, ODIHR, the World Bank, United Nations agencies (OHCHR, UNDP and UNHCR) and others.

Contacts and further information

The Council of Europe
Avenue de l'Europe
F-67075 Strasbourg Cedex

Tel: 33 3 88 41 20 00
Website: www.coe.int

Support Team of the Special Representative of the Secretary General for Roma issues
Council of Europe
Agora Building
1, Quai Jacoutot
F–67075 Strasbourg Cedex
France

Tel: 33 3 88 41 20 00
Fax: 33 3 90 21 40 53
Website: www.coe.int/roma

The Council publishes a great deal of material relevant to minority issues (see http://book.coe.int/EN).

[146] See www.coe.int/t/dg4/cultureheritage/culture/routes/roma_en.asp (accessed 4 December 2012).

CHAPTER XIII

THE ORGANIZATION FOR SECURITY AND CO-OPERATION IN EUROPE

Summary: The Organization for Security and Co-operation in Europe (OSCE) has played an important role in the development of normative and institutional instruments for the promotion and protection of minority rights. The Copenhagen Document on the Human Dimension contains one of the most comprehensive sets of international minority rights standards, and the OSCE High Commissioner on National Minorities is the only permanent international body for the prevention of inter-ethnic conflict within and between States. Other OSCE bodies are also relevant for the protection of minority rights. The Office for Democratic Institutions and Human Rights (ODIHR) conducts extensive human rights activities in the field of human rights education, monitoring and the promotion of tolerance and non-discrimination. It has a department dedicated to improving the lives of Roma and Sinti. OSCE field operations also engage in work which is relevant for minority groups, for example, through building Government and civil society capacity for good governance, economic participation and human rights.

The Organization for Security and Co-operation in Europe (OSCE) is a security body whose 56 participating States span the geographical area from Vancouver to Vladivostok.[147] Recognized as a regional arrangement under Chapter VIII of the Charter of the United Nations, OSCE is primarily an instrument for early warning, conflict prevention, crisis management and post-conflict rehabilitation. Prior to 1995, OSCE was known as the Conference on Security and Co-operation in Europe (CSCE) and was an intergovernmental diplomatic conference, also known as the "Helsinki process", begun during the 1970s as a forum for East–West dialogue during the cold war. As the descendant of this process, OSCE is still primarily a security organization, aimed at achieving security and stability for all its members through a process of cooperation. OSCE makes decisions by consensus; thus, all participating States may be considered to have made political commitments to respect OSCE resolutions, declarations and similar acts.

The OSCE approach regarding respect for human rights is embodied in the notion of "comprehensive security", which recognizes three main dimensions of security: politico-military, economic and environmental, and human. The organization therefore addresses a wide range of security-related concerns (e.g., arms control, non-proliferation, the destruction of weapons systems, military reforms, combating terrorism, and confidence- and security-building measures), economic and environmental issues (e.g., transport networks, water management, protection of land and good governance in economic matters) and the human dimension (human rights, national minorities, democratization, election observation, the rule of law, policing and humanitarian issues). The interdependence of military and political security and human rights, as well as economic and environmental concerns, was recognized in the 1975 Helsinki Final Act. This document established 10 fundamental principles governing the behaviour of participating

[147] The participating States are: Albania, Andorra, Armenia, Austria, Azerbaijan, Belarus, Belgium, Bosnia and Herzegovina, Bulgaria, Canada, Croatia, Cyprus, the Czech Republic, Denmark, Estonia, Finland, France, Georgia, Germany, Greece, the Holy See, Hungary, Iceland, Ireland, Italy, Kazakhstan, Kyrgyzstan, Latvia, Liechtenstein, Lithuania, Luxembourg, Malta, Monaco, Montenegro, the Netherlands, Norway, Poland, Portugal, the Republic of Moldova, Romania, the Russian Federation, San Marino, Serbia, Slovakia, Slovenia, Spain, Sweden, Switzerland, Tajikistan, the former Yugoslav Republic of Macedonia, Turkey, Turkmenistan, Ukraine, the United Kingdom of Great Britain and Northern Ireland, the United States of America, and Uzbekistan.

States towards those within their jurisdiction, as well as towards each other, which later became known as the Decalogue.

Overview of applicable standards

The inclusion of the principle of respect for human rights in the Helsinki Final Act was a major achievement. Together with the recommendations, principle VII of the Final Act represented the first acknowledgement of the direct link between human rights and security and has provided the foundation for the elaboration of new human rights standards, especially concerning the rights of persons belonging to national minorities. Principle VII stipulates:

> The participating States on whose territory national minorities exist will respect the right of persons belonging to such minorities to equality before the law, will afford them the full opportunity for the actual enjoyment of human rights and fundamental freedoms and will, in this manner, protect their legitimate interests in this sphere.

While cold war tensions blocked further progress in the 15 years following the adoption of the Helsinki Final Act, progress on minority issues greatly accelerated after 1989. In June 1990, the Copenhagen Document on the Human Dimension of the (then) CSCE was adopted; it is still regarded as the basic OSCE standard-setting instrument concerning human rights and minority rights and has inspired the adoption of other, legally binding international instruments on minority rights, such as the Council of Europe Framework Convention for the Protection of National Minorities (see chap. XII). The Copenhagen Document also includes a long list of provisions concerning democratic institution-building and the rule of law.

Taking individual human rights as its point of departure, paragraph 33 of the Copenhagen Document commits States to "protect the ethnic, cultural, linguistic and religious identity of national minorities on their territory ... in conformity with the principles of equality and non-discrimination". States also commit themselves, where necessary, to take special measures to ensure this equality. These special rights and measures do not constitute preferential treatment for persons belonging to national minorities. Rather, they aim to achieve equal and meaningful enjoyment of rights in fact as well as in law.

While the concept of minority rights grows out of the concept of individual human rights (e.g., art. 1 of the Council of Europe's Framework Convention for the Protection of National Minorities), it is only the shared exercise of these rights that enables persons belonging to a national minority to preserve their identity. The Copenhagen Document grants all persons belonging to national minorities a number of specific rights that may be exercised both individually and in community with other members of their group. These include the right to:

- "Express, preserve and develop" their identity and culture, free from any attempts at forced assimilation (para. 32);
- Use their mother tongue in private and in public and to exchange information in their mother tongue (paras. 32 (1) and 32 (5));
- Establish and maintain minority educational, cultural and religious institutions which can seek funding "in conformity with national legislation" (para. 32 (2));
- Practise their religion, including using religious materials and conducting religious educational activities in their mother tongue (para. 32 (3));
- Maintain "unimpeded contacts" with those with whom they share common origin, heritage or religious beliefs, within their country and across frontiers (para. 32 (4));
- "Effective participation in public affairs, including participation in the affairs relating to the protection and promotion of the identity of such minorities" (para. 35).

States are to "create conditions for the promotion of ... [minority] identity" (para. 33) and "will endeavour to ensure" that members of minorities "have adequate opportunities for instruction of their mother tongue or in their mother tongue, as well as, wherever possible and necessary, for its use before public authorities" (para. 34).

Although individuals may exercise their rights in community with others, there is no basis for collective rights per se within the OSCE framework. In particular, there is no connection with the right to self-determination (fear of which is sometimes expressed by Government authorities or the majority population), as paragraph 37 of the Copenhagen Document makes clear:

> None of these commitments [i.e., specified minority rights] may be interpreted as implying any right to engage in any activity or perform any action in contravention of the purposes and principles of the Charter of the United Nations, other obligations of international law or the provisions of the Final Act, including the principle of territorial integrity of States.

Additional minority-specific provisions are set forth in the 1990 Charter of Paris for a New Europe, which notes the determination of States to "foster the rich contribution of national minorities to the life of our societies", and the 1991 Report of the Geneva Meeting of Experts on National Minorities, which represents the conclusions of three weeks of discussion among experts from CSCE States on the issues of national minorities and the rights of persons belonging to them.

Furthermore, almost every relevant CSCE or OSCE document since 1990 has highlighted the situation of Roma, starting with the 1990 Copenhagen Document (para. 40 and subsections), which requires participating States to take measures to protect Roma and others against any acts that constitute incitement to violence and against threat or acts of discrimination, hostility or violence; the 1991 Report of the Geneva Meeting of Experts on National Minorities (chapter VI); and the 1992 Document of the Helsinki Follow-up Meeting (chapter VI, para. 35).

In addition to previous CSCE and OSCE commitments pertaining to Roma, OSCE participating States adopted the 2003 Action Plan at the 2003 Ministerial Council on Improving the Situation of Roma and Sinti within the OSCE Area. The Action Plan provides a set of principles to be followed in dealing with Roma and Sinti issues, as well as guidance in developing strategies to eliminate discrimination against Roma, Sinti and other related groups. Since its adoption, the Contact Point for Roma and Sinti Issues at the OSCE Office for Democratic Institutions and Human Rights (ODIHR, discussed below), in close cooperation with the High Commissioner on National Minorities, has been carrying out activities in support of participating States and NGOs in the implementation of the Action Plan and reporting on how participating States have been fulfilling the promises made in the Action Plan.

OSCE institutions and minority rights

OSCE monitors and promotes human rights through a variety of institutions, mechanisms and field operations. Particularly relevant for the protection of minority rights are the High Commissioner on National Minorities, ODIHR; the Special Representatives of the Chairman-in-Office to promote tolerance and combat racism, xenophobia and discrimination; and the field operations in several countries.

The High Commissioner on National Minorities

Almost all OSCE participating States have one or more national minority groups within their territories. In all those States, respect for the rights of minorities and the promotion of an integrated, multicultural society is not only desirable in itself but helps to ensure stability and peace both within and among States. Although armed conflict between States over territory or economic resources has diminished in the OSCE area in recent decades, tensions between different groups within States have risen. Too often, inter-ethnic conflicts within a State have spilled over to neighbouring countries and damaged relations between participating States. To address ethnic tensions and to prevent inter-State hostilities over national minority issues, the post of High Commissioner on National Minorities was established at the CSCE Helsinki Summit in 1992.

The High Commissioner on National Minorities is actively involved in several OSCE participating States, particularly those in Central and Eastern Europe and those which were previously part of the Soviet Union. The High Commissioner is supported by a small office of political and legal advisers and project officers, based in The Hague, the Netherlands. The mandate of the High Commissioner specifies that he or she is to be "an eminent international personality" who will act impartially and will "work in confidence and will act independently of all parties directly involved in the tensions". Max van der Stoel of the Netherlands served as the first High Commissioner from January 1993 until July 2001. He was succeeded by Rolf Ekéus of Sweden (2001-2007) and Knut Vollebaek of Norway (2007-present).

Mandate

As a conflict prevention instrument, the High Commissioner on National Minorities is placed firmly in the "security basket" of OSCE. The High Commissioner does not become engaged in all minority-related issues, instead focusing on those which have security implications. The High Commissioner has a two-fold mission: to try to contain and de-escalate tensions and to act as a "tripwire", alerting OSCE when the situation threatens to develop beyond a level which he or she is able to contain with the diplomatic means at their disposal. The original mandate states:

> The High Commissioner provides "early warning" and, as appropriate, "early action" at the earliest possible stage in regard to tensions involving national minority issues that have the potential to develop into a conflict within the CSCE area, affecting peace, stability or relations between participating States.[148]

Within the mandate, the transition from early warning to early action is rigidly structured. Most activities have concerned early action (e.g., multiple visits to the countries concerned), thereby avoiding the need for formal early warning. The mandate also contains an "exit strategy" under which the High Commissioner defers to the Chairman-in-Office (i.e., the foreign minister currently presiding over the Council of Ministers, the central decision-making and governing body) and the Senior Council, if he or she deems that scope for action is exhausted because the conflict has escalated. However, this option has never been employed.

The High Commissioner on National Minorities is, above all, a political instrument and is *not* intended to supervise States' compliance with their OSCE commitments or international obligations. The High Commissioner does not function as an advocate or ombudsman for minorities or as recourse for individuals belonging to national minorities. Of course, the subject matter addressed by the office (i.e., minority issues) is strongly linked with the human dimension: adequate protection of the rights of persons belonging to national minorities is essential for minimizing ethnic tensions which might otherwise threaten to create wider conflict. The High Commissioner therefore pays close attention to issues of human rights, especially freedom from discrimination, along with respect for minority rights.

Information-gathering

With the assistance of advisers, the High Commissioner collects and analyses information from all relevant sources (including wire services, the Internet and other media, Government representatives, independent experts, NGOs and secondary sources such as journals and

[148] CSCE 1992 Summit, Helsinki, 9-10 July 1992, CSCE Helsinki Document 1992: The Challenges of Change (para. 23), available from www.osce.org/mc/39530?download=true (accessed 4 December 2012).

reports), maintains contacts with OSCE missions and receives information through internal OSCE channels.

The mandate is unusual in terms of the authority granted to the High Commissioner to become directly involved in the affairs of a State. The High Commissioner enjoys a right of entry into, and freedom of movement within, any participating State. He or she may decide to become involved in a particular situation without the formal consent of the State concerned. However, having decided to visit, and in keeping with the OSCE principle of "cooperative security", the High Commissioner seeks the cooperation of the Government in facilitating a visit. He or she may receive and collect information from any source and maintain contact with anyone (except those who practise or publicly condone terrorism). The High Commissioner may also receive specific reports from and seek to communicate with the parties directly concerned, including Governments, associations, NGOs and other groups, for example, representatives of national minorities. Minority groups, human rights organizations and others may contact the High Commissioner on National Minorities to share information or to bring a particular situation or development to his or her attention, either prior to or during the course of their official visit.

In deciding to visit a country, the High Commissioner considers the degree to which issues concerning persons belonging to national minorities affect local or regional security and takes into account available information which might indicate potential conflict. Two main factors influence the decision: the extent to which he or she considers that their involvement is needed and the potential to have a positive impact. The High Commissioner will engage in a situation if there is a chance that this will influence the situation positively. When deciding whether to become involved, the High Commissioner also considers whether their involvement would bring added value, particularly where a number of international actors are already involved and efforts might be duplicated or even interfere with one another.

Confidentiality

While the High Commissioner enjoys wide access to information, the mandate prescribes that he or she work in a confidential manner. This discreet approach is designed to gain the trust and cooperation of all parties; it also helps avoid the inflammatory statements that public attention sometimes provokes. Parties are often more open to consider various options behind closed doors, when they know that they will not be subject to external pressures or be seen to be climbing down from declared positions. The commitment to confidentiality is intended to keep matters within the internal governmental framework of OSCE, but it does not preclude the High Commissioner from working in cooperation with other international bodies, such as the Council of Europe, the United Nations and the European Union, as often happens.

The High Commissioner has developed the practice of making recommendations to States through a formal exchange of letters with relevant ministers. While this correspondence usually remains confidential, regular statements to the Permanent Council[149] and academic publications give some insight into the activities of the High Commissioner. The High Commissioner generally avoids substantial contact with the press, except in specific situations where public statements are considered potentially beneficial.

International standards

The approach of the High Commissioner on National Minorities is firmly grounded in human dimension commitments and international human rights law, relying on the international standards by which States have already agreed to provide a framework for dialogue and recommendation. Since all OSCE participating States (except the Holy See) are members of the United Nations

[149] Available from www.osce.org/hcnm/documents (accessed 4 December 2012).

and all but nine are members of the Council of Europe, they are legally bound by treaties adopted under the aegis of those bodies, and by bilateral treaties, in addition to their politically binding OSCE commitments.

International standards for the protection of minorities may sometimes lack clarity, which leaves them open to interpretation and possible inconsistencies in application. In response to this, and in order to assist policymakers and legislators more generally, the High Commissioner on National Minorities has on several occasions sought the assistance of internationally recognized experts to clarify minority rights in specific areas and to offer generally applicable thematic recommendations. Six sets of thematic recommendations provide States with guidance in formulating policies for minorities within their jurisdiction:

- The Hague Recommendations regarding the Education Rights of National Minorities (1996);
- The Oslo Recommendations regarding the Linguistic Rights of National Minorities (1998);
- The Lund Recommendations on the Effective Participation of National Minorities in Public Life (1999);
- Guidelines on the Use of Minority Languages in the Broadcast Media (2003);
- Recommendations on Policing in Multi-Ethnic Societies (2006);
- The Bolzano/Bozen Recommendations on National Minorities in Inter-State Relations (2008).[150]

Furthermore, in cooperation with the High Commissioner on National Minorities, ODIHR adopted the Warsaw Guidelines to Assist National Minority Participation in the Electoral Process (2001), which serve as practical guidelines in respect of the four Lund recommendations (Nos. 7-10) concerning elections.

The two examples below illustrate the High Commissioner's involvement in individual countries.

Integrating the Armenian-speaking minority in Georgia

The Armenian-speaking minority in Georgia has traditionally been strongly oriented to its neighbouring kin-State. The programme of the High Commissioner on National Minorities aims to bring them into the mainstream of Georgian public life, for example, by translating Georgian television programmes into Armenian, a measure which has greatly increased local understanding of national affairs and raised the level of participation in national elections. It also includes training in the Georgian language for civil servants and first-year university students. In partnership with UNDP, the High Commissioner seeks to promote action on socioeconomic issues such as employment, for example, by upgrading transport links in the minority area.

[150] Available from www.osce.org/hcnm/66209 (accessed 4 December 2012).

Access to higher education in the former Yugoslav Republic of Macedonia

In the former Yugoslav Republic of Macedonia, the issue of access to (and funding of) Albanian language education has long been a source of concern for ethnic Albanians and a source of division within society. In response, the High Commissioner on National Minorities has been instrumental in setting up the private South East European University in Tetovo, which provides a curriculum not only in Albanian but also in Macedonian, English and other European languages. The University has proved to be a model of inter-ethnic cooperation, attracting large numbers of students from the Albanian and other communities. The High Commissioner has also set up a transition year programme, which seeks to increase the number of ethnic Albanians admitted to State universities. It provides intensive courses in Macedonian for Albanian-speaking, fourth-year secondary school students preparing for the university entrance examination. A supplementary programme focuses on Albanian and Macedonian professional terminology; through Saturday classes in seven different subjects in seven cities, students are taught in pairs by an ethnic Macedonian and an ethnic Albanian teacher. The long-term aim of the project is to contribute to the integration of the Albanian national minority within Macedonian society. On average, more than 90 per cent of the 1,000 or so participants in each academic year succeed in enrolling at university.

Involvement in Roma issues

Roma, the largest minority in Europe, are present throughout the OSCE region (see chap. XII). While the main competence for Roma and Sinti issues within OSCE rests with the ODIHR (discussed below), the 2003 Action Plan directs the High Commissioner on National Minorities to work on Roma and Sinti issues, in particular on combating racism and discrimination and reviewing legislation and law enforcement. It also encourages the High Commissioner to continue to work, within the conflict prevention mandate, on issues related to policing, education, media, and participation in public and political life.

In cooperation with the ODIHR Contact Point for Roma and Sinti Issues, the High Commissioner has conducted field visits to several OSCE States to assess the human rights situation of Roma. During normal bilateral visits, the High Commissioner raises Roma-related issues where it is considered necessary and offers expertise to combat the segregation and social exclusion of Roma and discrimination against Roma communities.

Tension-reducing projects

Although the High Commissioner on National Minorities is not primarily a project-implementing agency, its preventive diplomacy mandate is frequently backed up by targeted projects in support of education, language, participation in public life and media access and development, sometimes in cooperation with other agencies (e.g., OHCHR, UNHCR, other United Nations agencies, the Council of Europe and the European Union). The emphasis of these projects is always on early action and conflict prevention, and they aim to close gaps that otherwise would not necessarily be filled. The High Commissioner has also been trying to act as a catalyst by stimulating others, particularly relevant domestic authorities, to follow up on projects the office has completed or to develop their own. Projects are often implemented through local human rights NGOs, minority groups and other civil society actors, and these organizations are welcome to submit proposals for relevant projects to the High Commissioner.

Making submissions to the High Commissioner on National Minorities

While the High Commissioner on National Minorities does not act as a complaint mechanism, the office is open to direct approaches and submissions from concerned persons. There is no special format required for reports or information to be transmitted to the office, but any communication should be in writing, provide full names and addresses and be signed. It should contain a factual account of relevant developments and include only information that can be substantiated, to draw attention towards a situation that falls within the mandate of the High Commissioner.

Contacts and further information

The OSCE High Commissioner on National Minorities
Prinsessegracht 22
2515 AP The Hague
The Netherlands

Tel: 31 70 312 5500
Fax: 31 70 363 5910
E-mail: hcnm@hcnm.org
Website: www.osce.org/hcnm

Office for Democratic Institutions and Human Rights

The Office for Democratic Institutions and Human Rights (ODIHR) is the largest OSCE specialized body and is dedicated to building and supporting democracy and a culture that recognizes and respects human rights. Several of the activities of its five departments (Elections, Democratization, Human Rights, Tolerance and Non-discrimination, and the Contact Point for Roma and Sinti Issues) are highly relevant for minorities (e.g., the observation of elections, review of legislation or monitoring of human rights throughout the OSCE area).

ODIHR also conducts training programmes for Government and law enforcement officials, as well as NGOs, on how to uphold, promote and monitor human rights. A number of these activities are aimed at increasing the capacity of NGOs to monitor the human rights situation in their own countries in an objective and professional way. Support is also targeted at NGOs operating outside capital cities, where it is often harder to obtain international assistance. ODIHR is currently implementing a project in four countries in Central Asia, for example, focusing on human rights in pretrial detention, an issue of concern throughout the region. It has conducted training sessions on monitoring human rights in places of detention and has supported subsequent monitoring projects conducted by participants. NGOs interested in receiving human rights training can contact ODIHR directly to discuss the possibilities.

ODIHR also plays an important role in facilitating dialogue between States and civil society on human and minority rights, for example, through the two-week Human Dimension Implementation Meeting in Warsaw. This is Europe's largest annual human rights and democracy conference, attended by the 56 participating States of OSCE and up to 500 representatives of NGOs. Participation is open to human rights NGOs, minority groups and other civil society actors from all OSCE participating States, who can raise human rights issues with their Governments and the international community.[151]

The Tolerance and Non-discrimination Programme of ODIHR works to raise awareness and build Government capacity to prevent hate-based crime, monitor discrimination and combat various forms of intolerance. It does this through education programmes, legislative assistance,

[151] See www.osce.org/hdim_2012. To register for OSCE/ODIHR conferences, see http://meetings.odihr.pl/ (accessed 4 December 2012).

development and support of civil society networks and law enforcement training programmes. The Tolerance and Non-discrimination Information System, TANDIS, gives access to information received from the OSCE participating States, NGOs and other organizations; country pages covering country initiatives, legislation, national specialized bodies, statistics, and other information; thematic pages with information on key issues; international standards and instruments; and information from intergovernmental organizations, including country reports and annual reports.[152]

The ODIHR Contact Point for Roma and Sinti Issues addresses relevant issues either directly through its programmes or by promoting the establishment of local and national institutional frameworks for advising Governments on policymaking on Roma and Sinti affairs. It is also engaged in promoting the legalization of informal settlements, promoting civil registration and combating trafficking in human beings, and working to increase the participation of Roma and Sinti in public life at all levels and stages of decision-making. The Contact Point works in close coordination with other international organizations and NGOs and seeks to involve Roma and Sinti in all its activities. Human rights NGOs, Romani organizations and other civil society actors interested in cooperating with the Contact Point are encouraged to contact ODIHR directly.

Contacts and further information

OSCE Office for Democratic Institutions and Human Rights
Aleje Ujazdowskie 19
00-557 Warsaw
Poland

Tel: 48 22 520 06 00
Fax: 48 22 520 06 05
E-mail: office@odihr.pl
Website: www.osce.org/odihr

OSCE field operations

OSCE has 18 field operations in Central and Eastern Europe, the Caucasus and Central Asia. The size, character and activities of the field operations vary considerably depending on the mandate of the mission, which is available through the website of each field operation. In several cases, the activities undertaken by field operations (e.g., Government and civil society capacity-building in good governance, economic participation and human rights) are highly relevant for local minority groups. Missions also provide legislative assistance, monitor human rights and train judiciary and law enforcement officials.

Contacts and further information

Organization for Security and Co-operation in Europe Secretariat
Wallnerstrasse 6
1010 Vienna
Austria

Tel: 43 1 514 360
Fax: 43 1 514 36 6996
E-mail: info@osce.org
Website: www.ocse.org

152 See http://tandis.odihr.pl/ (accessed 4 December 2012).

A great number of works have been written on the OSCE Helsinki process generally and on the High Commissioner on National Minorities in particular. Since 2001, an annual account of the activities of the High Commissioner can be found in *The European Yearbook of Minority Issues* (Leiden, Boston, Martin Nijhoff). For an account of the activities of the first High Commissioner, Mr. Max van der Stoel, see Walter Kemp (ed.), *Quiet Diplomacy in Action: The OSCE High Commissioner on National Minorities* (The Hague, Kluwer Law International, 2001), and Yeorgios I. Diacofotakis, *Expanding Conceptual Boundaries: The High Commissioner on National Minorities and the Protection of Minority Rights in the OSCE* (Brussels, Athens, Ant. N. Sakkoulas and Bruylant, 2002).

A useful compilation of international standards on minority rights (in Russian and in English) is *OSCE and Council of Europe: National Minority Standards: A Compilation of OSCE and Council of Europe Texts* (Council of Europe, 2007).

CHAPTER XIV

THE EUROPEAN UNION

Summary: The Treaty on European Union states explicitly that the rights of persons belonging to minorities are among the values upon which the Union is founded and which it is explicitly committed to promote inside the Union and in its relations with the wider world. This chapter identifies specific European Union (EU) initiatives regarding the rights of persons belonging to minorities and explains how minority issues may be addressed in EU activities which promote human rights in general. The European Union has put in place a legal framework to fight discrimination, racism and xenophobia and contributes financially to programmes which support activities aimed at combating these on the ground. The European Union raises minority issues in its political dialogues with third countries and cooperates actively at United Nations forums to promote and protect the rights of persons belonging to minorities. In addition, the European Union uses a wide range of financial and technical cooperation instruments, including bilateral cooperation with Governments and direct support to civil society, to promote and protect the rights of persons belonging to minorities.

Treaty on European Union

According to the Treaty on European Union,[153] "The Union is founded on the values of respect for human dignity ..., equality ... and respect for human rights, including the rights of persons belonging to minorities" (art. 2). Article 3 commits the Union to promote these values, combat social exclusion and discrimination, respect its cultural and linguistic diversity, and ensure that Europe's cultural heritage is safeguarded and enhanced.

Article 6 states that the Union pursues its objectives according to the competences conferred upon it in relevant treaties. This encompasses the rights, freedoms and principles set out in the Charter of Fundamental Rights of the European Union.[154] Article 21 of the Charter includes the prohibition of discrimination on the basis of membership of a national minority.

The European Union and its bodies, as well as the member States when implementing EU law, are bound by these provisions. However, this does not provide the European Union with powers to adopt measures beyond those areas over which it has competence. In non-EU areas, it is up to EU member States to ensure the protection of fundamental rights, through the application of their own legislation and implementation of their international obligations.

Minorities in the European Union

In the European Union, too many persons belonging to minorities still face threats, discrimination and racism. They are confronted with the risk of being excluded from fully taking part in the economic, political, social and cultural life available to majorities in the countries or societies in which they live. The Treaty on European Union gives the European Union powers to adopt a number of instruments which contribute to the protection of the rights of persons belonging to minorities. In applying these powers, the European Union has put in place a legal framework to fight discrimination, racism and xenophobia and has contributed financially to programmes to support activities aimed at combating these phenomena on the ground.

[153] OJ 2008/C 115/13.

[154] OJ 2000/C 364/1.

Legal framework to fight discrimination, racism and xenophobia

Discrimination on grounds such as racial or ethnic origin, religion or belief is incompatible with the basic principles on which the European Union is founded and must be combated by the Union while defining and implementing its policies and activities (see art. 2 of the Treaty on European Union and art. 10 of the Treaty on the Functioning of the European Union[155]). The European Union has been working hard in recent years to complete its internal legislative framework to fight racism and discrimination.[156]

The Governments of member States are required under EU anti-discrimination law to enact national legislation which prohibits discrimination on grounds of race or ethnic origin in areas including employment, education, social protection and access to and supply of goods and services (Council Directive 2000/43/EC).[157] Protection against discrimination applies to every person living in the European Union, not only EU citizens. The Directive allows member States to adopt positive measures. Moreover, member States are obliged to designate or set up an independent body to help persons who have been discriminated against on the grounds of their racial or ethnic origin to receive advice and support to pursue their complaints. Most of these bodies are part of Equinet, the European Network of Equality Bodies, which develops cooperation and facilitates the exchange of information and good practice among national organizations.[158]

The Council Framework Decision on combating certain forms and expressions of racism and xenophobia by means of criminal law was adopted in 2008 (2008/913/JHA).[159] Requiring domestic adoption of appropriate laws, it aims to ensure that racist and xenophobic offences are sanctioned in all EU member States by effective, proportionate and dissuasive criminal penalties. Punishable offences include intentional public incitement to violence or hatred against a group of persons or a member of such a group, defined by reference to race, colour, religion, descent or national or ethnic origin. Such incitement is also punishable if committed through public dissemination or distribution of tracts, pictures or other material. The public condoning, denial or gross trivialization of Nazi crimes, crimes of genocide, crimes against humanity or war crimes, when carried out in a manner likely to incite violence or hatred, are also to be punished. For any criminal offences other than those covered by the Framework Decision, member States are obliged to ensure that racist and xenophobic motivation is considered as an aggravating circumstance or, alternatively, that such motivation may be taken into account in the determination of punishment. The Framework Decision provides for the liability of legal, as well as natural, persons. The investigation or prosecution of a crime referred to in the Framework Decision is not dependent on a report or accusation made by the victim.[160]

Information and awareness-raising about rights and obligations

Although legislation prohibiting discrimination against persons belonging to minorities is an absolute prerequisite to protection of their rights, on its own it cannot achieve the goal of creating a society free from discrimination. Prejudices and stereotypes faced by people because of their personal characteristics may impede them from fully participating and contributing at all levels of society. This is why the European Union seeks to improve knowledge about discrimination,

---

[155] OJ 2010/C 83/47.

[156] See http://ec.europa.eu/justice/discrimination/index_en.htm (accessed 4 December 2012).

[157] OJ 2000/L 180/22.

[158] See www.equineteurope.org.

[159] OJ 2008/L 328/55.

[160] See http://ec.europa.eu/justice/fundamental-rights/racism-xenophobia/framework-decision/index_en.htm (accessed 4 December 2012).

in particular on the grounds of sex, racial or ethnic origin, religion or belief, disability, age or sexual orientation, to fight against stereotypes and to raise awareness among the population of both their own and others' rights and the benefits of diversity.

To support the legislation and help change behaviours and attitudes, the European Union runs a Europe-wide information campaign, "For diversity. Against discrimination", featuring public events, journalism awards, movies and publications to raise awareness of people's rights and responsibilities. The film, *A Diverse Society: Tackling Discrimination across Europe*, for instance, explores equality and diversity under EU law and provides information about sources of assistance for those who have suffered discrimination.[161]

Cooperation with civil society

The European Commission consults with civil society organizations when formulating and implementing its policies on non-discrimination. It consults with the public before taking major policy initiatives and cooperates with social sector NGOs. Not least, public consultations serve the purpose of collecting ideas and suggestions from key stakeholders and experts on how to achieve the greatest possible impact of non-discrimination policies.

The European Union also financially supports intermediary actors (e.g., non-profit organizations, voluntary associations, foundations, NGOs and equality bodies) which are active in the fight against discrimination, racism and xenophobia. The European Union provides financial support to NGOs and other entities through the PROGRESS programme, for example, which aims at developing the capacity of key European networks to promote and further develop European Community policy goals and strategies to combat discrimination. In addition, the Specific Programme on Fundamental Rights and Citizenship focuses on the protection of the rights of the child, combating racism, xenophobia and antisemitism, the fight against homophobia, active participation in the democratic life of the European Union, data protection and privacy rights, training and networking among legal practitioners.[162]

Coordination of national policies for an inclusive society

Member States have competence in central policy areas, such as education, employment or social inclusion, for the inclusion of ethnic minorities. However, the European Union coordinates national policies by means of common objectives, policy guidelines and indicators. Member States draw up national reform programmes and action plans on which there is joint reporting and peer review, which encourages the transfer of good practices. The European Union's Structural Funds, and in particular the European Social Fund, serve as tools to implement the national programmes and action plans.

European Union Agency for Fundamental Rights

The European Union Agency for Fundamental Rights was established in 2007 through Council Regulation (EC) No. 168/2007.[163] Based in Vienna, it is an independent agency which cooperates with national and international bodies and organizations, in particular with the Council of Europe. When the relevant institutions and authorities of the European Union and its member States are implementing EU law, the Agency provides assistance and expertise relating to fundamental rights in order to support the institutions to formulate appropriate courses of action. While the Agency focuses on the situation regarding fundamental rights in the European

[161] See http://ec.europa.eu/justice/discrimination/awareness/index_en.htm (accessed 4 December 2012).

[162] See http://ec.europa.eu/justice/grants/programmes/fundamental-citizenship/index_en.htm (accessed 4 December 2012).

[163] OJ 2007/L 53/1.

Union and its 27 member States, candidate countries and countries which have concluded a stabilization and association agreement with the European Union can also be invited to participate in its activities.[164]

The Agency for Fundamental Rights is not empowered to examine individual complaints or exercise regulatory decision-making powers. It does not monitor the situation regarding fundamental rights in EU countries for the purposes of article 7 of the Treaty on European Union (which provides for the possibility of action against a member State in case of a serious fundamental rights violation), nor does it deal with the legality of EU acts and their legal transposition by member States into national law.

Information and data collection and analysis

The Agency for Fundamental Rights collects and analyses official and unofficial information and data on fundamental rights issues within the European Union. Given the differences in data availability and quality across the European Union, the Agency is also developing methods and standards to improve data quality and comparability. However, since such secondary data are often not available, it conducts its own EU-wide research and surveys and encourages others to do so.[165]

In its research work, the Agency examines contributory factors as well as development policies which affect fundamental rights. A very important part of its work is to identify positive initiatives which promote respect for and protection of fundamental rights. It publishes an annual report on fundamental rights in the European Union and thematic reports based on its research and surveys, highlighting examples of good practice regarding fundamental rights. It also regularly publishes reports and publications covering minority issues.[166]

Networking and cooperation

The Agency for Fundamental Rights works to support an environment in which the promotion and protection of fundamental rights at all levels of society will become a natural reflex. Engaging with stakeholders – the wider human rights community and both national and local service providers and users – is an essential part of its mandate. The Agency is adapting its work to make use of the new communications environment, including social networks and social media.

As an EU body, the Agency works with all relevant EU institutions and advisory bodies. It also works closely with the Council of Europe, OSCE, the United Nations and UNESCO.

Cooperation with civil society and awareness-raising

In accordance with its establishing regulation, the Agency promotes dialogue with civil society and works closely with NGOs and civil society institutions active in the field of fundamental rights. In 2008, in order to improve dialogue and coordination with all relevant stakeholders, the Agency launched the Fundamental Rights Platform, a network for cooperation and information exchange between itself and civil society.[167] The Platform is open to all interested and qualified civil society organizations based in any one of the EU member States, including human rights NGOs, trade unions, employers' organizations, relevant social and professional organizations, churches, religious, philosophical and non-confessional organizations, universities and experts from European and international bodies.

[164] The stabilization and association process is the framework for EU negotiations with Western Balkan countries which will lead to their eventual accession.

[165] See http://fra.europa.eu/fraWebsite/research/research_en.htm (accessed 4 December 2012).

[166] Available from http://fra.europa.eu/en/publications-and-resources/publications (accessed 4 December 2012).

[167] See http://fra.europa.eu/en/cooperation/civil-society/about-frp (accessed 4 December 2012).

The main tasks of the Fundamental Rights Platform are to:

- Involve civil society organizations as partners in various stages (from inception to evaluation) of the Fundamental Rights Agency's research, activities, education and awareness-raising projects. NGOs, for example, participate in the initial development of the Agency's projects and so help to shape project terms of reference and ensure that they contribute to practical solutions in the field. At a later stage, NGOs may act as researchers or external contractors. In order to facilitate synergies between the Agency's work and NGO activities, key stakeholders receive Agency research findings in advance (e.g., embargoed copies of reports), and they are important partners in disseminating research results;
- Provide feedback and suggestions for the Agency's annual work programme and annual report.

Members of the Fundamental Rights Platform meet annually. In November 2009, the Fundamental Rights Agency launched a drive to increase participation in the Platform, which is expected to expand to around 300 organizations.

European Union action for Roma

Of the estimated 10 million to 12 million Roma in Europe, six million live in the European Union. The European Union approach to Roma issues is "explicit, but not exclusive targeting", that is, Roma inclusion is not separated from mainstream EU activities. Instead, attention is paid to the specific situation of Roma within all EU policies and instruments aiming to improve the overall social and economic situation of people living in Europe.[168]

Legislation

EU legislation on discrimination, racism and xenophobia or freedom of movement (see above) fully applies to Roma, the majority of whom are EU citizens.

Coordination of national policies

The European Union has made an unprecedented commitment to making a tangible difference to the situation of Roma. Following the adoption on 5 April 2011 of the Commission's proposal for an EU Framework for National Roma Integration Strategies up to 2020,[169] the Council has adopted conclusions in which member States have expressed their commitment to follow the approach proposed by the Commission, and adopt or develop national Roma integration strategies or integrated sets of policy measures for Roma inclusion.[170] Four key priority areas have been identified: education, health, employment and housing.

Funding

The European Social Fund supports employment and helps people enhance their education and skills. The European Regional Development Fund supports regional development, economic change, enhanced competitiveness and territorial cooperation throughout the European Union. The European Agricultural Fund for Rural Development aims at improving living conditions in rural areas of the European Union. The PROGRESS programme (see above) funds awareness-raising activities to combat discrimination against Roma and support an EU-wide network of NGOs representing Roma and defending their rights. Other activities and funding mechanisms

---

[168] See http://ec.europa.eu/roma (accessed 4 December 2012).

[169] COM(2011) 173.

[170] EPSCO Council of 19 May 2011 and European Council of 23-24 June 2011.

can also be used to aid Roma inclusion, for example, the Lifelong Learning Programme, the Youth in Action Programme, the Culture Programme and the Health Programme.[171]

European Platform for Roma Inclusion

The European Commission promotes the active involvement of Roma in European decision-making, for example, through the European Platform for Roma Inclusion. Platform meetings bring together representatives of national Governments, the European Union, international organizations and Roma civil society to stimulate cooperation and exchange of experience on successful Roma inclusion policies and practices. Following the adoption of an EU Framework for National Roma Integration Strategies up to 2020, the European Platform for Roma Inclusion has been reformed, so as to give it a stronger role in connection with the Framework process and to give the Commission the leading role in its operation.[172]

Minority rights and the European Union enlargement process

A growing EU membership has been part of the development of European integration from the outset. In many countries which are currently candidates or potential candidates, persons belonging to minorities have been identified as being among the most vulnerable, which is why minority issues are a crucial element of the EU enlargement process. A number of resolutions of the European Parliament[173] have highlighted the protection of minorities, particularly Roma, as being essential in an enlarged European Union. In most countries of the Western Balkans, for example, there are large numbers of refugees or internally displaced persons. Ambitious laws and strategies often lack sufficient implementing procedures and resources, and most minorities still suffer from discrimination, segregation and limited participation in politics, administration and business.

An applicant country must meet certain political criteria, including respect for and protection of minorities.[174] Similar references are included in the framework of the pre-accession process. Minority issues are regularly raised in political dialogue with candidate countries and, during accession negotiations, are included within "judiciary and fundamental rights".[175]

The record of candidate and potential candidate countries on minority issues is also systematically assessed in annual progress reports published by the European Commission. For instance, the Croatia 2009 progress report[176] stated that, while there has been some progress in the area of minority rights, cultural rights and protection of minorities in Croatia, many problems remain. Minorities continue to face particular difficulties in the area of employment, in terms of under-representation in both the State administration, judiciary and police and the wider public sector. The report highlights the fact that most Roma remain excluded from mainstream Croatian society and face difficult living conditions.

NGOs and civil society organizations play a vital role in reforms carried out in candidate and potential candidate countries, and their work can prove crucial in determining the pace and quality of the accession process. The European Commission consults and cooperates closely with

---

171 Regularly updated information on funding opportunities is available from http://ec.europa.eu/social/main.jsp?langId=en&catId=86 (accessed 4 December 2012).

172 See http://ec.europa.eu/justice/discrimination/roma/roma-platform/index_en.htm (accessed 4 December 2012).

173 Available from www.europarl.europa.eu/comparl/afet/droi/others/default.htm (accessed 4 December 2012).

174 European Council in Copenhagen, 21-22 June 1993, Conclusions of the Presidency, DOC/93/3.

175 For the purpose of accession negotiations, EU legislation is divided into 35 subject-related chapters. Further information on the mandate and the framework of accession negotiations is available from http://ec.europa.eu/enlargement/index_en.htm (accessed 4 December 2012).

176 SEC(2009) 1333.

civil society, at both the European and local levels, to obtain the best possible information on progress and possible shortcomings in reform efforts.

The European Union provides focused pre-accession financial aid to candidate and potential candidate countries in order to help them introduce the necessary political, economic and institutional reforms to comply with EU standards. A key focus of such assistance is human rights, the protection of minorities and development of civil society. Considerable technical and financial assistance to vulnerable groups, including minorities, is provided under the Instrument for Pre-Accession Assistance, which covers a wide range of activities in areas such as education, social protection, non-discrimination and reconciliation. One example of such assistance is a multi-beneficiary project that addresses the widespread lack of personal documentation held by Roma in Western Balkans countries by assisting Roma to obtain identity papers – often a precondition for access to education, employment or social security.

Support to civil society development and dialogue focuses on three primary areas:

- Support to local civic initiatives and capacity-building to enforce the role of civil society;
- Visitor programmes to EU bodies for groups with influence over decision-making and society, such as journalists, young politicians, trade union leaders and teachers;
- Partnerships between the European Union and civil society organizations designed to lead to the transfer of knowledge and networks.

Another financial instrument with a clear focus on supporting civil society is the European Instrument for Democracy and Human Rights (EIDHR), which is discussed below. In the pre-accession context, the European Instrument projects for persons belonging to minorities are predominantly aimed at reducing social disparities; improving quality of life; and strengthening social cohesion through integrating disadvantaged people, combating discrimination and strengthening human capital, notably by reforming education systems. The European Instrument funded a project in Turkey, for example, to create the conditions to improve cooperation between majority and minority ethnic, linguistic and religious communities and to encourage the peaceful resolution of conflicts in Turkish society.

Information about the European Commission's support for civil society to participate in the enlargement process is available from the Commission's website.[177]

Minority rights and European Union external relations

The European Union has made human rights a central aspect of its external relations, through its political dialogues with third countries, actions in multilateral forums such as the United Nations and development policies and assistance. The promotion and protection of the rights of persons belonging to minorities is a key feature of its external human rights policy.

The European Union supports the Minorities Declaration, which it considers to be the key reference text on the rights of persons belonging to minorities at the global level. In Europe, the legal framework is influenced by the Council of Europe's Framework Convention for the Protection of National Minorities and the European Charter for Regional or Minority Languages (see chap. XII).

The European Union seeks to integrate human rights, including the rights of persons belonging to minorities, into all aspects of its external policies. In order to examine these issues in greater depth in its bilateral relations with certain countries, the European Union has initiated human rights dialogues[178] in which it regularly raises minority issues with third countries. Civil society is closely

[177] See http://ec.europa.eu/enlargement/tenders/support-for-civil-society/index_en.htm (accessed 4 December 2012).

[178] See http://eeas.europa.eu/human_rights/dialogues/index_en.htm . An update on the EU Guidelines on Human Rights Dialogues is available from www.consilium.europa.eu/uedocs/cmsUpload/16526.en08.pdf (accessed 4

involved, as the European Union regularly meets with local civil society representatives in the margins of these dialogues. The European Union also facilitates communication between human rights defenders and the authorities of the country in dialogue. Civil society actors interested in human rights dialogues should contact the EU delegation for the country concerned.[179]

The European Union also champions the promotion and protection of minority rights in multinational forums.[180] The European Union enjoys observer status at the United Nations. EU member States cooperate in forging common EU positions and the European Union reaches out to third countries in order to further improve respect for human rights generally and the rights of persons belonging to minorities in particular. The European Union attaches great importance to the work of United Nations special procedures, including the Independent Expert on minority issues (see chap. IV). The European Union considers the annual Forum on Minority Issues (see chap. III) to be a key process in the promotion of dialogue and cooperation on issues pertaining to the rights of minorities. The European Commission works closely with, inter alia, the United Nations High Commissioner for Human Rights, OSCE (in particular the High Commissioner on National Minorities), the Council of Europe and the World Bank.

Minority issues are also mainstreamed in cooperation strategies and action plans. The Commission's Colombia Country Strategy Paper 2007-2013, for example, specifically addresses the humanitarian and human rights situation of persons belonging to minorities.[181] It encourages peacebuilding through the participation of marginalized citizens in local governance and the economy, and through the promotion of human rights, good governance and the fight against impunity. Another example is the explicit reference to respect for the rights of persons belonging to national minorities in the European Neighbourhood Policy Action Plan with Ukraine.[182]

The European Union uses a wide range of financial and technical cooperation instruments, including bilateral cooperation with Governments and direct support to civil society, to promote and protect the rights of persons belonging to minorities. It supports Government programmes and policies which target minorities or have potential impact in this area, such as support for long-term solutions to the protracted refugee situation of Muslim minorities from Myanmar (Northern Rakhine State) in Bangladesh.

The European Union supports civil society organizations concerned with minorities through a number of thematic programmes, such as the European Instrument for Democracy and Human Rights (EIDHR, discussed above) and Non-State Actors and Local Authorities in Development Programme.

The European Instrument approaches minority issues with the aim of combating discrimination; promoting equal participation of men and women from minority communities in social, economic and political life; and strengthening human rights and democratic political participation.[183] In Kyrgyzstan, for example, the European Instrument has funded a project to strengthen minority group involvement with State bodies, NGOs, political representation at local and national levels and in democratic reforms. It also funded a three-year project entitled Global Advocacy Programme, implemented by Minority Rights Group International (in cooperation with OHCHR, the Council of Europe and Forum Asia). This is intended to build the capacity of 1,080 activists in 36 States in Europe, Asia and Africa to carry out advocacy nationally, regionally and at the

December 2012).

179 See http://eeas.europa.eu/delegations/web_en.htm (accessed 4 December 2012).

180 See http://eeas.europa.eu/human_rights/fora/index_en.htm (accessed 4 December 2012).

181 E/2007/484, available from http://eeas.europa.eu/colombia/csp/07_13_en.pdf (accessed 4 December 2012).

182 All European Neighbourhood Policy action plans, strategy papers, country reports and other documents are available from http://ec.europa.eu/world/enp/documents_en.htm#2 (accessed 4 December 2012).

183 See http://ec.europa.eu/europeaid/how/finance/eidhr_en.htm (accessed 4 December 2012).

United Nations on behalf of and with minority communities. Another example is the EU–Council of Europe Joint Programme, Minorities in Russia: Developing Languages, Culture, Media and Civil Society, which aims at facilitating ratification by the Russian Federation of the European Charter for Regional or Minority Languages. European Instrument projects are managed either from EU headquarters in Brussels or by one of over 130 EU delegations and offices around the world. While the projects' beneficiaries vary according to the objectives, calls for project proposals are generally open to civil society organizations based anywhere in the world.

The thematic programme "Non-State Actors and Local Authorities in Development" (NSA-LA) helps civil society organizations and local authorities build capacity in order to facilitate their involvement in the policymaking process and enhance their capacity to deliver basic services to the poorest people in developing countries.[184] Civil society organizations representing (or working on behalf of) minorities are eligible for funding, depending on the priorities established in calls for proposals. In Bangladesh, for instance, NSA-LA has funded Caritas France in partnership with Caritas Bangladesh for a project aimed at improving the living conditions of outcast and minority groups, with particular attention given to women's status. In Colombia, funding was provided to the international NGO Diakonie Katastrophenhilfe for a programme aimed at developing and applying a model of integrated and sustainable development to overcome poverty, promote human rights, and strengthen access to services in the Chocó Department, an area inhabited by a large Afro-Colombian population.

EU policies increasingly recognize the need to ensure the maximum involvement of all segments of civil society in the development cooperation process, including the participation of organizations promoting the rights of minorities in the formulation and implementation of development strategies and programmes. This happens mainly on the formulation and review of EU country strategy papers, national indicative programmes and European Neighbourhood Policy action plans; on the identification of priority areas for local calls for proposals under the European Instrument and NSA-LA programmes; and on the identification and formulation of Commission-funded Government programmes in social and human development, governance, environment and other relevant sectors. The EuropeAid Cooperation Office of the European Commission is responsible for implementing external aid programmes and projects across the world.[185]

Contacts and further information

European Commission
B-1049 Brussels
Belgium

Website: http://ec.europa.eu/index_en.htm

European Commission services particularly relevant to minority issues are:

Directorate-General Justice
Website: http://ec.europa.eu/justice/index_en.htm

Directorate-General for Employment, Social Affairs and Inclusion
Website: http://ec.europa.eu/social/home.jsp?langId=en

Directorate-General for Enlargement
E-mail: elarg-info@ec.europa.eu
Website: http://ec.europa.eu/enlargement/index_en.htm

Directorate-General Development and Cooperation – EuropeAid
Website: http://ec.europa.eu/europeaid/index_en.htm

---

184 See http://ec.europa.eu/europeaid/how/finance/dci/non_state_actors_en.htm (accessed 4 December 2012).

185 Further information about EuropeAid's initiatives to improve dialogue with civil society is available from http://ec.europa.eu/europeaid/who/partners/civil-society/dialogue_en.htm (accessed 4 December 2012).

Related agencies and services

European External Action Service
Website: http://eeas.europa.eu/contact/index_en.htm

European Union Agency for Fundamental Rights
Schwarzenbergplatz 11
1040 Wien
Austria

Tel: 43 1 580 30 634
E-mail: information@fra.europa.eu
Website: www.fra.europa.eu

CHAPTER XV

THE INTER-AMERICAN HUMAN RIGHTS SYSTEM

Summary: All 35 members of the Organization of American States fall within the jurisdiction of the Inter-American Commission on Human Rights, which has the authority to prepare reports on the human rights situation in any country in the Americas. It may also receive and consider complaints that a State party has violated the provisions of the American Convention on Human Rights or, with regard to those States which have not yet become a party, under the American Declaration of the Rights and Duties of Man. The American Convention on Human Rights creates an Inter-American Court of Human Rights, which is competent to issue binding judgements and to provide reparations when the Convention has been violated. This chapter describes the circumstances under which minorities can use the Commission and the Court to secure protection for their rights.

The Organization of American States (OAS) was founded in 1948 and has a membership of 35 States in the Western Hemisphere.[186] A regional organization, it encompasses a wide range of political, security and economic interests and has taken an active role in the promotion and protection of human rights since the 1960s. Its headquarters are in Washington, D.C.

All the OAS member States are bound by the OAS Charter and by the 1948 American Declaration of the Rights and Duties of Man. (Although the latter is only a declaration and not a treaty, OAS deems that all its members are politically bound to observe its provisions.) In addition, OAS has adopted a number of specific human rights treaties since 1969; these include the American Convention on Human Rights "Pact of San José, Costa Rica" (1969) and its Additional Protocol in the Area of Economic, Social and Cultural Rights "Protocol of San Salvador" (1988) and its Protocol to Abolish the Death Penalty (1990); the Inter-American Convention to Prevent and Punish Torture (1985); the Inter-American Convention on Forced Disappearance of Persons (1994); the Inter-American Convention on the Prevention, Punishment and Eradication of Violence against Women "Convention of Belem do Para" (1994) and the Inter-American Convention on the Elimination of All Forms of Discrimination against Persons with Disabilities (1999). Only those States which have formally ratified these treaties are bound by their provisions.

Members of minority groups, like anyone else, may become victims of torture, disappearance or violence. Such violations should be considered under the appropriate thematic mechanisms, whether the victims are members of the minority or majority. However, the most important OAS instruments for minorities are undoubtedly the American Declaration of the Rights and Duties of Man and the American Convention on Human Rights. Twenty-four OAS member States are parties to the Convention.[187] Sixteen of these are also parties to the Additional Protocol in the

[186] Antigua and Barbuda, Argentina, the Bahamas, Barbados, Belize, Bolivia (Plurinational State of), Brazil, Canada, Chile, Colombia, Costa Rica, Cuba, Dominica, the Dominican Republic, Ecuador, El Salvador, Grenada, Guatemala, Guyana, Haiti, Honduras, Jamaica, Mexico, Nicaragua, Panama, Paraguay, Peru, Saint Kitts and Nevis, Saint Lucia, Saint Vincent and the Grenadines, Suriname, Trinidad and Tobago, the United States of America, Uruguay, and Venezuela (Bolivarian Republic of). Cuba is a non-participating member State. Cuba was suspended from participation in 1962, but the suspension was lifted at the 2009 OAS General Assembly. In order for Cuba to participate again, Cuba must first seek a dialogue with OAS.

[187] The 24 member States of OAS that are parties to the American Convention on Human Rights are: Argentina, Barbados, Bolivia (Plurinational State of), Brazil, Chile, Colombia, Costa Rica, Dominica, the Dominican Republic, Ecuador, El Salvador, Grenada, Guatemala, Haiti, Honduras, Jamaica, Mexico, Nicaragua, Panama,

Area of Economic, Social and Cultural Rights, and 13 to the Protocol to Abolish the Death Penalty.

The two OAS bodies most directly concerned with human rights are the Inter-American Commission on Human Rights and the Inter-American Court of Human Rights, both of which are discussed below.

The substantive rights protected

The American Declaration of the Rights and Duties of Man applies to all OAS member States, while the 1969 American Convention on Human Rights is binding only on those States which have ratified it. The Declaration addresses a broad range of human rights, while the Convention is concerned primarily with civil and political rights (the 1988 Additional Protocol expanded its coverage to economic, social and cultural rights). It is important to bear in mind that minorities are entitled to *all* of the rights set forth in these documents, but among the rights of greatest interest to minorities are the following.

Article 2 of the Declaration guarantees equality before the law "without distinction as to race, sex, language, creed or any other factor". *Article 1 of the Convention* obliges States to respect Convention rights without discrimination based on "race, color, sex, language, religion, political or other opinion, national or social origin, economic status, birth, or any other social condition". *Article 24 of the Convention* provides broadly for equal protection of the law "without discrimination".

Article 3 of the Declaration guarantees freedom of religion. *Article 12 of the Convention* additionally provides that parents have the right to provide for the religious and moral education of their children in accord with their own convictions.

Article 4 of the Declaration guarantees freedom of expression. *Article 13 of the Convention* also prohibits any advocacy of national, racial or religious hatred that constitutes an incitement to lawless violence.

Article 5 of the Declaration guarantees that the law will protect everyone from attacks on their honour, reputation, and private and family life. *Articles 11 and 14 of the Convention* provide similar protections.

Article 8 of the Declaration protects freedom of movement and the right to choose one's residence. *Article 22 of the Convention* provides similar protection.

Article 12 of the Declaration sets forth the right to an education, including free primary education. There is no comparable right in the Convention itself, but the Protocol of San Salvador includes the right to education and specifies that education should foster "understanding, tolerance and friendship among all nations and all racial, ethnic or religious groups" (art. 13 (2)). The Protocol also affirms the right of parents to select the type of education to be given to their children and the right of everyone to establish educational institutions in accordance with domestic law.

Article 13 of the Declaration proclaims the right of everyone to take part in the cultural life of the community and to the protection of intellectual property. A similar provision is included in *article 14 of the Protocol of San Salvador.*

Article 18 of the Declaration guarantees the right to a fair trial. *Article 8 of the Convention* provides the same guarantee and specifies that an accused has the right to a translator or interpreter if necessary.

Paraguay, Peru, Suriname, Uruguay and Venezuela (Bolivarian Republic of). Trinidad and Tobago was a State party but denounced the Convention in 1998.

Article 20 of the Declaration guarantees the right to vote and to participate in the Government of one's country, although *article 23 of the Convention* permits these rights to be limited on the basis of, inter alia, language.

Article 22 of the Declaration guarantees freedom of association "to promote, exercise and protect [one's] legitimate interests of a political, economic, religious, social, cultural, professional, trade union or other nature". *Article 16 of the Convention* is a similar provision.

Inter-American Commission on Human Rights

The Commission consists of seven independent experts, nominated by States and elected by the OAS General Assembly.[188] It meets in Washington, D.C., in ordinary and special sessions several times a year (the length and frequency of meetings are determined by the members of the Commission and may change). It may hold hearings at any time on cases or subjects of concern. Many of the hearings include the participation of individuals, NGO representatives and Governments and are now broadcast on the Commission's website. The Commission holds thematic hearings (e.g., on climate change and the impact of large dam projects on human rights), although on an irregular basis. It may conduct on-site visits, but only with the consent or at the invitation of the State concerned.

The Commission's jurisdiction is very broad, covering every OAS member State and extending to the preparation of country-specific reports, the investigation of individual complaints about human rights violations and bringing cases to the Inter-American Court of Human Rights (if the State concerned has accepted the Court's jurisdiction). The Commission exercises similar authority under the Declaration (applicable to all OAS member States) and the Convention (applicable only to States parties). For a legal matter, it is important to know under which instrument the Commission is being asked to act, but practice and procedure are similar under both. The Commission's authority is governed by its statute and rules of procedure. Because of the small size of both the Commission and its staff, procedures may be subject to delay and may be less formal than, for example, those under the European Convention on Human Rights (see chap. XII).

Country reports

Perhaps the most unusual and effective authority of the Commission is its ability to initiate an investigation into the human rights situation in any OAS member State, either in response to information received or at its own initiative. Such an investigation is launched only when the Commission decides, by a majority, that it is warranted, and there is no way of mandating that the Commission initiate a study. Neither individuals nor NGOs have a formal role to play in this process, but information supplied by them generally provides the basis for the Commission's decision to initiate an investigation and report.

The Commission may gather information in any way it sees fit, including through hearings or direct testimony. It usually requests the State concerned to authorize an on-site visit, during which Commission members meet with individuals, NGOs and Government representatives. Such a visit usually garners a great deal of publicity within the country and thus provides an excellent opportunity for minorities to present their concerns directly to the Commission.

The Commission's reports are almost always published, and include information on the country's legal system and social condition, as well as on the human rights issues of concern. A report may address the conditions of minorities within a State, as did the March 2009 investigation into Afro-descendants in Colombia. In recent years, the Commission has focused on more targeted

[188] See www.cidh.oas.org/DefaultE.htm (accessed 6 December 2012).

investigations of the situation of certain groups, such as women, children, asylum seekers and migrants, rather than on the general human rights situation in a State. A State is not obligated to respond directly to the Commission's conclusions or recommendations, but a public report by the Commission can be a powerful means of exercising political pressure to improve human rights. In recent years, the Commission has published only one country report per year, on average; the most recent have concerned Honduras (2010, 2009), the Plurinational State of Bolivia (2009, 2007), the Bolivarian Republic of Venezuela (2009, 2003), Haiti (2008, 2005) and Guatemala (2003, 2001). Where discrimination against minorities is widespread, whether or not it is legally sanctioned, minority rights defenders should consider (in addition to filing a formal complaint) contacting the Commission and exploring the possibility of persuading the Commission to undertake an investigation.

Individual complaints of human rights violations

Any individual, group of individuals or NGO may file a complaint with the Commission alleging that human rights are being violated in an OAS member State. If the State is a party to the Convention, the Convention will be the governing law; if not, the rights protected are those set forth in the Declaration. In neither case is there a requirement that the petitioner be a victim of a violation, although the petition should refer to specific instances of alleged violations. The petition may concern a single incident and a single individual or may raise broader concerns which affect many people.

The complaint should set out the facts in as much detail as possible, including the Government acts or agents that are being challenged and the human rights considered to have been violated. The complainant must explain how any available domestic legal remedies have been exhausted. However, this may be excused if the State has no due process, access to remedies has been prevented, there is unwarranted delay in the domestic proceedings, or the complainant has been unable to obtain the necessary legal assistance. The mere fact of being unsuccessful in domestic proceedings is insufficient, unless the domestic procedure itself violated human rights guarantees – the Commission is not an appellate body whose task is to review the correctness of domestic judgements on factual issues. Of course, the case may be examined if the law itself is alleged to be incompatible with protected rights. The Commission is strict in requiring that a complaint be filed within six months of the date on which the decision from the highest domestic tribunal was notified to the victim (or within six months of the incident, if there are no remedies available).

The Commission delivers a formal opinion as to whether a complaint is admissible, that is, whether it meets all the formal requirements for submission. A preliminary analysis by the Commission Secretariat will normally result in one of three outcomes: (1) rejection of the petition as being "manifestly ill founded", which usually means that the alleged violation is not covered under the Declaration or Convention; (2) a request for further information; or (3) communication of the complaint to the State concerned. If the case is urgent and there is a possibility of irreparable harm to the life or physical integrity of the victim, the Commission may be asked to adopt "precautionary measures" by requesting the State to not act in a way that would prejudice the continued existence of the subject matter of the case. For example, the Commission may request that an execution or deportation be stayed or that the Government refrain from some other action that would render the complaint moot or cause irreparable damage.

If the State responds, the petitioner has the opportunity to present observations on the response in writing. If the State does not respond or merely offers a general denial, the Commission has the authority to deem the facts alleged to be true. At any time, the petitioner (or the State) may ask for an oral hearing, although the Commission will grant such a request only when it considers it to be necessary. The Commission will also offer to mediate or facilitate a "friendly settlement" between the complainant and the State, which must be agreed to by both parties.

Such a settlement might include, for example, the payment of compensation, release of a person from prison or even State agreement to amend a law or practice.

If there is no friendly settlement, the Commission deliberates in private and eventually prepares a report, including conclusions and recommendations, on the case. After a three-month waiting period, during which time the report is sent on a confidential basis to the State and the complainant, the report is either transmitted to the Court for consideration or published and printed in the Commission's annual report to the OAS General Assembly. The Commission's report is not legally binding on the State concerned, and the Commission cannot directly order the release of a prisoner, payment of compensation or amendment of a law that violates human rights. However, the Commission can (and does) give its opinion as to whether the Declaration or Convention has been violated and makes specific recommendations to States. Since States' records of compliance are far from consistent, the petitioner or an NGO may need to pressure the State to adopt the Commission's recommendations.

The process may take two years or longer, as a lack of resources makes it difficult to deal expeditiously with up to 1,000 pending cases. A favourable opinion from the Commission represents, at the very least, an important moral and political victory, and the process itself may encourage the State to consider meeting the complainant's demands even before a final report is adopted. Not many individual cases have dealt with minority issues per se, although cases concerning indigenous peoples are increasingly common.

Rapporteurship on the Rights of Afro-descendants and against Racial Discrimination

In 2005, the Commission created a Rapporteurship on the Rights of Afro-descendants and against Racial Discrimination to encourage, systematize, reinforce and consolidate the Commission's actions in this area.[189] The Rapporteur works with OAS member States in order to:

- Raise awareness of States' duties with respect to the human rights of Afro-descendants and the elimination of all forms of racial discrimination;
- Analyse the current challenges which confront countries of the region in this area, formulate recommendations designed to address those challenges and identify and share best practices;
- Monitor and provide technical assistance, upon the request of a member State.

Within the Commission, the Rapporteur seeks to ensure compliance with the mandates of the OAS General Assembly related to Afro-descendants, racism and racial discrimination. The Rapporteur supports the work of the Commission by:

- Preparing reports and special studies on the rights of Afro-descendants and on issues pertaining to the elimination of racial discrimination;
- Reviewing and analysing complaints of racism and racial discrimination received by the Commission and offering opinions and recommendations to the Commission;
- Making recommendations to the Commission regarding hearings to be granted and participating with the Commission in such hearings;
- Assisting the parties in reaching a settlement;
- Initiating consultations and presenting recommendations to member States regarding the modification of legislation related to the rights of Afro-descendants and racial discrimination;
- Accompanying the Commission in its on-site visits;
- Helping to draft admissibility decisions and reports on the merits in contentious cases, as

[189] See www.oas.org/en/iachr/afro-descendants/default.asp (accessed 6 December 2012).

well as thematic, country and annual reports.

The Rapporteur works with the other Commission rapporteurs on matters related to the mandate and also engages with civil society in order to raise awareness of the guarantees and mechanisms the inter-American human rights system offers. The Rapporteur also maintains a database of current information related to the mandate, and collaborates with relevant United Nations bodies, including the International Convention on the Elimination of All Forms of Racial Discrimination, the Working Group of Experts on People of African Descent, and the Special Rapporteur on contemporary forms of racism, racial discrimination, xenophobia and related intolerance.

Inter-American Court of Human Rights

Acceptance of the jurisdiction of the Inter-American Court of Human Rights is optional, even for those States which are parties to the Convention. In considering whether to approach the Court, therefore, it is necessary first to confirm whether the State in question has accepted the Court's jurisdiction. Currently, 22 of the 24 States parties to the Convention have done so. States which are not party to the Convention cannot be brought before the Court. The Court consists of seven judges, and its seat is in San José, Costa Rica.[190]

The Court is empowered to issue advisory opinions on various aspects of human rights, including the compatibility of domestic legislation with the Convention. Only member States and OAS organs can request advisory opinions. Although the Court's advisory opinions are not legally binding, they are important sources of jurisprudence and should be consulted whenever relevant to a particular case or issue. To date, over 20 such opinions have been rendered; of particular interest to minorities might be the advisory opinions on consular assistance (No. 16/99) and undocumented migrants (No. 18/03).

The Court has issued final decisions or judgements in over 200 contentious cases. These cases can reach the Court only after the Commission has issued its report on the merits of the case; either the Commission itself or the State concerned can refer the case to the Court. It is now normal practice for the Commission to refer all cases to the Court in which the Commission has found a violation of the Convention but the State has failed to comply with its recommendations. During its consideration the Court hears representatives of the petitioner as well as the Commission and the State, and the proceedings are formal. The Court may undertake its own investigation of the facts and hear witnesses, if it considers it necessary.

The Court's judgements are legally binding on the State concerned. The Court can order compensation or other relief, and it may also award attorney's costs and reimbursement of expenses. The Court's jurisprudence with respect to minority-specific issues has been relatively sparse, although it has ruled on such important issues as the responsibility of a State for forced disappearances, the death penalty and land rights of indigenous peoples.[191]

---

[190] See www.corteidh.or.cr/ (accessed 6 December 2012).

[191] The Court's jurisprudence is available from its website. Two illustrative cases are: *Yean and Bosico* v. *Dominican Republic*, Inter-American Court of Human Rights, Case 12.189 (2005), which affirmed the human right to nationality as a prerequisite to the equal enjoyment of all rights as civic members of a State; and *Aloeboetoe et al.* v. *Suriname*, Inter-American Court of Human Rights, Case 10.150 (1991 [merits], 1993 [reparations]), where the Court utilized, in part, the customary law and practices of the Saramaka tribe to determine appropriate reparations to be paid by the State for both "actual" and "moral" damages, after Suriname admitted human rights violations including torture and arbitrary execution.

Contacts and further information

Inter-American Commission on Human Rights
1889 F Street, N.W.
Washington, D.C. 20006
United States of America

Tel: 1 202 458 6000
Fax: 1 202 458 3992
E-mail: cidhdenuncias@oas.org
Website: www.oas.org/en/iachr

Inter-American Court of Human Rights
Avenue 10, Street 45-47 Los Yoses, San Pedro
P.O. Box 6906-1000
San José
Costa Rica

Tel: 506 2527 1600
Fax: 506 2234 0584
E-mail: coteidh@corteidh.0r.cr
Website: www.corteidh.or.cr

An article-by-article guide to the jurisprudence of the Inter-American system for the period 1980-1997, compiled by the Washington College of Law at American University (in Spanish), is available from www.wcl.american.edu/humright/repertorio.

There has been a great deal written about the inter-American system in both English and Spanish. Among the practical guides to the Commission and Court is: Jo M. Pasqualucci, *The Practice and Procedure of the Inter-American Court of Human Rights* (Cambridge, 2003).

ANNEX I

CORE DOCUMENTS

DECLARATION ON THE RIGHTS OF PERSONS BELONGING TO NATIONAL OR ETHNIC, RELIGIOUS AND LINGUISTIC MINORITIES

(Adopted by General Assembly resolution 47/135 of 18 December 1992)

The General Assembly,

Reaffirming that one of the basic aims of the United Nations, as proclaimed in the Charter, is to promote and encourage respect for human rights and for fundamental freedoms for all, without distinction as to race, sex, language or religion,

Reaffirming faith in fundamental human rights, in the dignity and worth of the human person, in the equal rights of men and women and of nations large and small,

Desiring to promote the realization of the principles contained in the Charter, the Universal Declaration of Human Rights, the Convention on the Prevention and Punishment of the Crime of Genocide, the International Convention on the Elimination of All Forms of Racial Discrimination, the International Covenant on Civil and Political Rights, the International Covenant on Economic, Social and Cultural Rights, the Declaration on the Elimination of All Forms of Intolerance and of Discrimination Based on Religion or Belief, and the Convention on the Rights of the Child, as well as other relevant international instruments that have been adopted at the universal or regional level and those concluded between individual States Members of the United Nations,

Inspired by the provisions of article 27 of the International Covenant on Civil and Political Rights concerning the rights of persons belonging to ethnic, religious or linguistic minorities,

Considering that the promotion and protection of the rights of persons belonging to national or ethnic, religious and linguistic minorities contribute to the political and social stability of States in which they live,

Emphasizing that the constant promotion and realization of the rights of persons belonging to national or ethnic, religious and linguistic minorities, as an integral part of the development of society as a whole and within a democratic framework based on the rule of law, would contribute to the strengthening of friendship and cooperation among peoples and States,

Considering that the United Nations has an important role to play regarding the protection of minorities,

Bearing in mind the work done so far within the United Nations system, in particular by the Commission on Human Rights, the Sub-commission on Prevention of Discrimination and Protection of Minorities and the bodies established pursuant to the International Covenants on Human Rights and other relevant international human rights instruments in promoting and protecting the rights of persons belonging to national or ethnic, religious and linguistic minorities,

Taking into account the important work which is done by intergovernmental and non-governmental organizations in protecting minorities and in promoting and protecting the rights of persons belonging to national or ethnic, religious and linguistic minorities,

Recognizing the need to ensure even more effective implementation of international human rights instruments with regard to the rights of persons belonging to national or ethnic, religious and linguistic minorities,

Proclaims this Declaration on the Rights of Persons Belonging to National or Ethnic, Religious and Linguistic Minorities:

Article 1

1. States shall protect the existence and the national or ethnic, cultural, religious and linguistic identity of minorities within their respective territories and shall encourage conditions for the promotion of that identity.

2. States shall adopt appropriate legislative and other measures to achieve those ends.

Article 2

1. Persons belonging to national or ethnic, religious and linguistic minorities (hereinafter referred to as persons belonging to minorities) have the right to enjoy their own culture, to profess and practise their own religion, and to use their own language, in private and in public, freely and without interference or any form of discrimination.

2. Persons belonging to minorities have the right to participate effectively in cultural, religious, social, economic and public life.

3. Persons belonging to minorities have the right to participate effectively in decisions on the national and, where appropriate, regional level concerning the minority to which they belong or the regions in which they live, in a manner not incompatible with national legislation.

4. Persons belonging to minorities have the right to establish and maintain their own associations.

5. Persons belonging to minorities have the right to establish and maintain, without any discrimination, free and peaceful contacts with other members of their group and with persons belonging to other minorities, as well as contacts across frontiers with citizens of other States to whom they are related by national or ethnic, religious or linguistic ties.

Article 3

1. Persons belonging to minorities may exercise their rights, including those set forth in the present Declaration, individually as well as in community with other members of their group, without any discrimination.

2. No disadvantage shall result for any person belonging to a minority as the consequence of the exercise or non-exercise of the rights set forth in the present Declaration.

Article 4

1. States shall take measures where required to ensure that persons belonging to minorities may exercise fully and effectively all their human rights and fundamental freedoms without any discrimination and in full equality before the law.

2. States shall take measures to create favourable conditions to enable persons belonging to minorities to express their characteristics and to develop their culture, language, religion, traditions and customs, except where specific practices are in violation of national law and contrary to international standards.

3. States should take appropriate measures so that, wherever possible, persons belonging to minorities may have adequate opportunities to learn their mother tongue or to have instruction in their mother tongue.

4. States should, where appropriate, take measures in the field of education, in order to encourage knowledge of the history, traditions, language and culture of the minorities existing within their territory. Persons belonging to minorities should have adequate opportunities to gain knowledge of the society as a whole.

5. States should consider appropriate measures so that persons belonging to minorities may participate fully in the economic progress and development in their country.

Article 5

1. National policies and programmes shall be planned and implemented with due regard for the legitimate interests of persons belonging to minorities.

2. Programmes of cooperation and assistance among States should be planned and implemented with due regard for the legitimate interests of persons belonging to minorities.

Article 6

States should cooperate on questions relating to persons belonging to minorities, inter alia, exchanging information and experiences, in order to promote mutual understanding and confidence.

Article 7

States should cooperate in order to promote respect for the rights set forth in the present Declaration.

Article 8

1. Nothing in the present Declaration shall prevent the fulfilment of international obligations of States in relation to persons belonging to minorities. In particular, States shall fulfil in good faith the obligations and commitments they have assumed under international treaties and agreements to which they are parties.

2. The exercise of the rights set forth in the present Declaration shall not prejudice the enjoyment by all persons of universally recognized human rights and fundamental freedoms.

3. Measures taken by States to ensure the effective enjoyment of the rights set forth in the present Declaration shall not prima facie be considered contrary to the principle of equality contained in the Universal Declaration of Human Rights.

4. Nothing in the present Declaration may be construed as permitting any activity contrary to the purposes and principles of the United Nations, including sovereign equality, territorial integrity and political independence of States.

Article 9

The specialized agencies and other organizations of the United Nations system shall contribute to the full realization of the rights and principles set forth in the present Declaration, within their respective fields of competence.

Commentary to the United Nations Declaration on the Rights of Persons Belonging to National or Ethnic, Religious and Linguistic Minorities of the Working Group on Minorities[1]

I. INTRODUCTION

1. In 1992, in its resolution 47/135, the United Nations General Assembly proclaimed the Declaration on the Rights of Persons Belonging to National or Ethnic, Religious and Linguistic Minorities. The Assembly requested that intensified efforts be made to disseminate information on the Declaration and promote understanding thereof.

2. This commentary has been prepared in the context of the Working Group on Minorities of the Sub-Commission on the Promotion and Protection of Human Rights. It is intended to serve as a guide to the understanding and application of the Declaration. The first draft, prepared by Asbjørn Eide as Chairperson-Rapporteur, was submitted to the Working Group on Minorities for discussion in 1998[2] and was subsequently circulated to Governments, intergovernmental and non-governmental organizations and individual experts for comments. A compilation of those comments was submitted to the Working Group at its fifth session in 1999.[3] Additional comments were made during that session and at the sixth session in 2000.[4] The Working Group requested Mr Eide on that basis to finalize the Commentary and to ensure its publication in the planned United Nations manual on minorities. The present final text therefore draws on written work or oral contributions by many experts, Governments and international and non-governmental organizations, and thus takes into account a broad body of opinion. The Working Group on Minorities, at its tenth session adopted the Commentary on the United Nations Declaration on the Rights of Persons Belonging to National or Ethnic, Religious and Linguistic Minorities originally drawn up by its former Chairperson, Asbjørn Eide, and contained in document E/CN.4/AC.5/2001/2, as a Commentary of the Working Group as a whole.

II. PURPOSES OF THE DECLARATION: ADVANCING HUMAN RIGHTS AND THE PRINCIPLES OF THE CHARTER OF THE UNITED NATIONS

3. The purposes of the Declaration, as set out in the General Assembly resolution 47/135 and the preamble to the Declaration, is to promote more effective implementation of the human rights of persons belonging to minorities and more generally to contribute to the realization of the principles of the Charter of the United Nations and of the human rights instruments adopted at the universal or regional level. The Declaration on Minorities is inspired by article 27 of the International Covenant on Civil and Political Rights. The General Assembly holds that the promotion and protection of the rights of minorities contribute to the political and social stability of the States in which minorities live and contribute to the strengthening of friendship and cooperation among peoples and States.

4. The Declaration builds on and adds to the rights contained in the International Bill of Human Rights and other human rights instruments by strengthening and clarifying those rights which make it possible for persons belonging to minorities to preserve and develop their group

[1] E/CN.4/Sub.2/AC.5/2005/2.

[2] E/CN.4/Sub.2/AC.5/1998/WP.1.

[3] E/CN.4/Sub.2/AC.5/1999/WP.1.

[4] E/CN.4/Sub.2/AC.5/2000/WP.1.

identity. The human rights set out in the Universal Declaration of Human Rights must at all times be respected in the process, including the principle of non-discrimination between individuals. The State is obliged to respect and ensure to every person within its territory and subject to its jurisdiction, without discrimination on any ground, including race, ethnicity, religion or national origin, the rights contained in the instruments to which that State is a party.

5. It is in the light of these purposes and principles that the articles of the Declaration on Minorities must be interpreted.

III. INTERPRETATION OF AND COMMENTS ON THE TITLE AND THE INDIVIDUAL ARTICLES

THE TITLE AND SCOPE OF THE DECLARATION

Declaration on the Rights of Persons Belonging to National or Ethnic, Religious and Linguistic Minorities

6. The beneficiaries of the rights under article 27 of the International Covenant on Civil and Political Rights, which has inspired the Declaration, are persons belonging to "ethnic, religious or linguistic minorities". The Declaration on Minorities adds the term "national minorities". That addition does not extend the overall scope of application beyond the groups already covered by article 27. There is hardly any national minority, however defined, that is not also an ethnic or linguistic minority. A relevant question, however, would be whether the title indicates that the Declaration covers four different categories of minorities, whose rights have somewhat different content and strength. Persons belonging to groups defined solely as religious minorities might be held to have only those special minority rights which relate to the profession and practice of their religion. Persons belonging to groups solely defined as linguistic minorities might similarly be held to have only those special minority rights which are related to education and use of their language. Persons who belong to groups defined as ethnic would have more extensive rights relating to the preservation and development of other aspects of their culture also, since ethnicity is generally defined by a broad conception of culture, including a way of life. The category of national minority would then have still stronger rights relating not only to their culture but to the preservation and development of their national identity.

7. The Declaration does not, in its substantive provisions, make such distinctions. This does not exclude the possibility that the needs of the different categories of minorities could be taken into account in the interpretation and application of the various provisions.

8. Regional European instruments on minority rights use only the concept "national minorities" and do not refer to "ethnic, religious or linguistic minorities". The most important among them are the instruments and documents of the Council of Europe[5] and the Organization for Security and Cooperation in Europe.[6] When applying those instruments it is important to define "national minority", but the same problem does not arise for the United Nations Declaration on Minorities: even if a group is held not to constitute a national minority, it can still be an ethnic, religious or linguistic minority and therefore be covered by the Declaration.

9. This can be important in several respects. In relation to the European regional instruments, some States argue that "national minorities" only comprise groups composed of citizens of the State. Even if that is accepted (at present it is a matter of some controversy), it would not apply to

5 The Framework Convention for the Protection of National Minorities, adopted by the Council of Europe in 1994.

6 Most important are the Helsinki Final Act of 1975 and the Document of the Copenhagen Meeting of the Conference on the Human Dimension of the Conference on Security and Cooperation in Europe, 1990, section IV, paragraphs 30 to 40.

the United Nations Declaration on Minorities because it has a much wider scope than "national minorities". As the Declaration is inspired by article 27 of the International Covenant on Civil and Political Rights, it may be assumed that the Declaration has at least as wide a scope as that article. In conformity with article 2 of the Covenant, States parties are under an obligation to respect and ensure the application of article 27 to everyone within its territory and under its jurisdiction, whether the person - or group of persons - are citizens of the country or not. This is also the view expressed by the Human Rights Committee in paragraphs 5.1 and 5.2 of its general comment No. 23 (fiftieth session, 1994). Persons who are not (yet) citizens of the country in which they reside can form part of or belong to a minority in that country.

10. While citizenship as such should not be a distinguishing criterion that excludes some persons or groups from enjoying minority rights under the Declaration, other factors can be relevant in distinguishing between the rights that can be demanded by different minorities. Those who live compactly together in a part of the State territory may be entitled to rights regarding the use of language, and street and place names which are different from those who are dispersed, and may in some circumstances be entitled to some kind of autonomy. Those who have been established for a long time on the territory may have stronger rights than those who have recently arrived.

11. The best approach appears to be to avoid making an absolute distinction between "new" and "old" minorities by excluding the former and including the latter, but to recognize that in the application of the Declaration the "old" minorities have stronger entitlements than the "new".

12. The word "minority" can sometimes be misleading in itself. Outside Europe, and particularly in Africa, countries are often composed of a large number of groups, none of which make up a majority.

13. The relevant factors differ significantly between States. What is required is to ensure appropriate rights for members of all groups and to develop good governance in heterogeneous societies. By good governance is here understood legal, administrative and territorial arrangements which allow for peaceful and constructive group accommodation based on equality in dignity and rights for all and which allows for the necessary pluralism to enable the persons belonging to the different groups to preserve and develop their identity.

14. The Declaration sets out rights of persons belonging to minorities mainly in article 2 and spells out the duties of the States in which they exist in articles 1, 4 and 5. While the rights are consistently set out as rights of individuals, the duties of States are in part formulated as duties towards minorities as groups. This is most clearly expressed in article 1 (see below). While only individuals can claim the rights, the State cannot fully implement them without ensuring adequate conditions for the existence and identity of the group as a whole.

15. The rights of persons belonging to minorities differ from the rights of peoples to self-determination. The rights of persons belonging to minorities are individual rights, even if they in most cases can only be enjoyed in community with others. The rights of peoples, on the other hand, are collective rights. While the right of peoples to self-determination is well established under international law, in particular by common article 1 of the two International Covenants on Human Rights, it does not apply to persons belonging to minorities. This does not exclude the possibility that persons belonging to an ethnic or national group may in some contexts legitimately make claims based on minority rights and, in another context, when acting as a group, can make claims based on the right of a people to self-determination.

16. Within the United Nations and also within the Organization of American States, a distinction is drawn between the rights of persons belonging to minorities and those of indigenous peoples. The latter have particular concerns which are not properly addressed in the Declaration

on Minorities. The main instrument at the global level relating to indigenous peoples is the Convention concerning Indigenous and Tribal Peoples in Independent Countries (No. 169) of the International Labour Organization (ILO), which has been ratified by only a small number of States. The draft declaration on the rights of indigenous peoples, adopted by the Working Group on Indigenous Populations and transmitted by the Sub-Commission on the Prevention of Discrimination and Protection of Minorities in 1993 to the Commission on Human Rights, is still under consideration by the Commission.

17. Persons belonging to indigenous peoples are of course fully entitled, if they so wish, to claim the rights contained in the instruments on minorities. This has repeatedly been done under article 27 of the International Covenant on Civil and Political Rights. Persons belonging to indigenous peoples have made several submissions under the Optional Protocol to that Covenant.

18. That protocol does not generally make it possible to claim the group-oriented rights sought by indigenous peoples, but some modification of that point follows from general comment No. 23 of the Human Rights Committee (fiftieth session, 1994). The Committee noted that, especially in the case of indigenous peoples, the preservation of their use of land resources can become an essential element in the right of persons belonging to such minorities to exercise their cultural rights (para. 7). Since the indigenous peoples very often have collective rights to land, individual members of the group may be in a position to make claims not only for themselves, but for the indigenous group as a whole.

19. Some see a link between the right of persons belonging to minorities to effective political participation and the right of peoples to self-determination. The issue of effective participation is addressed below in the comments on articles 2.2 and 2.3. If participation is denied to a minority and its members, this might in some cases give rise to a legitimate claim to self-determination. If the group claims a right to self-determination and challenges the territorial integrity of the State, it would have to claim to be a people, and that claim would have to be based on article 1 common to the Covenants and would therefore fall outside the Declaration on Minorities. This follows also from article 8.4 of the Declaration (see below). The same would apply in other contexts where the collective right to self-determination is claimed. The Declaration neither limits nor extends the rights to self-determination that peoples have under other parts of international law.[7]

20. While the Declaration does not provide group rights to self-determination, the duties of the State to protect the identity of minorities and to ensure their effective participation might in some cases be best implemented by arrangements for autonomy in regard to religious, linguistic or broader cultural matters. Good practices of that kind can be found in many States. The autonomy can be territorial, cultural and local, and can be more or less extensive. Such autonomy can be organized and managed by associations set up by persons belonging to minorities in accordance with article 2.4. But the Declaration does not make it a requirement for States to establish such autonomy. In some cases, positive measures of integration (but not assimilation) can best serve the protection of minorities.

7 Reference can also be made here to general comment No. 23 (1994), adopted by the Human Rights Committee at its fiftieth session. It deals with article 27 of the International Covenant on Civil and Political Rights (the minority rights provision), and points out, in paragraph 3.1, the distinction between the right of peoples to self-determination and the rights of persons belonging to minorities, which are protected under article 27.

ARTICLE 1

1.1 States shall protect the existence and the national or ethnic, cultural, religious and linguistic identity of minorities within their respective territories and shall encourage conditions for the promotion of that identity.

21. The relationship between the State and its minorities has in the past taken five different forms: elimination, assimilation, toleration, protection and promotion. Under present international law, elimination is clearly illegal. The Declaration is based on the consideration that forced assimilation is unacceptable. While a degree of integration is required in every national society in order to make it possible for the State to respect and ensure human rights to every person within its territory without discrimination, the protection of minorities is intended to ensure that integration does not become unwanted assimilation or undermine the group identity of persons living on the territory of the State.

22. Integration differs from assimilation in that while it develops and maintains a common domain where equal treatment and a common rule of law prevail, it also allows for pluralism. The areas of pluralism covered by the Declaration are culture, language and religion.

23. Minority protection is based on four requirements: protection of the existence, non-exclusion, non-discrimination and non-assimilation of the groups concerned.

24. The protection of the existence of minorities includes their physical existence, their continued existence on the territories on which they live and their continued access to the material resources required to continue their existence on those territories. The minorities shall neither be physically excluded from the territory nor be excluded from access to the resources required for their livelihood. The right to existence in its physical sense is sustained by the Convention on the Prevention and Punishment of the Crime of Genocide, which codified customary law in 1948. Forced population transfers intended to move persons belonging to minorities away from the territory on which they live, or with that effect, would constitute serious breaches of contemporary international standards, including the Rome Statute of the International Criminal Court. But protection of their existence goes beyond the duty not to destroy or deliberately weaken minority groups. It also requires respect for and protection of their religious and cultural heritage, essential to their group identity, including buildings and sites such as libraries, churches, mosques, temples and synagogues.

25. The second requirement is that minorities shall not be excluded from the national society. Apartheid was the extreme version of exclusion of different groups from equal participation in the national society as a whole. The Declaration on Minorities repeatedly underlines the rights of all groups, small as well as large, to participate effectively in society (arts. 2.2 and 2.3).

26. The third requirement is non-discrimination, which is a general principle of human rights law and elaborated by, inter alia, the International Convention on the Elimination of All Forms of Racial Discrimination, which also covers discrimination on ethnic grounds. The Declaration on Minorities elaborates the principle of non-discrimination in its provision that the exercise of their rights as persons belonging to minorities shall not justify any discrimination in any other field, and that no disadvantage shall result from the exercise or non-exercise of these rights (art. 3).

27. The fourth requirement is non-assimilation and its corollary, which is to protect and promote conditions for the group identity of minorities. Many recent international instruments use the term "identity", which expresses a clear trend towards the protection and promotion of cultural diversity, both internationally and internally within States. Relevant provisions are articles 29 and 30 of the Convention on the Rights of the Child, article 31 of the International Convention on the Protection of the Rights of All Migrant Workers and Members of Their Families, article 2.2 (b) of

ILO Convention No. 169, which refers to respect for the social and cultural identity, customs and traditions and institutions of indigenous peoples, as well as provisions of regional instruments such as those of the Organization on Security and Cooperation in Europe, including its 1990 Copenhagen Conference on the Human Dimension and its 1991 Geneva Meeting of Experts on National Minorities. Another recent instrument in the same direction is the European Framework Convention for the Protection of National Minorities.

28. Minority group identity requires not only tolerance but a positive attitude towards cultural pluralism on the part of the State and the larger society. Not only acceptance but also respect for the distinctive characteristics and contribution of minorities to the life of the national society as a whole are required. Protection of their identity means not only that the State should abstain from policies which have the purpose or effect of assimilating minorities into the dominant culture, but also that it should protect them against activities by third parties which have an assimilatory effect. The language and educational policies of the State concerned are crucial in this regard. Denying minorities the possibility of learning their own language and of receiving instruction in their own language, or excluding from their education the transmission of knowledge about their own culture, history, tradition and language, would be a violation of the obligation to protect their identity.

29. Promotion of the identity of minorities requires special measures to facilitate the maintenance, reproduction and further development of their culture. Cultures are not static; minorities should be given the opportunity to develop their own culture in the context of an ongoing process. That process should be an interaction between the persons belonging to the minority themselves, between the minority and the State, and between the minority and the wider national society. The measures required to achieve this purpose are set out in greater detail in article 4 of the Declaration.

1.2 States shall adopt appropriate legislative and other measures to achieve those ends.

30. Article 1.2 requires "appropriate legislative and other measures". Legislation is needed and it must be complemented by other measures in order to ensure that article 1 can be effectively implemented. Both process and content are important here. In terms of process, it is essential that the State consult the minorities on what would constitute appropriate measures. This follows also from article 2.3 of the Declaration. Different minorities may have different needs that must be taken into account. Any differences in policy, however, must be based on objective and reasonable grounds in order to avoid discrimination.

31. "Other measures" include, but are not limited to, judicial, administrative, promotional and educational measures.

32. In general terms, the content of the measures which have to be adopted are set out in the other provisions of the Declaration, particularly articles 2 and 4, which will be discussed below. One set of measures stems directly from article 1.1: States must adopt laws protecting against acts or incitement to acts which physically threaten the existence of groups or threaten their identity. This obligation also follows from the International Convention on the Elimination of All Forms of Racial Discrimination. Under article 4 of that Convention, States are required to adopt legislative measures intended to protect groups against hatred and violence on racial or ethnic grounds. A comparable obligation is contained in article 20 of the International Covenant on Civil and Political Rights.

ARTICLE 2

2.1 Persons belonging to national or ethnic, religious and linguistic minorities (hereinafter referred to as persons belonging to minorities) have the right to enjoy their own culture, to profess and practise their own religion, and to use their own language, in private and in public, freely and without interference or any form of discrimination.

33. Article 27 of the International Covenant on Civil and Political Rights has almost the same language, but the Declaration is more explicit in requiring positive action. Article 27 of the Covenant requires that persons belonging to minorities "shall not be denied the right to ...", whereas article 2 of the Declaration uses the positive expression "have the right to ...". Article 27 has been interpreted by the Human Rights Committee as requiring more than mere passive non-interference.[8] The Declaration on Minorities makes it clear that these rights often require action, including protective measures and encouragement of conditions for the promotion of their identity (art. 1) and specified, active measures by the State (art. 4).

34. The words "freely and without interference or any form of discrimination" at the end of article 2.1 show that it is not enough for the State to abstain from interference or discrimination. It must also ensure that individuals and organizations of the larger society do not interfere or discriminate.

2.2 Persons belonging to minorities have the right to participate effectively in cultural, religious, social, economic and public life.

35. The right to participate in all aspects of the life of the larger national society is essential, both in order for persons belonging to minorities to promote their interests and values and to create an integrated but pluralist society based on tolerance and dialogue. By their participation in all forms of public life in their country, they are able both to shape their own destinies and to contribute to political change in the larger society.

36. The words "public life" must be understood in the same broad sense as in article 1 of the International Convention on the Elimination of All Forms of Racial Discrimination, though much is covered already by the preceding words "cultural, religious, social and economic". Included in "public life" are, among other rights, rights relating to election and to being elected, the holding of public office, and other political and administrative domains.

37. Participation can be ensured in many ways, including the use of minority associations (see also article 2.4), membership in other associations, and through their free contacts both inside the State and across borders (see article 2.5).

2.3 Persons belonging to minorities have the right to participate effectively in decisions on the national, and where appropriate, regional level concerning the minority to which they belong or the regions in which they live, in a manner not incompatible with national legislation.

38. While article 2.2 deals generally with the right to participation in all aspects of the public life of a society, article 2.3 deals specifically with the right of persons belonging to minorities to effective participation "in decisions ... concerning the minority to which they belong or the regions in which they live". As such decisions have a particular impact on persons belonging to minorities, the emphasis on effective participation is here of particular importance.

[8] Human Rights Committee, general comment No. 23, adopted at the fiftieth session, 1994, paragraphs 6.1 and 6.2.

Representatives of persons belonging to minorities should be involved beginning at the initial stages of decision-making. Experience has shown that it is of little use to involve them only at the final stages where there is very little room for compromise. Minorities should be involved at the local, national and international levels in the formulation, adoption, implementation and monitoring of standards and policies affecting them.

39. In 1991, the Conference on Security and Cooperation in Europe held a Meeting of Experts on National Minorities in Geneva. The States there assembled noted approaches used with positive results in some of the participating States. These included advisory and decision-making bodies - in particular with regard to education, culture and religion - on which minorities were represented. Also mentioned were assemblies for national minority affairs, local and autonomous administration, as well as autonomy on a territorial basis, including the existence of consultative, legislative and executive bodies chosen through free and periodic elections. Reference was further made to forms of self-administration by a national minority of aspects concerning its identity in situations where autonomy on a territorial basis did not apply, and decentralized or local forms of government.[9]

40. In early May 1999, a group of independent experts met in Lund, Sweden, to draw up a set of recommendations on the effective participation of national minorities in public life. The recommendations are built upon fundamental principles and rules of international law, such as respect for human dignity, equal rights and non-discrimination, as they affect the rights of national minorities to participate in public life and to enjoy other political rights.[10] At its fifth session, at the end of May 1999, the Working Group on Minorities adopted a set of recommendations on the same topic.[11]

41. The following commentary draws extensively on these recommendations. The purpose is not to set out only the minimum rights under article 2.3 of persons belonging to minorities, but also to provide a list of good practices which may be of use to Governments and minorities in finding appropriate solutions to issues confronting them.

42. Effective participation provides channels for consultation between and among minorities and Governments. It can serve as a means of dispute resolution and sustain diversity as a condition for the dynamic stability of a society. The number of persons belonging to minorities is by definition too small for them to determine the outcome of decisions in majoritarian democracy. They must as a minimum have the right to have their opinions heard and fully taken into account before decisions which concern them are adopted. A wide range of constitutional and political measures are used around the world to provide access for minorities to decision-making.

43. The variety in the composition, needs and aspirations of different types of minority groups requires identification and adoption of the most appropriate ways to create conditions for effective participation in each case. The mechanisms chosen have to take into account whether the persons belonging to the minority in question live dispersed or in compactly settled groups, whether the minority is small or large, or an old or a new minority. Religious minorities may also require different types or contexts of participation than ethnic or national minorities. It should be noted, however, that in some cases religion and ethnicity coincide.

9 Report of the CSCE Meeting of Experts on National Minorities, Geneva, 19 July 1991, Part IV. See also the second progress report of Special Rapporteur A. Eide on possible ways and means of facilitating the peaceful and constructive solution of problems involving minorities (E/CN.4/Sub.2/1992/37), paragraphs 122-155.

10 The Lund recommendations can be found on the website of the OSCE High Commissioner on National Minorities, www.osce.org/hcnm/documents/lund.htm.

11 Report of the Working Group on Minorities on its fifth session (E/CN.4/Sub.2/1999/21), paragraphs 81-88.

44. Effective participation requires representation in legislative, administrative and advisory bodies and more generally in public life. Persons belonging to minorities, like all others, are entitled to assemble and to form their associations and thereby to aggregate their interests and values to make the greatest possible impact on national and regional decision-making. They are entitled not only to set up and make use of ethnic, cultural and religious associations and societies (see commentary to article 2.4 below), but also to establish political parties, should they so wish. In a well-integrated society, however, many persons belonging to minorities often prefer to be members of or vote for parties which are not organized on ethnic lines but are sensitive to the concerns of the minorities.

45. Where minorities are concentrated territorially, single-member districts may provide sufficient minority representation. Proportional representation systems, where a political party's share in the national vote is reflected in its share of the legislative seats, may assist in the representation of minorities. Some forms of preference voting, where voters rank candidates in order of choice, may also facilitate minority representation and promote inter-communal cooperation.

46. Decentralization of powers based on the principle of subsidiarity, whether called self-government or devolved power, and whether the arrangements are symmetrical or asymmetrical, would increase the chances of minorities to participate in the exercise of authority over matters affecting themselves and the entire society in which they live.

47. Public institutions should not, however, be based on ethnic or religious criteria. Governments at local, regional and national levels should recognize the role of multiple identities in contributing to open communities and in establishing useful distinctions between public institutional structures and cultural identities.

48. States should also establish advisory or consultative bodies involving minorities within appropriate institutional frameworks. Such bodies or round tables should be attributed political weight and effectively consulted on issues affecting the minority population.

49. There should be equal access to public sector employment across the various ethnic, linguistic and religious communities.

50. Citizenship remains an important condition for full and effective participation. Barriers to the acquisition of citizenship for members of minorities should be reduced. Forms of participation by resident non-citizens should also be developed, including local voting rights after a certain period of residence and inclusion of elected non-citizen observers in municipal, regional and national legislative and decision-making assemblies.

2.4 Persons belonging to minorities have the right to establish and maintain their own associations.

51. Persons belonging to minorities are entitled, in the same way as other members of society, to set up any association they may want,[12] including educational or religious institutions, but their right to association is not limited to concerns related to their cultural, linguistic or religious identity. The right to associate of persons belonging to minorities extends both to national and to international associations. Their right to form or join associations can be limited only by law and the limitations can only be those which apply to associations of majorities: limitations must be those necessary in a democratic society in the interests of national security or public safety, public order, the protection of public health or morals, or the protection of rights and freedoms.

---

[12] Universal Declaration of Human Rights, article 20; International Covenant on Civil and Political Rights, article 22.

2.5 Persons belonging to minorities have the right to establish and maintain, without any discrimination, free and peaceful contacts with other members of their group and with persons belonging to other minorities, as well as contacts across frontiers with citizens of other States to whom they are related by national or ethnic, religious or linguistic ties.

52. The right to contacts has three facets, permitting intra-minority contacts, inter-minority contacts, and transfrontier contacts. The right to intra-minority contacts is inherent in the right of association. Inter-minority contacts make it possible for persons belonging to minorities to share experience and information and to develop a common minority platform within the State. The right to transfrontier contacts constitutes the major innovation of the Declaration, and serves in part to overcome some of the negative consequences of the often unavoidable division of ethnic groups by international frontiers. Such contacts must be "free" but also "peaceful". The latter limitation has two aspects: contacts must not involve the use of violent means or preparation of the use of such means; and the aims must be in conformity with the Declaration and generally with the purposes and principles of the Charter of the United Nations, as set out also in article 8.4 of the Declaration.

ARTICLE 3

3.1 Persons belonging to minorities may exercise their rights, including those set forth in the present Declaration, individually as well as in community with other members of their group, without any discrimination.

53. The main point here is that persons can exercise their rights both individually and collectively, the most important aspect being the collective exercise of their rights, be it through associations, cultural manifestations or educational institutions, or in any other way. That they can exercise their rights in community with other members of the group applies not only to the rights contained in the Declaration, but any human right. They shall not be subject to any discrimination as a consequence of exercising their rights. This principle is important, because Governments or persons belonging to majorities are often tolerant of persons of other national or ethnic origins until such time as the latter assert their own identity, language and traditions. It is often only when they assert their rights as persons belonging to a group that discrimination or persecution starts. Article 3.1 makes it clear that they shall not be subjected to discrimination for manifesting their group identity.

3.2 No disadvantage shall result for any person belonging to a minority as a consequence of the exercise or non-exercise of the rights set forth in the present Declaration.

54. While article 3.1 provides that persons belonging to minorities shall not be subjected to discrimination for exercising, individually or collectively, their minority rights, article 3.2 makes it clear that they shall also not be disadvantaged in any way for choosing not to belong to the minority concerned. This provision is directed both towards the State and the agencies of the minority group. The State cannot impose a particular ethnic identity on a given person (which is what the apartheid regime in South Africa sought to do) by the use of negative sanctions against those who do not want to be part of that group; nor can persons belonging to minorities subject to any disadvantage persons who on objective criteria may be held to form part of their group but who subjectively do not want to belong to it. While, under conventional law, responsibility for human rights compliance normally rests with the State, the Declaration in this respect implies duties - at least morally - for persons representing minorities. Furthermore, States would be under a duty to prohibit the taking of measures by minorities to impose their particular rules on any

person who did not want to be part of the minority concerned and therefore did not want to exercise her or his rights.

ARTICLE 4

4.1 States shall take measures where required to ensure that persons belonging to minorities may exercise fully and effectively their human rights and fundamental freedoms without any discrimination and in full equality before the law.

55. Article 4 sets out the State measures that should be taken in order to achieve the purpose of the Declaration and is its most important part, together with article 2, which sets out the rights. While States are generally obliged under international law to ensure that all members of society may exercise their human rights, States must give particular attention to the human rights situation of persons belonging to minorities because of the special problems they confront. They are often in a vulnerable position and have, in the past, often been subjected to discrimination. In order to ensure equality in fact, it may under some circumstances be necessary for the State to take transitional affirmative action, as provided for in article 2.2 of the International Convention on the Elimination of All Forms of Racial Discrimination, which is applicable to ethnic as well as racial minorities, provided these measures do not disproportionately affect the rights of others.

4.2 States shall take measures to create favourable conditions to enable persons belonging to minorities to express their characteristics and to develop their culture, language, religion, traditions and customs, except where specific practices are in violation of national law and contrary to international standards.

56. This paragraph of article 4 calls for more than mere tolerance of the manifestation of different cultures within a State. The creation of favourable conditions requires active measures by the State. The nature of those measures depends on the situation of the minority concerned, but should be guided by the purpose set forth in article 4.2, which is twofold. On the one hand, individual members of the minority shall be enabled to express the traditional characteristics of the group, which may include a right to use their traditional attire and to make their living in their own cultural ways. On the other hand, they shall be enabled, in community with other persons belonging to the group, to develop their culture, language and traditions. These measures may require economic resources from the State. In the same way as the State provides funding for the development of the culture and language of the majority, it shall provide resources for similar activities of the minority.

57. The words "except where specific practices are in violation of national law and contrary to international standards" require some comment. The meaning of the words "contrary to international standards" is simple enough. In particular, it is intended that the practices must not be contrary to international human rights standards. This, however, should apply to practices of both majorities and minorities. Cultural or religious practices which violate human rights law should be outlawed for everyone, not only for minorities. The qualification contained in the final words of article 4.2 is therefore only a specific application of a universal principle applicable to everyone.

58. The first part of the phrase "in violation of national law" raises somewhat more difficult questions. It is clear that the State is not free to adopt whatever prohibitions against minorities' cultural practices that it wants. If that were the case, the Declaration, and article 4.2 in particular, would be nearly empty of content. What is intended, however, is to respect the margin of appreciation which any State must have regarding which practices it wants to prohibit, taking

into account the particular conditions prevailing in that country. As long as the prohibitions are based on reasonable and objective grounds, they must be respected.

4.3 States should take appropriate measures so that, wherever possible, persons belonging to minorities may have adequate opportunities to learn their mother tongue or to have instruction in their mother tongue.

59. Language is among the most important carriers of group identity. In line with the general requirement in article 1 that States shall encourage the promotion of the linguistic identity of the minority concerned, measures are required for persons belonging to minorities to learn their mother tongue (which is a minimum) or to have instruction in their mother tongue (which goes some steps further).

60. The steps required in these regards depend on a number of variable factors. Of significance will be the size of the group and the nature of its settlement, i.e., whether it lives compactly together or is dispersed throughout the country. Also relevant will be whether it is a long-established minority or a new minority composed of recent immigrants, whether or not they have obtained citizenship.

61. In cases where the language of the minority is a territorial language traditionally spoken and used by many in a region of the country, States should to the maximum of their available resources ensure that linguistic identity can be preserved. Pre-school and primary school education should ideally in such cases be in the child's own language, i.e., the minority language spoken at home. Since persons belonging to minorities, like those belonging to majorities, have a duty to integrate into the wider national society, they need also to learn the official or State language(s). The official language(s) should gradually be introduced at later stages. Where there is a large linguistic minority within the country, the language of the minority is sometimes also an official language of the State concerned.

62. At the European regional level, educational rights relating to minority languages are developed at greater length in the European Charter for Regional or Minority Languages, adopted by the Council of Europe. On this subject, a group of experts elaborated the Hague Recommendations regarding the Education Rights of National Minorities (October 1996), prepared under the auspices of the Foundation on Inter-Ethnic Relations.

63. In regard to non-territorial languages spoken traditionally by a minority within a country, but which are not associated with a particular region of that country, a uniform solution is more difficult to find. The principles stated above should be applied where appropriate, but where the persons belonging to the minority live dispersed, with only a few persons in each particular place, their children need to learn the language of the surrounding environment more fully at an earlier stage. Nevertheless, they should always also have an opportunity to learn their mother tongue. In this regard, persons belonging to minorities have a right, like others, to establish their private institutions, where the minority language is the main language of instruction. However, the State is entitled to require that the State language also be taught. One question to be addressed is whether the State is obliged to provide subsidies for such teaching. It would be a requirement that the State does ensure the existence of and fund some institutions which can ensure the teaching of that minority language. It follows from the general wording of article 4.3 that everyone should have adequate opportunities "wherever possible". How far the obligation to fund teaching of minority languages for persons belonging to dispersed groups goes would therefore depend on the resources of the State.

64. Greater difficulties arise in regard to languages used solely by persons belonging to new minorities. These are usually more dispersed than are the older and settled minorities, and the

number of languages spoken at home by migrants in a country of immigration can be quite large. Furthermore, the children have a great need to learn to use the language of the country of immigration as quickly and as effectively as possible. Should, however, some new minorities settle compactly together in a region of the country and in large number, there is no reason to treat them differently from old minorities. It should be noted, however, that the European Charter for Regional or Minority Languages does not cover the languages of migrants. In any case, persons belonging to new minorities are entitled to set up their own private educational institutions allowing for the teaching of and instruction in their mother tongue. The State is entitled to demand that the official language also be taught.

4.4 States should, where appropriate, take measures in the field of education, in order to encourage knowledge of the history, traditions, language and culture of the minorities existing within their territory. Persons belonging to minorities should have adequate opportunities to gain knowledge of the society as a whole.

65. Experience has shown that in societies where different national, ethnic, religious or linguistic groups coexist, the culture, history and traditions of minority groups have often been neglected and the majorities are frequently ignorant of those traditions and cultures. Where there has been conflict, the minority groups' culture, history and traditions have often been subject to distorted representations, resulting in low self-esteem within the groups and negative stereotypes towards members of the group on the part of the wider community. Racial hatred, xenophobia and intolerance sometimes take root.

66. To avoid such circumstances, there is a need for both multicultural and intercultural education. Multicultural education involves educational policies and practices which meet the separate educational needs of groups in society belonging to different cultural traditions, while intercultural education involves educational policies and practices whereby persons belonging to different cultures, whether in a majority or minority position, learn to interact constructively with each other.

67. Article 4.4 calls for intercultural education, by encouraging knowledge in the society as a whole of the history, tradition and culture of the minorities living there. Cultures and languages of minorities should be made accessible to the majorities as a means of encouraging interaction and conflict prevention in pluri-ethnic societies. Such knowledge should be presented in a positive way in order to encourage tolerance and respect. History textbooks are particularly important in this regard. Bias in the presentation of the history and neglect of the contributions of the minority are significant causes of ethnic tension. The United Nations Educational, Scientific and Cultural Organization has concerned itself with the need to eliminate such prejudices and misrepresentations in history textbooks, but much remains to be done.

68. This paragraph of article 4 also emphasizes the complementary duty to ensure that persons belonging to minorities gain knowledge of the society as a whole. This provision should counteract tendencies towards fundamentalist or closed religious or ethnic groups, which can be as much affected by xenophobia and intolerance as the majorities.

69. The overall purpose of article 4.4 is to ensure egalitarian integration based on non-discrimination and respect for each of the cultural, linguistic or religious groups which together form the national society. The formation of more or less involuntary ghettos where the different groups live in their own world without knowledge of, or tolerance for, persons belonging to the other parts of the national society would be a violation of the purpose and spirit of the Declaration.

70. A concern similar to that of article 4.4 is expressed in the International Convention on the Elimination of All Forms of Racial Discrimination (art. 7) and in the Convention on the Rights of the Child (art. 29).

4.5 States should consider appropriate measures so that persons belonging to minorities may participate fully in the economic progress and development of their country.

71. There is often a risk that minorities, owing to their limited number compared to the majority and for other reasons, may be subjected to exclusion, marginalization or neglect. In the worst cases, the land and resources of minorities are taken over by the more powerful sectors of society, with consequent displacement and marginalization of persons belonging to the minorities. In other cases, persons belonging to minorities are neglected in the economic life of the society. Article 4.5 requires steps being taken to ensure that this does not happen. It should also prevent minorities being made into museum pieces by a misguided requirement that they remain at their traditional level of development while the members of the surrounding society experience significant improvements in their standard of living.

72. Article 4.5 calls for the integration of everyone in the overall economic development of society as a whole, while ensuring that this integration takes place in ways which make it possible for persons belonging to minorities to preserve their own identity. The balancing act required by these two separate aims can be difficult, but is facilitated by the existence of active and free associations of minorities which are fully consulted in regard to all development activities which affect or can affect their minority. Measures taken under article 2 to ensure participation facilitate this process.

ARTICLE 5

5.1 National policies and programmes shall be planned and implemented with due regard for the legitimate interests of persons belonging to minorities.

73. The participation of persons belonging to minorities in the economic progress and development of their country (art. 4.5) can be achieved only if their interests are taken into account in the planning and implementation of national policies and programmes. Their interests go beyond purely economic aspects, however. Planning of educational policy, health policy, public nutrition policy or housing and settlement policies are among the many aspects of social life in which the interests of the minorities should be taken into account. While the authorities are required to take only "legitimate" interests into account, this is no different from what is required in relation to majorities: an accountable Government should not promote "illegitimate interests" of any group, whether majority or minority. The interests of minorities should be given "due regard", which means that they should be given reasonable weight compared with other legitimate interests that the Government has to take into consideration.

5.2 Programmes of cooperation and assistance among States should be planned and implemented with due regard for the legitimate interests of persons belonging to minorities.

74. This provision is of particular interest for development assistance, but relates also to other economic cooperation among States, including trade and investment agreements. There have been many instances in the past where such cooperation has neglected or directly violated the interests of minorities. Development agencies, financial institutions and others involved in international cooperation have a dual task: firstly, to ensure that legitimate interests of minorities

are not negatively affected by the measures implied in the cooperation envisaged; and secondly, to ensure that persons belonging to minorities can benefit as much as members of majorities from that cooperation. The notion of "due regard" means that proper weight should be given to the interests of the minorities, all factors taken into account. An assessment should be made of the likely impact of the cooperation on the affected minorities. This should be an integral part of any feasibility study.

ARTICLE 6

States should cooperate on questions relating to persons belonging to minorities, inter alia by exchanging information and experiences, in order to promote mutual understanding and confidence.

75. Two sets of considerations underlie this provision. One is to share and exchange knowledge about good practices, whereby States can learn from each other. The other is to promote mutual understanding and trust. The latter is of particular importance.

76. Situations involving minorities often have international repercussions. Tensions between States have arisen in the past and in some cases continue in the present over the treatment of minorities, particularly in relations between the home State of a given minority and other States where persons belonging to the same ethnic, religious or linguistic group reside. Such tensions can affect the security of the countries involved and create a difficult political atmosphere, both internally and internationally.

77. Article 6 encourages States to cooperate in order to find constructive solutions to situations involving minorities. In accordance with the Charter of the United Nations, States should observe the principle of non-intervention in their bilateral relations. They should abstain from any use of force and also from any encouragement of the use of violence by parties to group conflicts in other States, and should take all necessary measures to prevent incursion by any armed group or mercenaries into other States in order to participate in group conflicts. On the other hand, they should, in their bilateral relations, engage in constructive cooperation to facilitate, on a reciprocal basis, the protection of equality and promotion of group identities. One approach, much used in Central and Eastern Europe, is for States to conclude bilateral treaties or other arrangements concerning good neighbourly relations based on the principles of the Charter and on international human rights law, combining commitments of strict non-intervention with provisions for cooperation in promoting conditions for the maintenance of group identities and transborder contacts by persons belonging to minorities. Provisions on minorities contained in such treaties and other bilateral arrangements should be based on universal and regional instruments relating to equality, non-discrimination and minority rights. Such treaties should include provisions for the settlement of disputes regarding their implementation.

ARTICLE 7

States should cooperate in order to promote respect for the rights set forth in the present Declaration.

78. The cooperation called for in article 7 can be undertaken at the regional and subregional levels, as well as at the level of the United Nations. At the European level, a number of intergovernmental mechanisms and procedures have been established whose purpose, at least partially, is to promote in a peaceful way the rights of minorities and achieve constructive group accommodation. These mechanisms include the Council of the Baltic Sea States and its Commissioner on Democratic Institutions and Human Rights, including the Rights of Persons belonging to Minorities; the OSCE, with its Office of the High Commissioner on National

Minorities; and the Council of Europe, which has adopted several instruments of relevance for minorities. In the United Nations, cooperation can take place through the Working Group on Minorities.

79. The treaty bodies, in particular the Committee on the Elimination of All Forms of Racial Discrimination, the Human Rights Committee and the Committee on the Rights of the Child, can also play important roles in this regard. (See also below under article 9.)

ARTICLE 8

8.1 Nothing in the present Declaration shall prevent the fulfilment of international obligations of States in relation to persons belonging to minorities. In particular, States shall fulfil in good faith the obligations and commitments they have assumed under international treaties and agreements to which they are parties.

80. The Declaration does not replace or modify existing international obligations in favour of persons belonging to minorities. It is an addition to, not a substitute for, commitments already made.

8.2 The exercise of the rights set forth in the present Declaration shall not prejudice the enjoyment by all persons of universally recognized human rights and fundamental freedoms.

81. The rights of specific categories of persons are supplementary to the universally recognized rights of every person. The Declaration is intended to strengthen the implementation of human rights in regard to persons belonging to minorities, but not to weaken for anyone the enjoyment of universal human rights. Consequently, the exercise of rights under the Declaration must not negatively affect the enjoyment of human rights for persons who do not belong to a minority, nor for persons who belong to the minority. In their efforts to preserve the collective identity of the minority, agencies of the minority concerned cannot on the basis of the Declaration adopt measures which interfere with the individual human rights of any person belonging to that minority.

8.3 Measures taken by States to ensure the effective enjoyment of the rights set forth in the present Declaration shall not prima facie be considered contrary to the principle of equality contained in the Universal Declaration of Human Rights.

82. In accordance with article 1 of the Universal Declaration of Human Rights, all human beings are born free and equal in dignity and rights. Article 2 of the Universal Declaration provides that everyone is entitled to all the rights set out in that declaration without distinction of any kind such as race, language, religion or national origin. The question has been raised as to whether special measures in favour of national or ethnic, religious or linguistic minorities constitute a distinction in the enjoyment of human rights. The same question could be put with even greater emphasis with respect to the definition of racial discrimination contained in article 1.1 of the International Convention on the Elimination of All Forms of Racial Discrimination, which reads: "The term 'racial discrimination' shall mean any distinction, exclusion, restriction or preference based on race, colour, descent, or national or ethnic origin which has the purpose or effect of nullifying or impairing the recognition, enjoyment or exercise, on an equal footing, of human rights and fundamental freedoms in the political, economic, social, cultural or any other field of public life." The question would then be whether special measures under the Declaration on Minorities, which would indeed be taken on the basis of "national or ethnic origin", would constitute a preference and therefore constitute impermissible discrimination.

83. Article 8.3 answers this question by pointing out that such measures shall not prima facie be considered to be contrary to the principle of equality. Under normal circumstances, measures to ensure effective participation, or to ensure that minorities benefit from economic progress in society or have the possibility to learn their own language will not be a privilege vis-à-vis other members of the society. It is essential, however, that such measures do not go beyond what is reasonable under the circumstances and are proportional to the aim sought to be realized.

8.4 Nothing in the present Declaration may be construed as permitting any activity contrary to the purposes and principles of the United Nations, including sovereign equality, territorial integrity and political independence of States.

84. As stated in the preamble, the Declaration is based on the principles of the Charter of the United Nations. Note should also be taken of the conviction expressed in the preamble that the promotion and protection of the rights of minorities contribute to the political and social stability of States. Article 8.4 serves as a reminder that nothing in the Declaration can be construed as permitting any activity which is contrary to the purposes of the Charter. Particular mention is made of activities that are contrary to the sovereign equality, territorial integrity and political independence of States. As pointed out above, the rights of persons belonging to minorities are different from the rights of peoples to self-determination, and minority rights cannot serve as a basis for claims of secession or dismemberment of a State.

ARTICLE 9

The specialized agencies and other organizations of the United Nations system shall contribute to the full realization of the rights and principles set forth in the present Declaration, within their respective fields of competence.

85. Wherever possible, the agencies and bodies of the United Nations system shall contribute to the full realization of the Declaration. Projects of technical cooperation and assistance shall take the standards contained in the Declaration fully into account. The Working Group on Minorities established by the United Nations in July 1995 serves as a stimulus for such cooperation. This article should be seen in the light of the Charter of the United Nations (Arts. 55 and 56), according to which the Organization shall promote respect and observance for human rights and fundamental freedoms. Promotion of the rights of persons belonging to minorities form[s] part of that obligation. United Nations organs and specialized agencies should give special consideration to requests for technical cooperation and assistance that are designed to achieve the aims of this Declaration.

ANNEX II

USEFUL WEBSITES

Contact information for the main bodies discussed in this *Guide* is given in each chapter. The following websites may also be of interest to minority rights advocates. While not comprehensive, this list includes key global and regional intergovernmental and non-governmental bodies which operate programmes relevant to minority issues.[1]

Disclaimer: OHCHR does not endorse and cannot assume responsibility for the accuracy or reliability of the information contained in the websites listed below. The views expressed in these websites do not necessarily reflect the views of the United Nations or of OHCHR. Any issues pertaining to the contents of the websites listed below should be addressed directly to the organization concerned.

UNITED NATIONS SYSTEM

Main website	Subordinate and related websites
Food and Agriculture Organization of the United Nations (FAO) Rome, Italy www.fao.org	Right to Food http://www.fao.org/righttofood/right-to-food-home/en/
International Fund for Agricultural Development (IFAD) Rome, Italy www.ifad.org	Indigenous peoples www.ifad.org/english/indigenous/index.htm
International Labour Organization (ILO) Geneva, Switzerland www.ilo.org	Labour standards www.ilo.org/public/english/standards/norm/index.htm
United Nations www.un.org	Office of the Special Adviser on the Prevention of Genocide www.un.org/preventgenocide/adviser
United Nations Children's Fund (UNICEF) New York, United States of America www.unicef.org	Convention on the Rights of the Child www.unicef.org/crc The State of the World's Children reports www.unicef.org/sowc/
United Nations Development Programme (UNDP) New York, United States of America www.undp.org	Human development reports http://hdr.undp.org/en/reports

[1] All websites listed in this annex were accessed on 13 December 2012.

United Nations Educational, Scientific and Cultural Organization (UNESCO) Paris, France www.unesco.org	Dialogue www.unesco.org/new/en/culture/themes/dialogue/ Indigenous peoples www.unesco.org/new/en/indigenous-peoples/ Management of Social Transformations Programme (MOST) www.unesco.org/new/en/social-and-human-sciences/themes/most-programme/ Enhancing intercultural dialogue www.unesco.org/new/en/venice/culture/intercultural-dialogue International migration and multicultural policies www.unesco.org/most/most1.htm Linguistic rights www.unesco.org/most/ln1.htm Religious rights www.unesco.org/most/rr1.htm
United Nations Entity for Gender Equality and the Empowerment of Women (UN-Women) New York, United States of America www.unwomen.org	
Office of the United Nations High Commissioner for Refugees (UNHCR) Geneva, Switzerland www.unhcr.org	Refworld www.refworld.org
United Nations Institute for Training and Research (UNITAR) Geneva, Switzerland www.unitar.org	Peace, Security, and Diplomacy Unit www.unitar.org/pmcp
United Nations Office at Geneva (UNOG) Geneva, Switzerland www.unog.ch	The United Nations and civil society: NGO liaison www.unog.ch/80256EE60057E07D/(httpPages)/AA57E3C5A169F6EA80256EF4002C4A1E?OpenDocument
United Nations Office for the Coordination of Humanitarian Affairs (OCHA) Geneva, Switzerland www.unocha.org	Reliefweb An online archive of humanitarian, human rights and development reference documents http://reliefweb.int
Office of the United Nations High Commissioner for Human Rights (OHCHR) Geneva, Switzerland www.ohchr.org Information relating to the entire range of OHCHR activities (e.g., relating to minorities, indigenous peoples, Afro-descendants, internally displaced persons, migrant workers, racism and racial discrimination, religious intolerance and the World Conference Against Racism)	

United Nations regional commissions: Economic Commission for Africa (ECA) Addis Ababa, Ethiopia www.uneca.org Economic Commission for Europe (ECE) Geneva, Switzerland www.unece.org Economic Commission for Latin America and the Caribbean (ECLAC) Santiago, Chile www.eclac.org Economic and Social Commission for Asia and the Pacific (ESCAP) Bangkok, Thailand www.unescap.org Economic and Social Commission for Western Asia (ESCWA) Beirut, Lebanon www.escwa.org.lb	
United Nations University (UNU) Tokyo, Japan www.unu.edu	
Womenwatch New York, the United States of America www.un.org/womenwatch	
World Bank Group Washington, D.C., United States of America www.worldbank.org	Human rights http://web.worldbank.org/WBSITE/EXTERNAL/EXTSITETOOLS/0,,contentMDK:20749693~pagePK:98400~piPK:98424~theSitePK:95474,00.html
World Health Organization (WHO) Geneva, Switzerland www.who.int	Health and human rights www.who.int/hhr/en/
World Intellectual Property Organization (WIPO) Geneva, Switzerland www.wipo.int	Traditional knowledge, genetic resources and traditional cultural expressions/folklore www.wipo.int/tk/en

REGIONAL ORGANIZATIONS AND MECHANISMS

AFRICA African Union Established in 2002, the African Union is the successor to the Organization of African Unity.	www.africa-union.org

INTERNATIONAL ORGANIZATIONS	
Amnesty International A worldwide movement of people, based in London, who campaign for internationally recognized human rights	www.amnesty.org
Association for the Prevention of Torture Offers guidelines for national NGOs on alternative reporting to United Nations treaty bodies, including the Committee against Torture	www.apt.ch
Centre for Housing Rights and Evictions Guidance to assist NGOs in using the Committee on Economic, Social and Cultural Rights	www.cohre.org
Commonwealth Human Rights Initiative (CHRI) An independent, non-partisan, international NGO mandated to ensure the practical realization of human rights in the countries of the Commonwealth	www.humanrightsinitiative.org
Defence for Children International Offers guidance for NGOs reporting to the Committee on the Rights of the Child	www.defenceforchildren.org
Child Rights International Network A global network coordinating information and promoting action on child rights	www.crin.org/NGOGroupforCRC/about.asp
Derechos Human Rights General human rights organization	www.derechos.org
Global Rights Human rights advocacy group that partners with local activists to challenge injustice and amplify new voices within the global discourse; based in Washington, D.C.	www.globalrights.org
Human Rights First Founded in 1978 as the Lawyers Committee for International Human Rights to promote laws and policies that advance universal rights and freedoms	www.humanrightsfirst.org
Human Rights Internet Canadian-based consulting and capacity-building organization committed to social justice, good governance and conflict prevention	www.hri.ca
Human Rights Watch Global human rights organization, based in New York	www.hrw.org
International Conflict Research Institute A joint project of the United Nations University and the University of Ulster, combining research, education and comparative analysis	www.incore.ulst.ac.uk
International Alert An independent peacebuilding organization that works to lay the foundations for lasting peace and security in communities affected by violent conflict, including ethnic conflict	www.international-alert.org
International Centre for the Legal Protection of Human Rights (INTERIGHTS) London-based legal organization focusing on litigation that offers advice to lawyers, human rights defenders and other partners	www.interights.org
International Commission of Jurists Geneva-based NGO with national sections worldwide	www.icj.org
International Federation of Human Rights Leagues Based in Paris	www.fidh.org
International Institute of Human Rights A research and education organization, based in Strasbourg, France; offers annual courses and training sessions on human rights	www.iidh.org
International League for Human Rights New York-based NGO that seeks to raise human rights issues and cases before the United Nations and other intergovernmental regional organizations	www.ilhr.org

International Movement Against All Forms of Discrimination and Racism (IMADR) Founded in 1988 by one of Japan's largest minorities, the Buraku people; devoted to eliminating discrimination and racism, forging international solidarity among discriminated minorities and advancing the international human rights system	www.imadr.org
Minority Rights Group International London-based NGO working to secure rights for ethnic, religious and linguistic minorities and indigenous people around the world	www.minorityrights.org
Minorities at Risk Project University-based research project that monitors and analyses the status and conflicts of politically active communal group	www.cidcm.umd.edu/mar
Open Society Justice Initiative Pursues law reform activities grounded in the protection of human rights, and contributes to the development of legal capacity for open societies worldwide	www.soros.org/initiatives/justice
World Organisation Against Torture Global network of nearly 300 local, national and regional organizations which share the common goal of eradicating torture and enabling the respect of human rights for all	www.omct.org
AMERICAS and the CARIBBEAN	
Organization of American States	www.oas.org
Inter-American Court of Human Rights	www.corteidh.or.cr/index.cfm
Inter-American Commission on Human Rights	www.cidh.oas.org
Inter-American Institute of Human Rights	www.iidh.ed.cr/default_eng.htm
EUROPE	
Central European Initiative	www.ceinet.org
Commonwealth of Independent States	www.cis.minsk.by
Council of the Baltic Sea States	www.cbss.org
Council of Europe Directorate General Human Rights and Rule of Law	www.coe.int/t/dghl/Default_en.asp
Council of Europe Commissioner for Human Rights	www.coe.int/t/commissioner/default_EN.asp
Council of Europe, Roma and Travellers	www.coe.int/T/DG3/RomaTravellers/Default_en.asp
Council of Europe, European Charter for Regional or Minority Languages	
European Commission against Racism and Intolerance (ECRI)	www.coe.int/t/dg4/education/minlang/default_en.asp
European Court of Human Rights	www.coe.int/t/dghl/monitoring/ecri/default_en.asp
OSCE High Commissioner on National Minorities	www.echr.coe.int
OSCE Office for Democratic Institutions and Human Rights (ODIHR) www.osce.org/odihr	www.osce.org/hcnm Roma and Sinti issues http://www.osce.org/odihr/roma Tolerance and non-discrimination www.osce.org/odihr/44450
European Union Agency for Fundamental Rights	TANDIS (Tolerance information system) http://tandis.odihr.pl/
European Union and European Community http://europa.eu/index_en.htm	http://fra.europa.eu/fraWebsite/home/home_en.htm
	Employment, social affairs and inclusion http://ec.europa.eu/social/main.jsp?langId=en&catId=423

REGIONAL ORGANIZATIONS	
AFRICA	
African Centre for the Constructive Resolution of Disputes	www.accord.org.za
African Commission on Human Rights	www.achpr.org
African Court on Human and Peoples' Rights	www.aict-ctia.org/courts_conti/achpr/achpr_home.html
African Centre for Democracy and Human Rights Studies Promotes human rights and democracy through training, action-oriented research, legal service, publications, documentation and networking	www.acdhrs.org
MIDDLE EAST AND NORTH AFRICA	
Alkarama Foundation Swiss-based foundation that seeks to ensure the promotion and protection of human rights, especially in the Arab world	www.alkarama.org
Habitat International Coalition MENA Works on housing and land rights	www.hic-mena.org
AMERICAS	
Latin American Network Information Center (LANIC) Guide to human rights resources throughout Latin America, based at the University of Texas	http://lanic.utexas.edu/la/region/hrights
ASIA AND PACIFIC	
Asian Human Rights Commission Seeks to protect and promote human rights by monitoring, investigation, advocacy, and taking solidarity actions; based in Hong Kong	www.humanrights.asia
Asia-Pacific Forum Australian-based regional human rights organization that seeks to advance human rights in the Asia-Pacific region through its member organizations	www.asiapacificforum.net
South Asia Human Rights Documentation Centre Regional network based in New Delhi that seeks to investigate, document and disseminate information about human rights	www.hrdc.net/
EUROPE	
The Balkan Human Rights Webpages Includes country-specific topics, organizations and publications	www.greekhelsinki.gr/bhr/english/index.html
Consortium of Minority Resources (COMIR) Cooperative project that aims at promoting the free flow of information and dialogue in the field of ethnic relations, multicultural politics and minority rights	http://lgi.osi.hu/comir
Constitutional and Legal Policy Institute (COLPI) A legal reform support programme of the Open Society Institute-Budapest whose mission is to contribute to the development of open societies in the countries of Central and Eastern Europe, Central Asia, and Mongolia through strengthening the rule of law and respect for human rights	www.osi.hu/colpi/indexie.html
European Centre for Minority Issues (ECMI) Conducts practice-oriented research, provides information and documentation, and offers advisory services concerning minority-majority relations in Europe	www.ecmi.de
European Roma Rights Centre (ERRC) International public interest law organization engaging in a range of activities aimed at combating anti-Romani racism and human rights abuse of Roma	www.errc.org

Federal Union of European Nationalities (FUEN) Independent union of organizations of national minorities in Europe, based in Flensburg, Germany	www.fuen.org
Human Rights in Russia General human rights NGO	www.hro.org
Local Government and Public Service Reform Initiative The LGI Managing Multiethnic Communities Project (LGI/MMCP), established in 1997, supports the Open Society Institute mission by working to promote democratic and effective local government and public administration	http://lgi.osi.hu
Minority Electronic Resources (MINELRES) Directory of resources on minority rights and related problems of the transition period in Eastern and Central Europe	www.minelres.lv/
Minority Rights Information System Database on minority issues, primarily European	http://miris.eurac.edu/mugs2/index.jsp?TopBarItem=Home
Statewatch Monitors civil liberties in the European Union	www.statewatch.org